PHILIP'S

STRE

CW00340976

Bournemouth

www.philips-maps.co.uk

First published in 2006 by

Philip's, a division of
Octopus Publishing Group Ltd
www.octopusbooks.co.uk
2-4 Heron Quays, London E14 4JP
An Hachette Livre UK Company
www.hachettelivre.co.uk

First edition 2006
Second impression 2008

ISBN 978-0-540-08992-5

© Philip's 2006

Photographic acknowledgements:
VIII Denny Rowland / Alamy
IX top Ivor Toms / Alamy
IX bottom Mark Bird / Alamy

Printed by Toppan, China

Contents

II **Key to map symbols**

III **Key to map pages**

IV **Route planning**

VIII **Sights of Bournemouth**

2 **Street maps** at 4½ inches to 1 mile

112 **Street maps of Bournemouth town centre**
at 7 inches to 1 mile

113 **Index**

134 **List of numbered locations**

Key to map symbols

Roads

(12) **Motorway** with junction number

A42 **Primary route** – dual, single carriageway

A42 **A road** – dual, single carriageway

B1289 **B road** – dual, single carriageway

Through-route – dual, single carriageway

Minor road – dual, single carriageway

Rural track, private road or narrow road in urban area

Path, bridleway, byway open to all traffic, road used as a public path

Road under construction

Pedestrianised area

Gate or obstruction to traffic restrictions may not apply at all times or to all vehicles

P P&R **Parking, Park and Ride**

Railways

Railway

Miniature railway

Metro station, private railway station

Emergency services

Ambulance station, coastguard station

Fire station, police station

H ✚ **Hospital, Accident and Emergency entrance to hospital**

General features

✚ PO **Place of worship, Post Office**

i **Information centre** (open all year)

Bus or coach station, shopping centre

Important buildings, schools, colleges, universities and hospitals

Woods, built-up area

Tumulus FORT **Non-Roman antiquity, Roman antiquity**

Leisure facilities

⚠ 🚐 **Camping site, caravan site**

▶ ✕ **Golf course, picnic site**

Boundaries

• • • • • • • **Postcode boundaries**

— · — **County and unitary authority boundaries**

Water features

 Tidal water, water name

Non-tidal water – lake, river, canal or stream

< | **Lock, weir**

Enlarged mapping only

Railway or bus station building

Place of interest

Parkland

Scales

Blue pages: 4½ inches to 1 mile 1:14 080

| 0 | 220 yds | ¼ mile | 660 yds | ½ mile |
| 0 | 125m | 250m | 375m | ½ km |

Red pages: 7 inches to 1 mile 1:9051

| 0 | 110 yds | 220 yds | 330 yds | ¼ mile |
| 0 | 125m | 250m | 375m | ½ km |

44 **Adjoining page indicators** The colour of the arrow and the band indicates the scale of the adjoining page (see above)

Abbreviations

Acad	Academy		Mkt	Market
Allot Gdns	Allotments		Meml	Memorial
Cemy	Cemetery		Mon	Monument
C Ctr	Civic Centre		Mus	Museum
CH	Club House		Obsy	Observatory
Coll	College		Pal	Royal Palace
Crem	Crematorium		PH	Public House
Ent	Enterprise		Recn Gd	Recreation Ground
Ex H	Exhibition Hall		Resr	Reservoir
Ind Est	Industrial Estate		Ret Pk	Retail Park
IRB Sta	Inshore Rescue Boat Station		Sch	School
Inst	Institute		Sh Ctr	Shopping Centre
Ct	Law Court		TH	Town Hall/House
L Ctr	Leisure Centre		Trad Est	Trading Estate
LC	Level Crossing		Univ	University
Liby	Library		Wks	Works
			YH	Youth Hostel

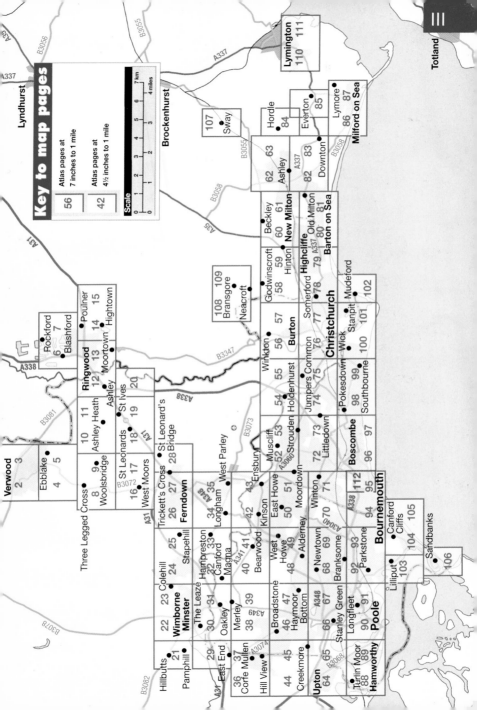

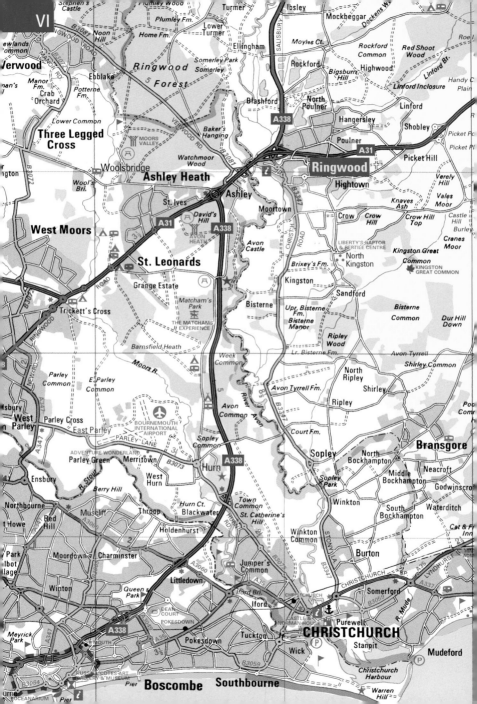

Sights of Bournemouth

▲ Sandbanks

Museums and Galleries

Atrium Gallery *Talbot Campus, Fern Barrow, Bournemouth University* Variety of exhibitions with private viewings available.
🖳www.bournemouth.ac.uk
☎01202 524111 70 C4

Bournemouth Aviation Museum *Hangar 600, Bournemouth International Airport, Christchurch* A flying museum featuring military jets from the 50's and 60's. Access the cockpits and visit the model room containing over 600 models on display. Picnic area to watch the aircraft. ☎01202 580858 🖳www.aviation-museum.co.uk

Christchurch Motor Museum *Machismo Lane, Hurn* Vintage and classic cars and other motoring memorabilia on display.
🖳www.tourism.bournemouth.com ☎01202 882533 30 B4

Museum of Electricity *The Old Power Station, Bargates, Christchurch* A unique collection of electrical memorabilia, in an Edwardian power station. Regular demonstrations available. ☎01202 480467 76 B2

The Priest's House Museum and Garden *23-27 High Street, Wimborne* Elizabethan town house with collections of local history, Georgian Parlour period room, 17th century Hall and Victorian kitchen, with a secret garden. 🖳www.aboutbritain.com/priestshousemuseum.htm☎01202 488100 30 B4

Red House Museum and Gardens *Quay Road, Christchurch* A 1764 warehouse now housing a very fine collection of objects reflecting the social and natural history of the area, with costume gallery and walled gardens. 🖳www.hants.gov.uk/museum/redhouse ☎01202 482860 76 B1

Ringwood Town & Country Experience *Gouldings Farm, Salisbury Road, Ringwood* A fascinating insight into times gone by with real life size village shops, steam train, vintage cars, an original Bouncing Bomb, RAF display and model air crafts, radio shop and a toy shop. ☎01425 472746 🖳www.rtce.co.uk 6 A1

RNLI Headquarters and Display Museum *West Quay Road, Poole* Displays of the history and development of the RNLI from its foundation in 1824 to today. Details of heroism, paintings, photographs and models.
☎01202 663000
🖳www.rnli.org.uk 90 C2

Russell-Cotes Art Gallery & Museum *East Cliff, Bournemouth* World famous collections of Victorian art and sculpture in a rich and colourful Victorian House. The Japanese garden overlooks Poole Bay.☎01202 451858 🖳www.russell-cotes.bournemouth.gov.uk 96 A1

Sammy Miller Motorcycle Museum *Bashley Manor, New Milton* Houses a very fine collection of fully restored motorcycles spanning seven decades.
🖳www.sammymiller.co.uk
☎01425 616446 61 B4

The Shelley Rooms *Beechwood Avenue, Boscombe* A collection of resources relating to the poet Shelley, concentrating on the last few months of her life (1822). Library of romantic literature. Costume and textile collection. ☎01202 303571
97 C3

Verwood Heathland Heritage Centre *Manor Way, Verwood* Mini-museum of the last remaining workshop of Verwood's once numerous potteries. Fully restored with exhibitions of local interest.
🖳www.verwoodheritage.net
2 C3

Waterfront Museum *High Street, Poole* The history of Poole over 2000 years showing Roman occupation, Poole Pottery and Studland Bay Wreck with research facilities.
🖳www.poole.gov.uk
☎01202 262600 90 B1

Historic Sites

Badbury Rings *Shapwick nr Wimborne Minster* An iron age hill fort dating from 150BC in the estates of Kingston Lacy House. 🖳www.nationaltrust.org.uk

Christchurch Castle and Norman House *Christchurch* Originally known as Twynham Castle with the remains of the 12th century Constable's House attached.
🖳www.english-heritage.org.uk 76 B1

Clouds Hill *Clouds Hill, near Wareham* An isolated brick and tile cottage owned by T E Lawrence as a retreat. The rooms are as he left them, the furniture and interior decor were designed by Lawrence.
☎01929 405616
🖳www.nationaltrust.org.uk

Compton Acres *Canford Cliffs Road, Poole* Fine Georgian house standing in 266 acre parkland. Fashioned in 18th century style, the state rooms contain ornate plasterwork, extensive family portrait collection, fine furniture and original wallpaper.
🖳www.comptonacres.co.uk
☎01793 700778 104 B4

Highcliffe Castle *Rothesay Drive, Highcliffe* Built by Lord Stuart de Rothesay in 19th century. Now a heritage centre with cliff-top walk, tranquil grounds, stateroom galleries and family detective trail. ☎01425 278807 🖳www.highcliffecastle.co.uk 79 B2

Throop Mill *Throop Road, Bournemouth* Mentioned in the Doomsday Book it has ancient stone foundations along with coins from the reigns of George III and IV. Now disused, it contains some fine early 20th century milling machinery.
🖳www.bournemouth.gov.uk
☎01202 451451 (Bournemouth Council) 53 B3

Places of Worship

Christchurch Priory Church *Quay Road, Christchurch* 11th century church with special tours to the tower, crypts and roof. Contains a small museum.
🖳www.christchurchpriory.org
☎01202 488645 76 B1

St Peters Parish Church *Hinton Road, Bournemouth* Grade 1 listed Victorian church with spectacular chancel and famous tombs including that of Mary Shelley, author of Frankenstein. ☎01202 290986 🖳www.stpetersbournemouth.org 112 B2

Wimborne Minster *High Street, Wimborne Minster* Historic, mainly Norman, minster church. Unique chained library founded in 1686. Contains an astronomical clock and a quarterjack on the west tower who strikes the quarter hours.
🖳www.wimborneminster.org.uk ☎01202 884753 30 B4

Other Sights

Bournemouth Eye *Lower Gardens, Bournemouth* A spherical helium-filled balloon with an enclosed gondola. Carries up to 30 passengers 500ft above Bournemouth. ☎0845 051 1701 🖳www.bournemouth.gov.uk 112 B2

Bournemouth International Centre *Exeter Road, Bournemouth* Venue for conferences, entertainment and events ranging from musicals to party political conferences. The BIC operates alongside The Pavilion Theatre, Ballroom and The Pier Theatre.
🖳www.bic.co.uk
☎01202 456400 112 B1

Cliff Lifts *Fisherman's Walk, East Cliff and West Cliff* Three funicular railways from the cliff top to beach level built between 1908 and 1935 ☎01202 451781 🖳www.bournemouth.gov.uk/Visitors/Seafront/Getting_Around/Cliff_Lifts.asp
98 B2, 96 B1, 112 A1

The Court House *Castle Street, Christchurch* 14th century with thatched roof where the mayor and officers of the town were annually sworn in, now houses

New Forest Perfumery and Tea Rooms. 🖳 www.dorsetforyou.com 76 C1

Kingston Lacy *Wimborne Minster* Home of the Bankes family for over 300 years, all floors are open to visitors. Contain lavish interiors. Edwardian laundry gives a fascinating insight into life below stairs 100 years ago. ☎ 01202 883402 🖳 www.nationaltrust.org.uk

Oceanarium *West Beach, Bournemouth* A fully interactive experience, with feeding demonstrations, walk-through underwater tunnel and exhibits. 🖳 www.oceanarium.co.uk ☎ 01202 311993 112 B1

Stapehill Abbey, Crafts and Gardens *Wimborne Road West, Wimborne Minster* A 19th century Abbey with award winning gardens, Victorian parlour, museum and farmyard, showing rural England in Victorian times. ☎ 01202 861686 🖳 www.aboutbritain.com/stapehillabbey.htm 25 B1

Walford Mill Craft Centre *Stone Lane, Wimborne Minster* A converted mill with an exhibition gallery featuring contemporary British textiles, ceramics, glass, with stained glass and jewellery workshops. ☎ 01202 841400 🖳 www.walfordmillcrafts.co.uk 22 B2

Wimborne Market *Station Road / New Borough Road, Wimborne Minster* The largest open and covered market in the south of England. 400 stalls of antiques, collectables, crafts, fresh produce, plants and clothing. Farmers market every Friday morning. ☎ 01202 841212 🖳 www.wimbornemarket.co.uk 31 A3

Wimborne Model Town and Gardens *King Street, Wimborne Minster* Lifelike models of 1950s Wimborne Minster town

centre. Fantastic attention to detail with prize-winning gardens. ☎ 01202 881924 🖳 www.wimborne-modeltown.com 30 B4

Tivoli Theatre *West Borough, Wimborne Minster* Art-Deco theatre showing live productions of musicals, rock and jazz. Also shows latest film releases. 🖳 www.tivoliwimborne.co.uk ☎ 01202 848014 22 B1

Green Spaces

Alum Chine and Argyll Gardens *West Cliff, Bournemouth* Tropical garden walk with spectacular views and unusual plantings. Wooded walk up the Chine valley, with a bowls club. Awarded the prestigious Green Flag Award in 2000. ☎ 01202 451451 🖳 www.bournemouth.gov.uk 94 C1

Avon Heath Country Park *Brooks Pine, St Leonards* 580 acres of heathland and woodland popular with cyclists and walkers. Rangers offer guided walks, exhibitions and activity trails for families. ☎ 01425 478470 🖳 www.aboutbritain.com/avonheathcountrypark.htm 19 C3

Deans Court Garden *Deans Court Lane, Wimborne Minster* 13 acres of partly wild gardens, specimen trees, herb garden, rose garden, peacocks and monastery fish pond. ☎ 01202 886116 (Wimborne TIC) 30 C4

Farrs Lodge *Cowgrove Road, Wimborne Minster* Gravel gardens, bulb lawns, buddleia walk, wild flower meadow, artist's studio and old rifle range. ☎ 01202 885130 21 B1

Knoll Gardens *Stapehill Road, Wimborne Minster* Mature framework of unusual trees, shrubs and tumbling waterfalls. Mediterranean style gravel garden, exotic summer garden with a nationally acclaimed specialist nursery. ☎ 01202 873931 🖳 www.knollgardens.co.uk 33 C4

MacPenny's Woodland Gardens & Nursery *Burley Road, Bransgore, Christchurch* 4 acres

◄ *The Cliff Lift at Fisherman's Walk*

▲ *Wimborne Minster*

of established woodland gardens created from gravel pits in 1950s. Canopy of indigenous trees with rare plants. Large nursery. ☎ 01425 672348 109 B3

Moors Valley Country Park *Horton Road, Ashley Heath* Country park of 750 acres, with walk and cycle paths, tree top trail, steam railway, lakes and high ropes course. Restaurant, shop and 19 hole golf course. 🖳 www.moors-valley.co.uk ☎ 01425 470721 10 A4

Spinners Garden *School Lane, Boldre, nr Lymington* Woodland garden with internationally known nursery. ☎ 01590 673347 🖳 www.hants.gov.uk

Tuckton Tea Gardens *Belle Vue Road, Tuckton* Beautiful gardens with a small cafe, stunning views of River Stour. Putting green and crazy golf. Fourteen flavours of locally made ice cream. ☎ 01202 429119 99 C4

Upton Lacy Country Park *Upton Road, Upton* 100 acres of gardens, woodland and bird hide near Poole Harbour. 🖳 www.poole.gov.uk ☎ 01202 262748 65 C2

Activities

Farmer Palmer's Farm Park *Wareham Road, Organford, Poole* Family owned and run specially designed for families and children. A farm park with animal barn events and tractor trailer rides. Caters for large groups and parties. ☎ 01202 622022 🖳 www.farmerpalmer.co.uk

Lighthouse *Kingland Road, Poole* The largest arts centre outside London with cinema, theatre and workshops. 🖳 www.lighthousepoole.co.uk ☎ 0870 066 8701 91 A3

Littledown Centre *Chaseside, Bournemouth* Situated in 47 acres of parkland, the leisure facilities offered include swim-

ming pools with waterslides, spa, gym, studios, squash courts, football pitches, creche and miniature railway. 🖳 www.littledowncentre.co.uk ☎ 01202 417600 74 A3

Queens Park *Queens Park West Drive, Bournemouth* One of the oldest municipal courses in the UK. 18 hole Championship Course through many acres of heathers and gorse. No handicap required. ☎ 01202 437807 🖳 www.littledowncentre.co.uk/qpgolf 73 B3

Splashdown Water Park *Yarrow Road, Poole* Indoor and outdoor family water park with pools and 12 waterslides. 🖳 www.splashdownpoole.co.uk ☎ 01202 716123 48 B1

Tower Park *Mannings Heath Road, Poole* Brand new total entertainment centre with 24 computerised bowling lanes, Video World and the American Pool Pit. 🖳 www.towerparkcentre.co.uk ☎ 01202 723671 48 B1

Information

Tourist Information
🖬 *Westover Road, Bournemouth*
🖳 www.bournemouth.co.uk
☎ 0845 051 1701 112 B2

Bournemouth Borough Council
🖬 *Town Hall, Bourne Avenue*
🖳 www.bournemouth.gov.uk
☎ 01202 451451 112 A2

Car Parking City Council
🖳 www.bournemouth.gov.uk
☎ 01202 451451

Car Parking NCP
☎ 0870 606 7050
🖳 www.ncp.co.uk

National Rail Enquiries
☎ 0845 748 4950
🖳 www.nationalrail.co.uk

Local Bus and Rail
☎ 0870 608 2608
🖳 www.traveline.org.uk

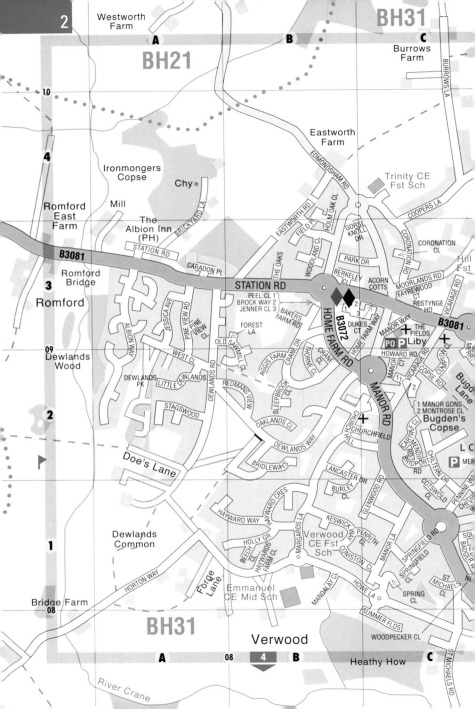

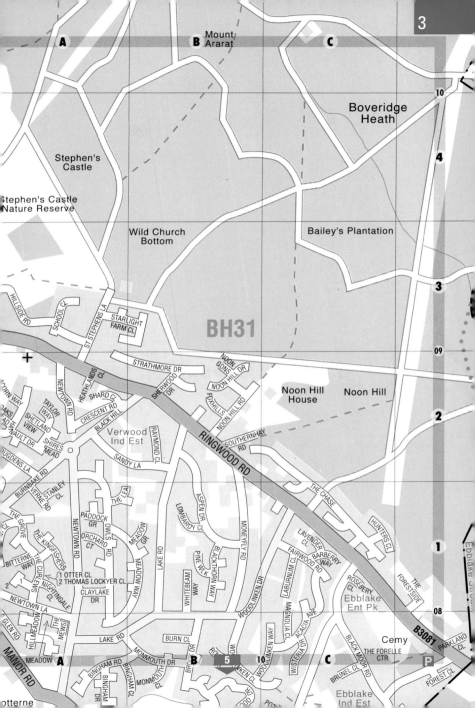

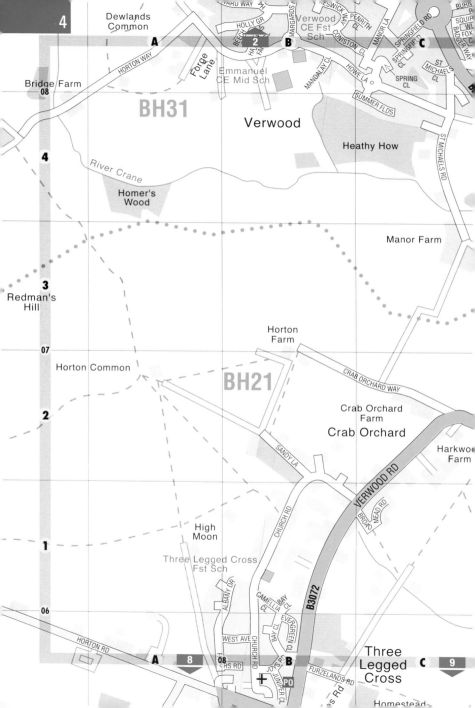

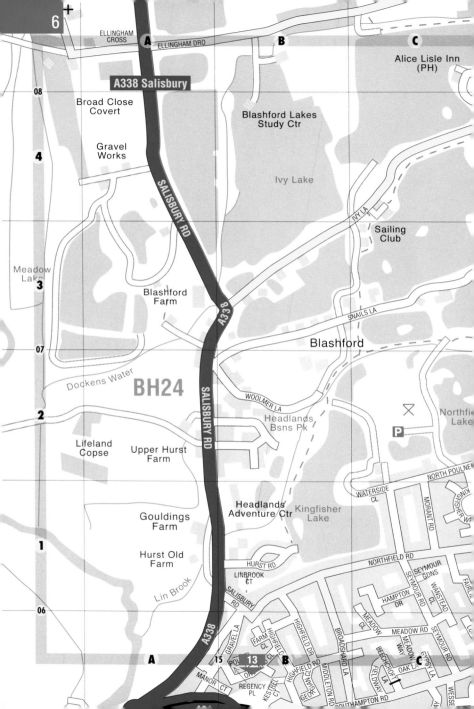

Little Whitemoor
Bottom

A P

B

C

Rockford

08

ckford
Green

BH24

Waterslade
Farm

4

Bigsburn
Hill

Water Slade Bottom

Rockford
Farm

Highwood

Highwood
Copse

3

Bracken
Hill

Forest Edge
Farm

HIGHWOOD LA

Linbrook
Almshouses

Highwood
Farm

07

Linbrook
View

Lin Brook

Linbank
Farm

2

MORE CT 1
FARM CL 2

COWPITTS LA

LIN BROOK DR

LWATER
PK

North
Poulner

Hangersley

ST AUBYNS LA

Burcomb

SHAW
RD

LAWRENCE
RD

ulner
& Jun
Schs

ROSS
RD

DENE CL

CROFT RD

PADGET
RD

DENHOLM CL

Hangersley
Hill

BURCOMBE LA

1

FOREST SIDE GDNS

BH24

PO

HOLM CL

BUTLERS LA

LINFORD RD

Forest Corner
Farm

FAIRIE

PARKERS CL

GORLEY RD

5

NARROW LA

1 GRENVILLE CL
2 DRAKE CL
3 FROBISHER CL
4 CHICHESTER RD
5 POULNER PK

06

HAWKINS
CL

4

2

1

3

LINK
RD

FAIRIE
RD

COOK CL

CUNNINGHAM
CL

ANSON CL

BEATTY CL

THE LONDON TAVERN
CVN PK

Forest
Corner

GORLEY RD

LEIGH

SOMERVILLE
RD

HUDSON
CL

A

B

14

17

C

FIELD LA

THE MOUNT

NARROW LA

Poulner

Dunain
Farm

A31 POULNER HILL

Moors River

A
B
C

Moors Valley
Railway

Kings
Farm
CH

Moors Valley
Country Park

Kingsmere

06

4

Moors Valley
Country Park

Visitor
Centre
P

neland
arm

Ashley Heath
Ind Est

BH21

9
3

05

BH24

Woolsbridge Manor
Farm

oolsbridge

Y CL

Y CL

2

Wools
Bridge

ASHLEY HEATH
CVN PK

Ashley
Heath

Woolsbridge
Farm

A CL

HORTON RD

FOREST EDGE DR

WEBBS CL

EMERALD CL

WEBBS
WAY

ELMORE
DR

EVANS CL

EVERGRE

PINE MANOR RD

FOREST
EDGE CL

BURTON CL

1

Little Lions
Farm

GROSVENOR CL

LIONS LA

SHELLEY CL

DRYDEN CL

BUSHMEAD DR

THE GLADE

WOOLSBRIDGE RD

Castleman Trailway

Lions
Hill

ST LEONARDS WAY

NORRIS
CL

04

Lions Hill
Farm

Lions Hill Way

BRACKEN CL

FERNLEA CL

10
A
B
11
C

LIONS WOOD

Moors River

WILLOW CL

HEATH

SYLVAN CL

HOLLY
CL

GARTH CL
SPIN

06

Baker's
Hanging

4

VERWOOD RD

B3081

Watchmoor
Wood

3

Ashley Heath

BH24

12

Ashley Trailway
Castleman Trailway

05

Holly Grove
Farm

THE SPINNEY

STRUAN GDNS

STRUAN DR

STRUAN CT

STRUAN CL

ASHLEY PK

+

The Sheiling
Sch

2

Ashley

PEVERIL CL

HORTON RD

HORTON RD

ASHLEY DR W

ASHLEY DR N

MONKWORTHY
DR

BADGERS
CL

WHITFIELD
PK

St Ives
House

St Ives
Fst
Sch

STRODE
GDNS

St Ives Wood

RUSSELL
GDNS

1

SUNNYSIDE
PK

ASHLEY DR S

LANGLEY
CHASE

ST IVES PK

HESKETH CL

SANDY LA

FERNWOOD CL

St Ives

POST OFFICE LA

PINEHOT CL

A31 RINGWOOD RD

A338

WINDSOR CL

PADDOCK
CL

COPPICE
CL

SANDY LA

COMPTON BEECHES

SCHOOL LA

LARCH CL

AZALEA CL

ST IVES
THE
CLOSE

PO

David's
Hill

04

Whitehouse
Wood

WOODLANDS
WAY

KNOLL GDNS

PINEWOOD RD

GLENIVES
CL

ST IVES
CRES

The
Rowans

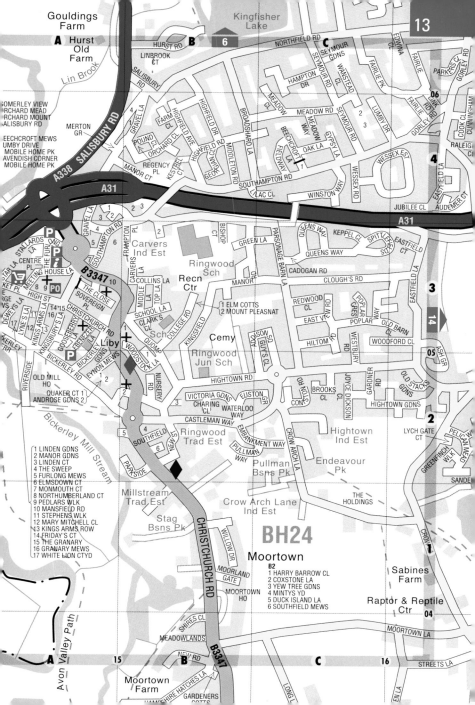

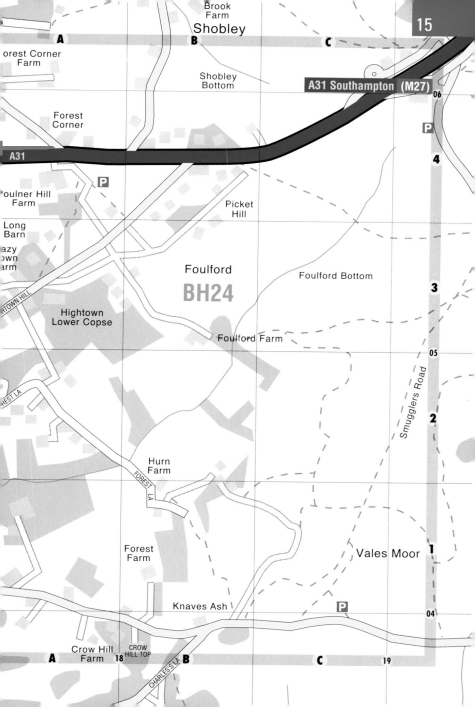

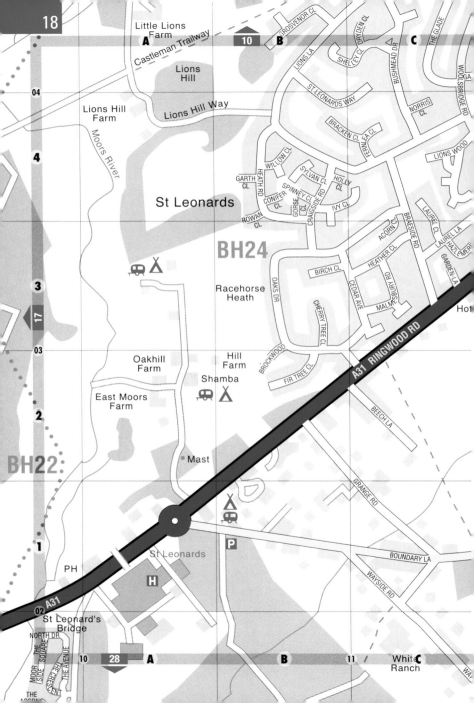

Little Lions
Farm

Castleman Trailway

A 10 **B** GROSVENOR CL **C** THE GLADE

Lions
Hill

LIONS LA

SHELLEY CL DRYDEN CL

BUSHMEAD DR

WOOLSBRIDGE RD

GA

04

Lions Hill
Farm

Lions Hill Way

ST LEONARDS WAY

NORRIS CL

Moors River

4

BRACKEN CL LA

FERNLEA CL

LIONS WOOD

LAUREL CL

GARTH CL

HEATH RD

WILLOW CL

SYLVAN CL

HOLLY CL

CRAIGSIDE RD

LAUREL LA

St Leonards

CONIFER CL

SPINNEY CL

GORSE CL

IVY CL

BRAESIDE RD

HAZEL LA

EMER

BH24

ROWAN CL

ACORN CL

LIONS WOOD

LAUREL CL

3

Racehorse
Heath

BIRCH CL

HEATHER CL

MALMESBURY RD

GARDEN LA

17

03

OAKS DR

CEDAR AVE

Oakhill
Farm

CHERRY TREE CL

Hill
Farm

BROCKWOOD

FIR TREE CL

A31 RINGWOOD RD

Hot

Shamba

East Moors
Farm

2

BEECH LA

BH22

• Mast

GRANGE RD

1

BOUNDARY LA

St Leonards

WAYSIDE RD

P

PH

H

A31

02

St Leonard's
Bridge

NORTH DR

10 **28** **A** **B** **11** White
Ranch **C**

THE SQUARE

MOORSIDE

CRESCENT

THE AVENUE

WA

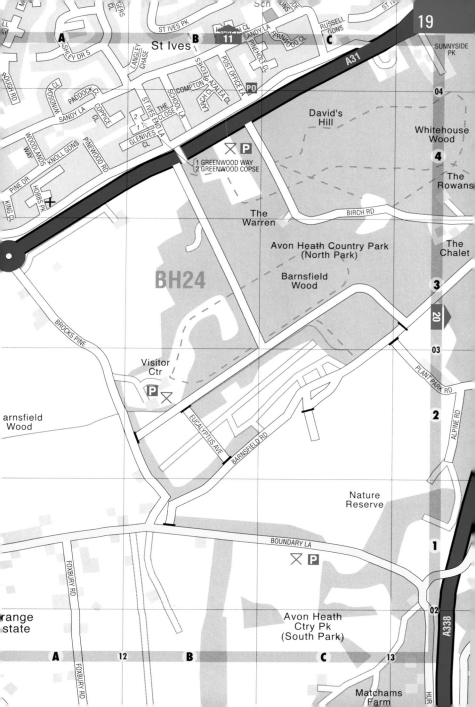

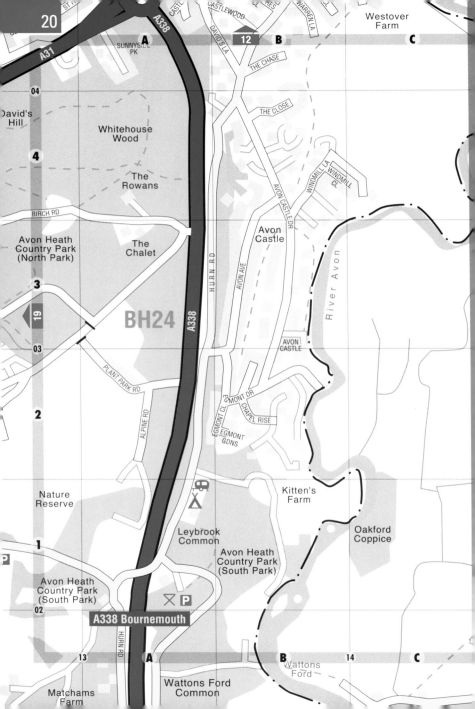

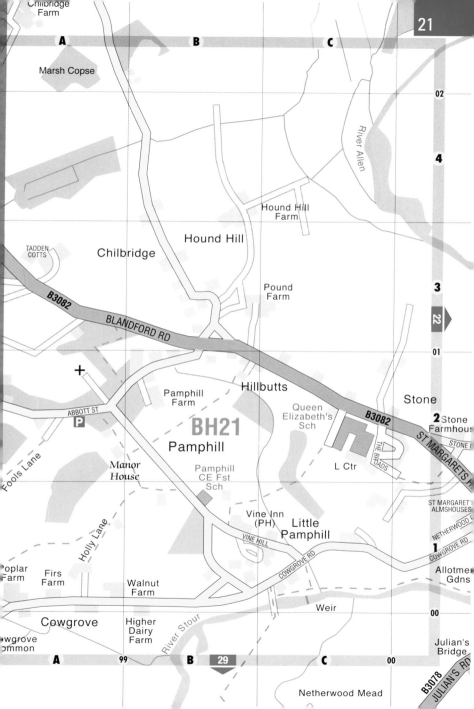

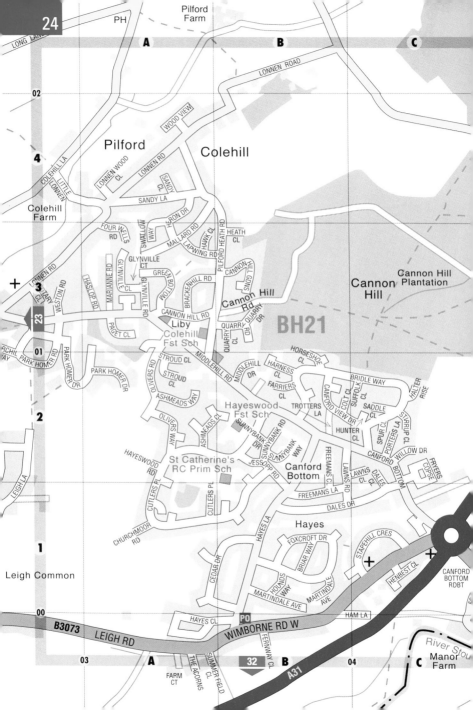

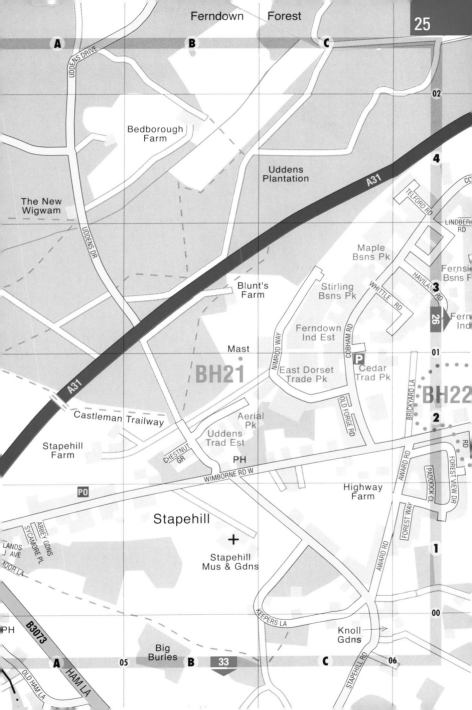

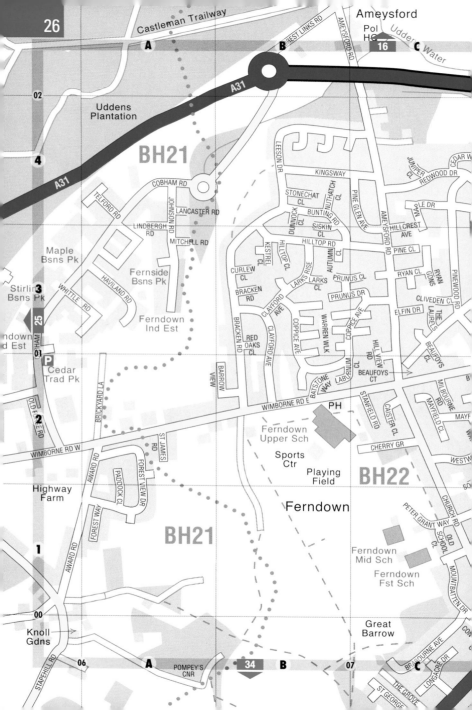

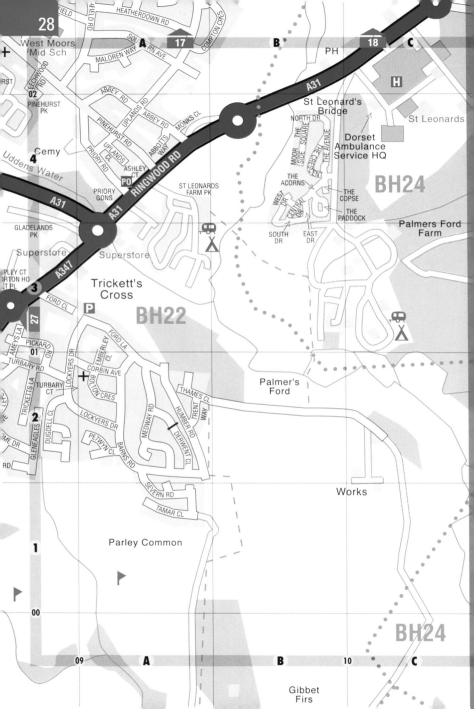

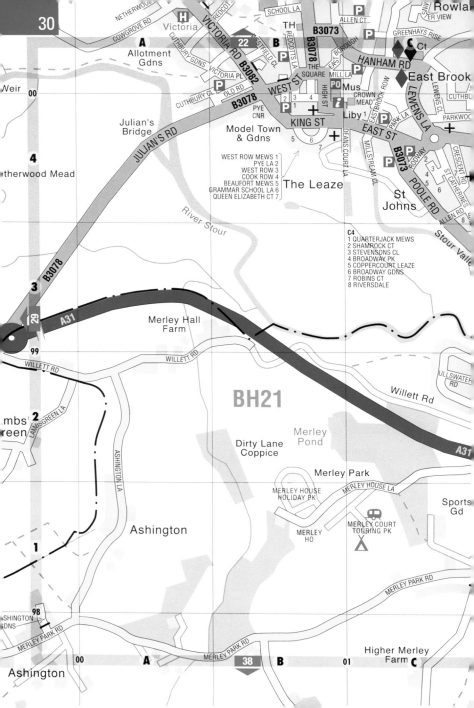

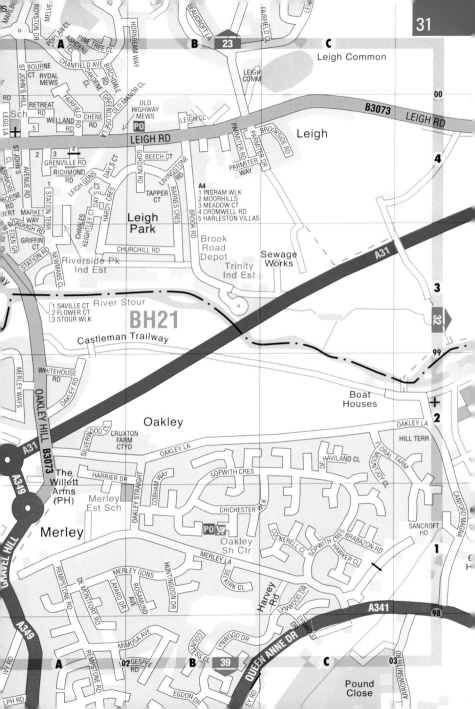

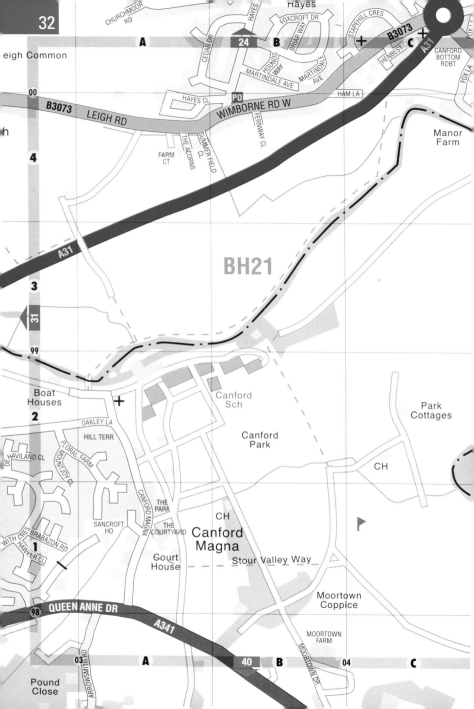

YELANDS
AVE

ABBEY GDNS

SYCAMORE PL

RAYMOOR LA

B3073

PH

OLD HAM LA

STOUR CL

Little
Canford

River Stour

Stapehill
Mus & Gdns

KEEPERS LA

Big
Burles

Little Moors
Farm

HAM LA

SQUARE
CL

Stourbank
Nurseries

BH21

Hampreston
CE Fst Sch

NEW
COTTS

Hampreston

Manor Farm
House

Manor
Farm

AWARD RD

Knoll
Gdns

STAPEHILL RD

00

4

The
Roughs

Big
Copse

3

34

99

B3073

BH22

HIGH MEAD LA

HIG

2

1

98

River Stour

Knighton
House

Bartlett's
Cliff

King's

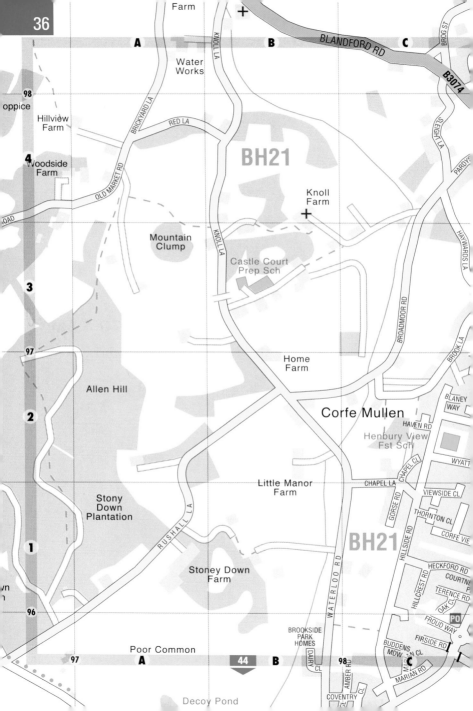

Farm

A

Water
Works

BLANDFORD RD

BROG ST

B3074

KNOLL LA

BRICKYARD LA

RED LA

98

oppice

Hillview
Farm

S.LEIGH LA

PARDYS

BH21

4

Woodside
Farm

OLD MARKET RD

OAD

Knoll
Farm

HAYWARDS LA

Mountain
Clump

KNOLL LA

Castle Court
Prep Sch

3

BROADMOOR RD

97

Home
Farm

BROOK LA

Allen Hill

BLANEY
WAY

2

Corfe Mullen

HAVEN RD

Henbury View
Fst Sch

WYATT

CHAPEL CL

Little Manor
Farm

CHAPEL LA

GORSE RD

VIEWSIDE CL

THORNTON CL

CORFE VIE

Stony
Down
Plantation

RUSHALL LA

BH21

HILLSIDE RD

HILLCREST RD

HECKFORD RD

COURTNE

TERENCE RD

1

OAK CL

CORFE VIE

Stoney Down
Farm

WATERLOO RD

FROUD WAY

PO

96

FIRSIDE RD

BROOKSIDE
PARK
HOMES

BUDDENS
MDW

Poor Common

97 A 44 B 98 C

DAIRY
CL

AMBER CL

N CL

MARIAN RD

COVENTRY

Decoy Pond

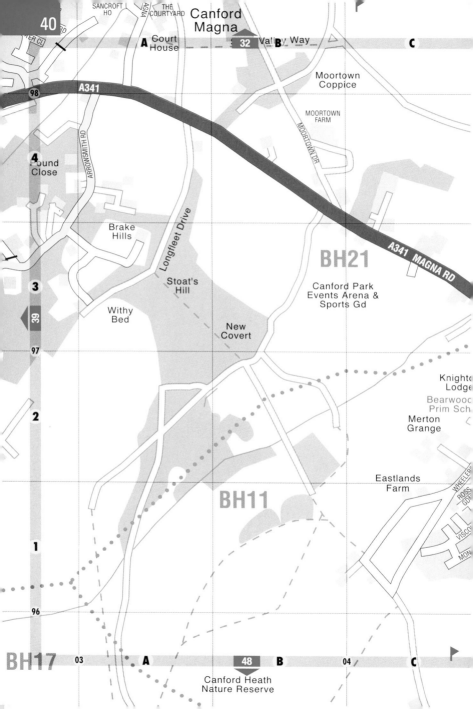

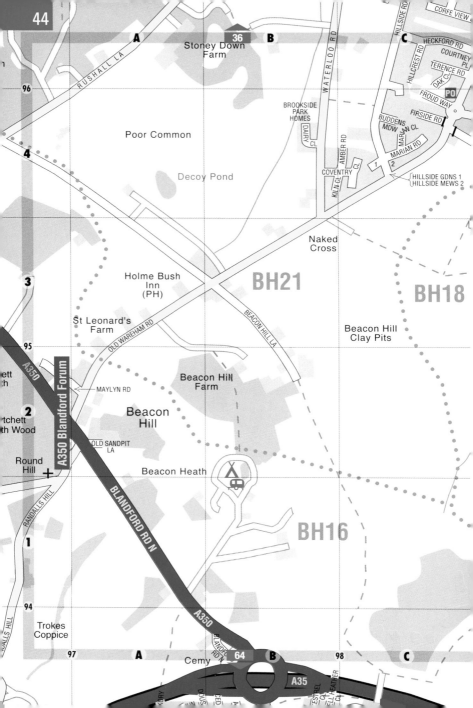

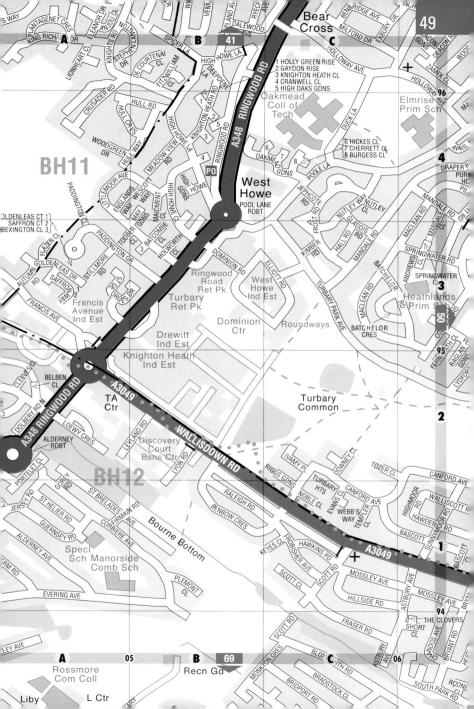

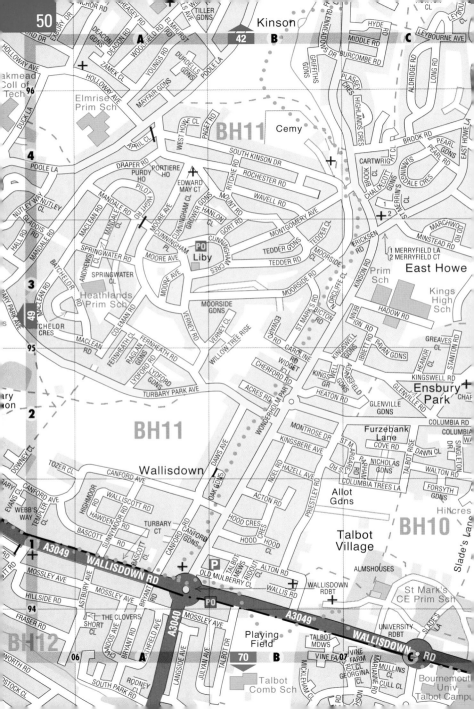

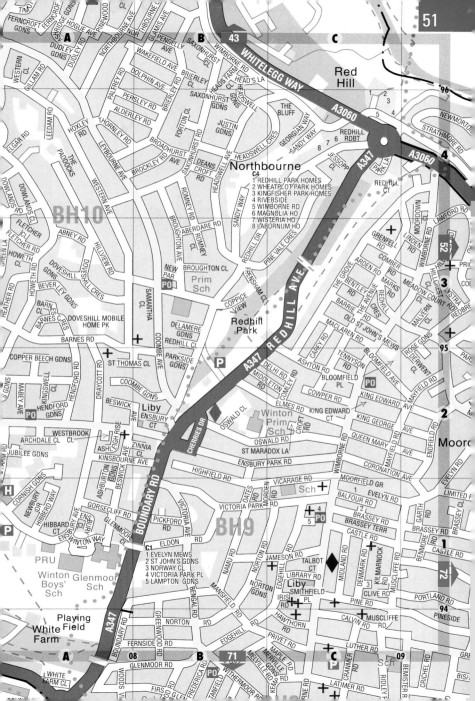

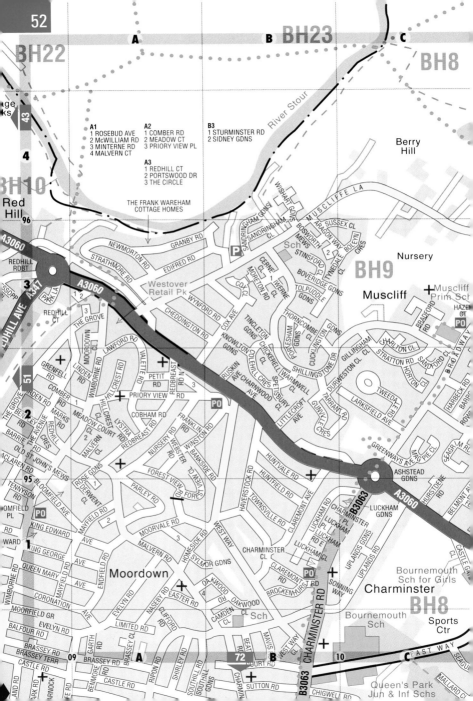

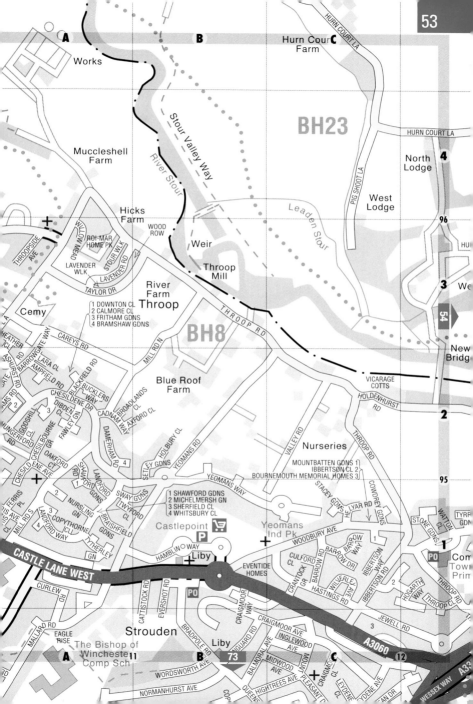

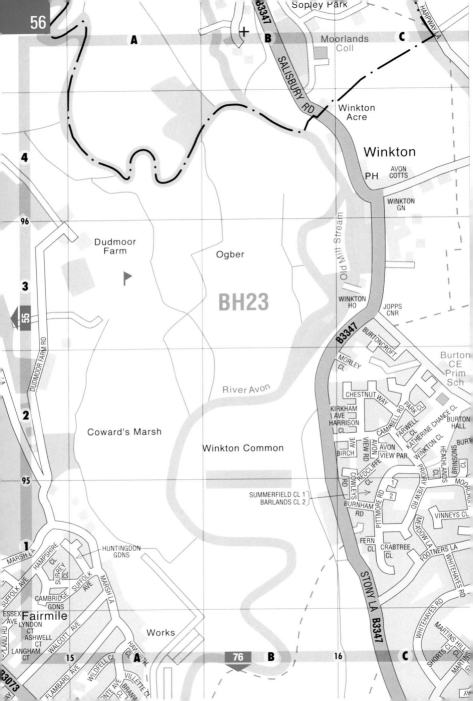

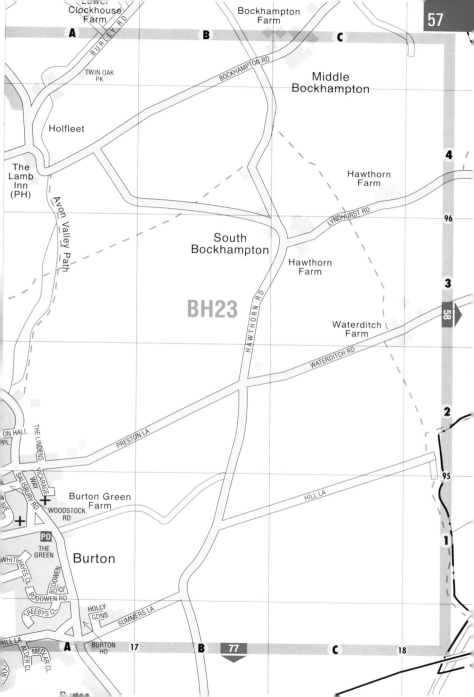

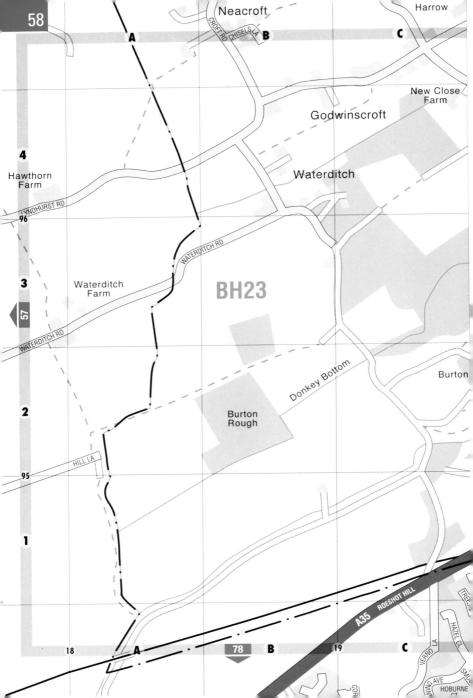

Neacroft

Harrow

A

CROFT RD CHISELS LA **B**

C

New Close
Farm

Godwinscroft

4

Waterditch

Hawthorn
Farm

YNDHURST RD

96

WATERDITCH RD

3

Waterditch
Farm

BH23

57

WATERDITCH RD

Donkey Bottom

Burton

2

Burton
Rough

95

HILL LA

1

A35 ROESHOT HILL

VERNO LA

HAZEL CL

HOBURNE

18

A

78

B

19

C

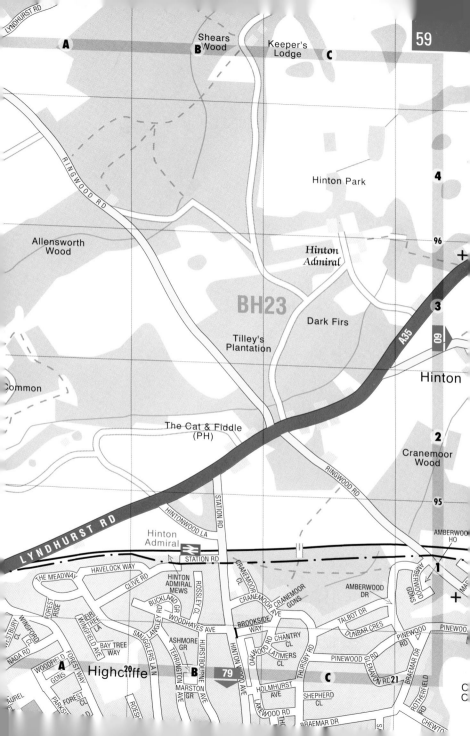

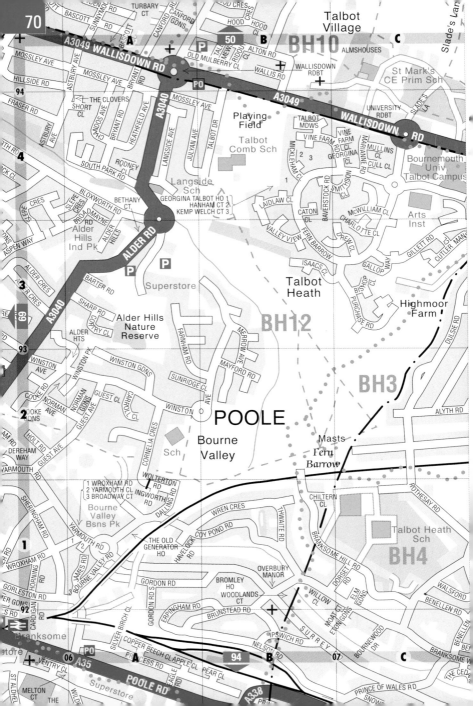

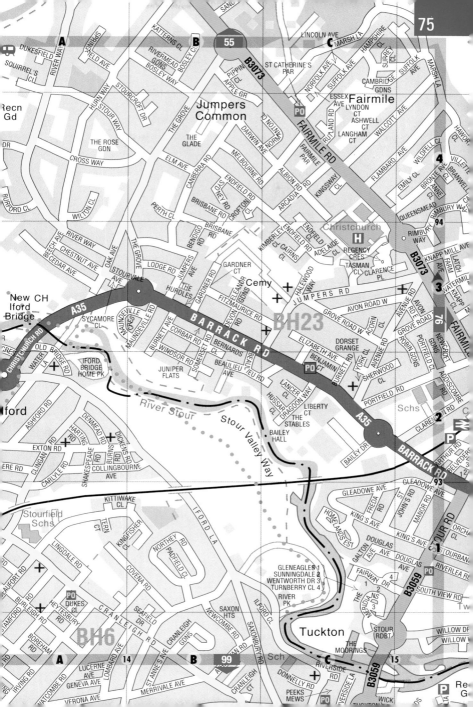

A1
1 DEVEREL CL
2 BLENHEIM CT
3 CLARENCE PL
4 OSTERLEY CT
5 TIDEMILL CL

A1
1 HOMESTOUR HO
2 ORCHARD MEWS
3 ST ANDREWS
4 RIVERLAND CT

A2
1 WINSTON CT
2 KENILWORTH CT
3 ARTHUR LA
4 MULBERRY CT
5 MITRE CT

B1
1 POUND LA
2 MILLHAMS STREET N
3 THE CLOISTERS
4 PRIORY VIEW CT
5 SILVER ST

1 TENON CT
2 CENTENARY HO

BH23

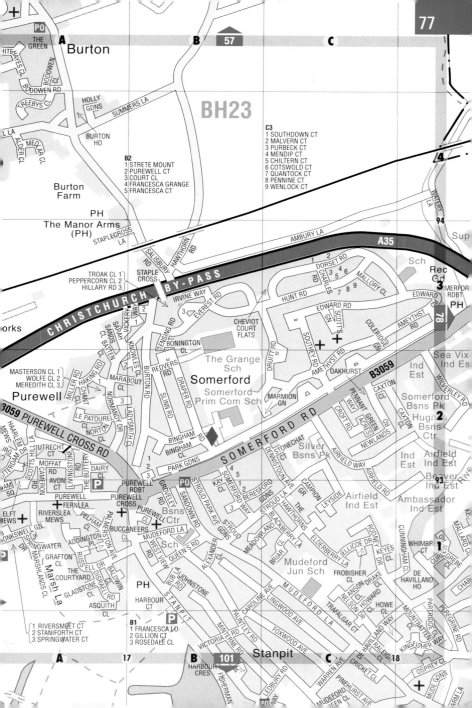

LYNDHURST RD

Hinton
Admiral
STATION RD
A HAVELOCK WAY **B** **59** **C**

THE MEADWAY
FOREST RISE
CLIVE RD
HINTON
ADMIRAL
MEWS
ROSSLEY CL
CRANEMOOR AVE
AMBERWOOD DR
ERWOOD GDNS

WESTBURY CL
WINSFORD CL
NADA RD
EIB TREE LA
WINGFIELD AVE
BAY TREE WAY
BUCKLAND GR
LANGLEY RD
WOODHAYES AVE
MILVERTON CL
BROOKSIDE WAY
CRANEMOOR GDNS
TALBOT DR
DUNBAR CRES
PINEWOOD RD
PINEWOOD

FOREST WAY
WOODFIELD GDNS
FOREST CL
PARKSIDE
FIELD WAY
SMUGGLERS LA N
ASHMORE GR
TERRINGTON AVE
HURSTBOURNE AVE
OAKWOOD RD
CHANTRY CL
LATIMERS CL
THURSBY RD
PINEWOOD RD
GLENAVON RD
BRAEMAR RD
CROTHERFIELD
Chewton
Common

LAUREL CL
BALFOUR CL
FARMDENE CL
RIDGEFIELD GDNS
NEA CL
HARRIERS CL
MARSTON GR
HINTON WOOD AVE
HOLMHURST AVE
LAKWOOD RD
SHEPHERD CL
BRAEMAR DR
CHEWTON COMMON RD
4
94
HASLEMERE PL

Highcliffe
Sch
MOONRAKERS WAY
BIRCHWOOD CL
FIRSHILL
CARISBROOKE WAY
DENHAM DR
Sch
GREENWAYS
KINGSBERE GDNS
HASLEMERE AVE
MERLEY DR

SMUGGLERS LA N
ROWAN CL
ROWAN DR
SMUGGLERS LAS
NEA RD
AMBERLEY CL
COLEMERE GDNS
FELTON CRES
HASLEMERE AVE
IMBER DR
BH23
Highcliffe
3

ULFLAND DR
ULFLAND HO
PRESTON WAY
KNIGHTWOOD CL
COPSE WAY
NORLEYWOOD
QUINTIN CL
JULIA CL
EARLS CL
SUDAN WAY
ANGELINE CL
CRISPIN CL
GERMAINE CL
GREENWAYS
JESMOND AVE
BUCE CL
80

BARNFELD
RNFORD WAY
BURN SIDE
CURZON
WOODLAND WAY
KILMINGTON WAY
LYME CRES
PO
P

IZABETH GDNS
ST GEORGE'S CL
PINE CRES
SILVER WAY
CASTLE AVE
ABBOTS CL
A337
WORT

SHELLEY HILL
HIGH PINES
SHELLEY HAMLETS
SOMERFORD CT
CH
ROTHESAY DR
LYMINGTON RD
OAKLEIGH WAY
MAPLE CL
RANELAGH RD
BEACON DR
REDAN CL
WHARNCLIFFE RD
ELMWOOD WAY
WHARNCLIFFE GDNS
WATERF

riars
Cliff
ER RD
Highcliffe
Castle
P
ARUNDEL WAY
1 2 3
BEACON CT 1
HARRINGTON CT 2
WHARNCLIFFE CT 3
MARINA CT
PALMA CT
High
2

Groynes
93
Groyn

1

CHURCH

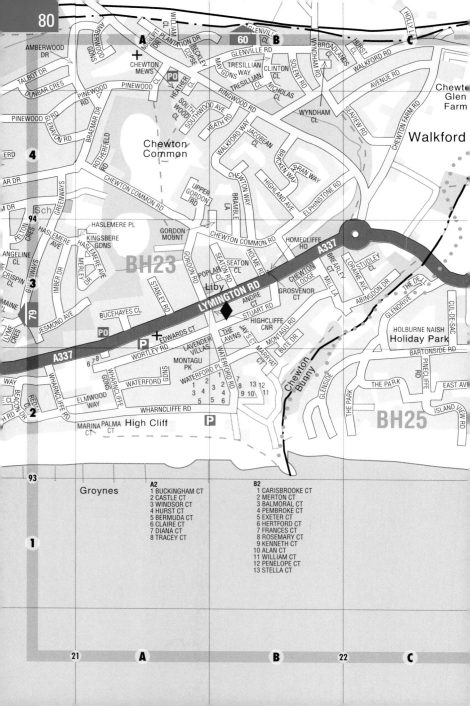

WICK CL
WICK DR
HAMILTON WAY
GORE RD
CETT RD
FIELD
GORE GRANGE
COMPTON RD
Recn Ctr

61

PH
CULVER RD
WELL CL
MILTON MEAD
The Arnewood Sch Cemy
HOBART RD
CHURCH LA
OLD MILTON RD

P

OLD MILTON RD
FURZE CFT
DAWKING AVE
WAY
GARD

CONNAUGHT CL 7
CEDAR GDNS 8
INGLEGREEN CL 9
SOUTHLAWNS WLK 10
PRESTWOOD CL 11
CHILTERN CL 12
CHAUCOMBE PL 13
THE DORMERS 14
MIDDLETON MEWS 15
ELEANOR CT 16

King George
MOBILE HOME PK
OLD MILTON RD
Arts Ctr
New Milton Schs

Old Milton

GN
LYMINGTON RD
A337

4

Chewton Glen Hotel

CHRISTCHURCH RD

DUNFORD CL
PO THE PARADE
14
13 15
16 CL
LAKE
BOUVERIE

MOORE RD
MANOR FARM CL

CHRISTCHURCH RD
A337

DUNFORD CL
CHILTERN DR
PENN CL
7
8
CHILTERN DR
WENDOVER CL
PARK RD
10
12
SOUTHERN OAKS
ALBANY CL
SOUTHERN LA
MOAT LA
FRIARS WLK

94

FARM LA N

82

GLEN CL
EAST CL
KNIGHTON PK
BYRON
SEAR RD
CHILTERN DR
11
HEATH
HWOOD AVE
ELDON CL
ELDON AVE
THREE ACRE DR
PARKLAND DR
SOUTHERN LA
WOOD LAWN
MOORLAND AVE
BARTON DR
SUNNYFIELD
HLANDS

3

HURST CL
BRANSHAW WAY
STUDLEY CT
FIELD PL
BURLEY
ELLINGHM RD
SOPLEY CL
BOLDRE CL
NEACROFT CL
WESTERN AVE
CARLTON AVE
BARTON LA
SEACROFT AVE
PINE CL
COASTGUARD COTTS
WAVENDON AVE
KEYSWORTH AVE
HENGISTBURY RD
HEATHY CL
BARTON WAY
ARNOLDS CL
BARTON COURT AVE
DILLY LA
FARM LA S
BARTON CROFT

BH25

LWOOD WAY
KBOURNE GDNS
CENT

SEAFIELD RD
6
BLYTHSWOOD CT

VECTIS RD
NAISH RD
FAIRFIELD RD
SEAFIELD CL
CLEEVE HO
WHITE KNIGHTS

SALENT RD
CLEVELAND CL
PURBECK RD
POWERSCOURT RD
CLIFFE RD
CHANNEL CT
WOODLANDS RD
SEAWARD AVE
GROVE RD

MARINE CT
MARINE DRIVE W
CLIFFE RD
BARTON WOOD RD
BROOK HO
CHRISTCHURCH BAY RD
BEACH AVE DR
4
3

SOUTHCLIFFE RD

JANIRED CT
BARTON HO
WHITE HORSES
SANDMARTIN CL
CRESCENT DR
5
GROVE RD
MARINE

HARBOUR CT
MARINE DR
CLIFF CRES
1
93

Barton Cliff
PEARCE-SMITH CT
P
FIRST MARINE AVE
DOLPHIN MANS

Groynes
PO
P

WESTMINSTER CT 1
CRESCENT CT 2
MARINE PROSPECT 3
MARINE POINT 4
BARTON CHASE 5
BRACKLESHAM PL 6

Barton on Sea

A 23
B
C 24

A
23
B
C
24

1

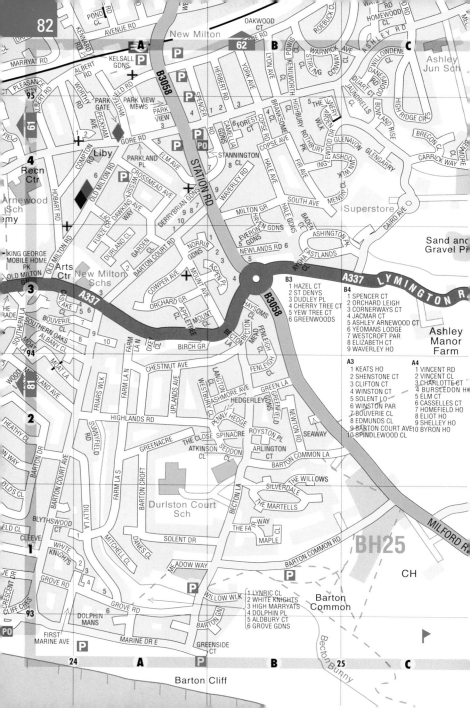

A New Milton **62 B** **C**

Ashley Jun Sch

B3
1 HAZEL CT
2 ST DENYS
3 DUDLEY PL
4 CHERRY TREE CT
5 YEW TREE CT
6 GREENWOODS

B4
1 SPENCER CT
2 ORCHARD LEIGH
3 CORNERWAYS CT
4 JACMAR CT
5 ASHLEY ARNEWOOD CT
6 YEOMANS LODGE
7 WESTCROFT PAR
8 ELIZABETH CT
9 WAVERLEY HO

A3
1 KEATS HO
2 SHENSTONE CT
3 CLIFTON CT
4 WINSTON CT
5 SOLENT LO
6 WINSTON PAR
7 BOUVERIE CL
8 EDMUNDS CL
9 BARTON COURT AVE
10 SPINDLEWOOD CL

A4
1 VINCENT HO
2 VINCENT CL
3 CHARLOTTE CT
4 BURSLEDON HO
5 ELM CT
6 CASSELLES CT
7 HOMEFIELD HO
8 ELIOT HO
9 SHELLEY HO
10 BYRON HO

Ashley Manor Farm

Sand and Gravel Pi

Superstore

BH25

CH

Barton Common

1 LYNRIC CL
2 WHITE KNIGHTS
3 HIGH MARRYATS
4 DOLPHIN PL
5 ALDBURY CT
6 GROVE GDNS

Durlston Court Sch

24 **A** **B** **25** **C**

Barton Cliff

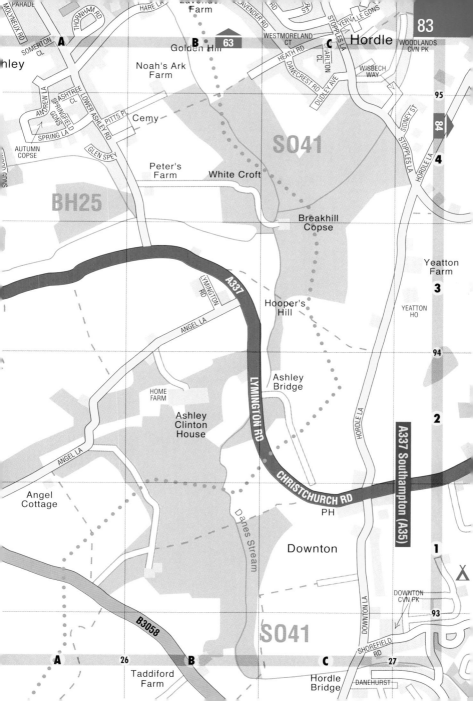

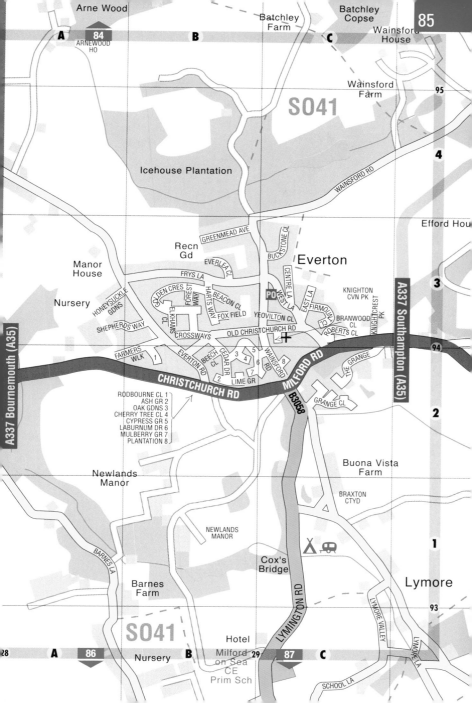

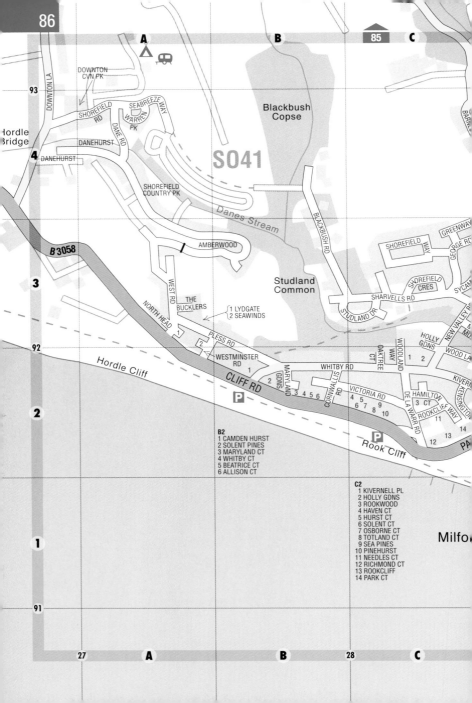

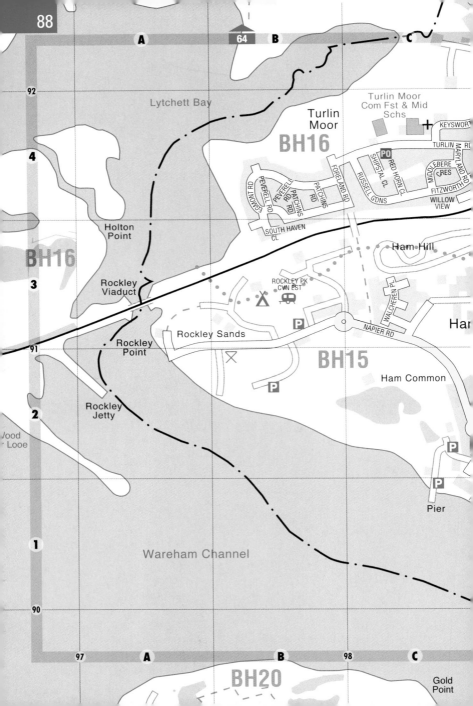

64

A   B

Lytchett Bay

92

Turlin Moor
Com Fst & Mid
Schs

Turlin
Moor

KEYSWOR

BH16

TURLIN RD

4

MARYLAND RD

PO   RED HORN CL

MIDDLEBERE

CRES

SHIPSTAL CL

FITZWORTH

RUSSELL GDNS

WILLOW
VIEW

CANNOT RD

PEVERELL RD

PEVERELL
RD

PATCHINS RD

PATCHINS
RD

FORELAND RD

Holton
Point

BH16

3

SOUTH HAVEN
CL

Ham Hill

ROCKLEY PK
CVN EST

Rockley
Viaduct

WALCHEREN PL

P

Rockley Sands

NAPIER RD

Ha

P

91

Rockley
Point

BH15

Ham Common

P

2

Rockley
Jetty

Vood
Looe

P

1

Wareham Channel

P

Pier

90

A   B   C

97   98

BH20

Gold
Point

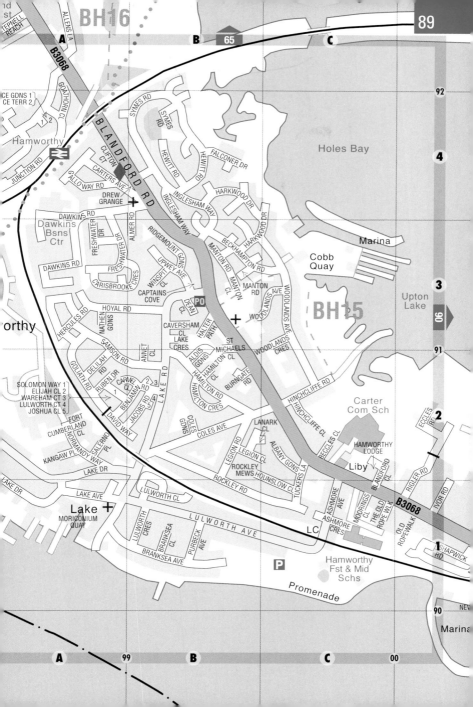

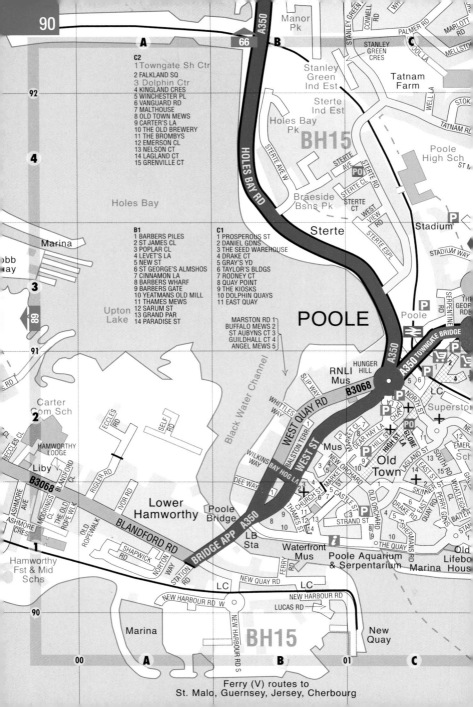

C2
1 Towngate Sh Ctr
2 FALKLAND SQ
3 Dolphin Ctr
4 KINGLAND CRES
5 WINCHESTER PL
6 VANGUARD RD
7 MALTHOUSE
8 OLD TOWN MEWS
9 CARTER'S LA
10 THE OLD BREWERY
11 THE BROMBYS
12 EMERSON CL
13 NELSON CT
14 LAGLAND CT
15 GRENVILLE CT

B1
1 BARBERS PILES
2 ST JAMES CL
3 POPLAR CL
4 LEVET'S LA
5 NEW ST
6 ST GEORGE'S ALMSHOS
7 CINNAMON LA
8 BARBERS WHARF
9 BARBERS GATE
10 YEATMANS OLD MILL
11 THAMES MEWS
12 SARUM ST
13 GRAND PAR
14 PARADISE ST

C1
1 PROSPEROUS ST
2 DANIEL GDNS
3 THE SEED WAREHOUSE
4 DRAKE CT
5 GRAY'S YD
6 TAYLOR'S BLDGS
7 RODNEY CT
8 QUAY POINT
9 THE KIOSKS
10 DOLPHIN QUAYS
11 EAST QUAY

MARSTON RD 1
BUFFALO MEWS 2
ST AUBYNS CT 3
GUILDHALL CT 4
ANGEL MEWS 5

Manor Pk

Stanley Green Ind Est

Sterte Ind Est

Holes Bay Pk

BH15

Tatnam Farm

Poole High Sch

Stadium

Holes Bay

Sterte

Marina

Cobb ay

Upton Lake

POOLE

RNLI Mus

Poole

Hunger Hill

Superstor

Carter Com Sch

Black Water Channel

Old Town

HAMWORTHY LODGE

Liby

B3068

Lower Hamworthy

Poole Bridge

Mus

New Orchard

Poole Aquarium & Serpentarium

Old Lifebo Marina Hous

Hamworthy Fst & Mid Schs

BLANDFORD RD

BRIDGE APP A350

LB Sta

Waterfront Mus

Marina

BH15

New Quay

Ferry (V) routes to
St. Malo, Guernsey, Jersey, Cherbourg

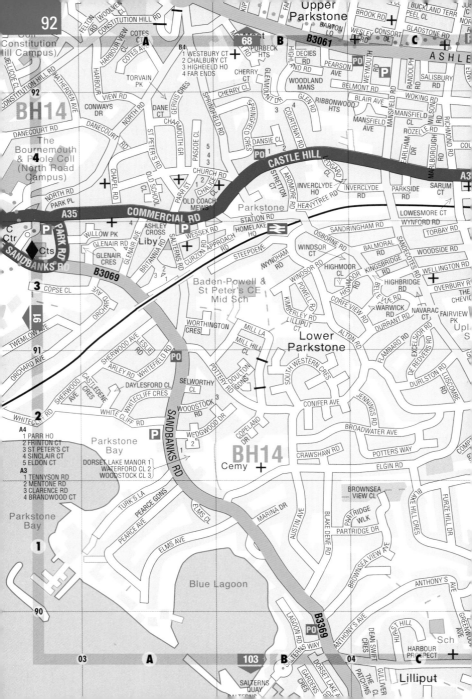

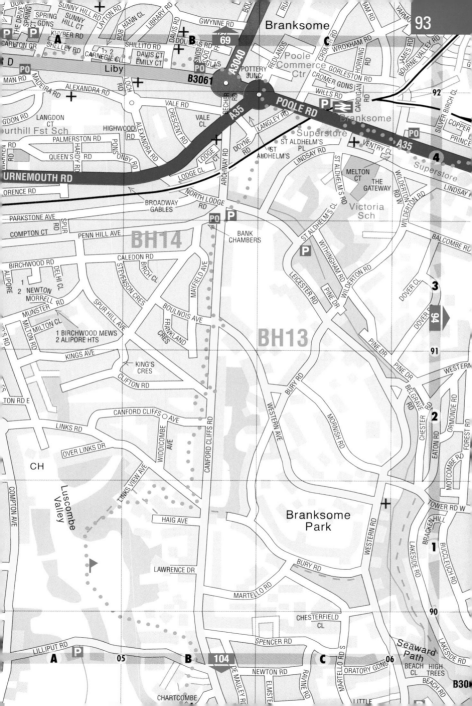

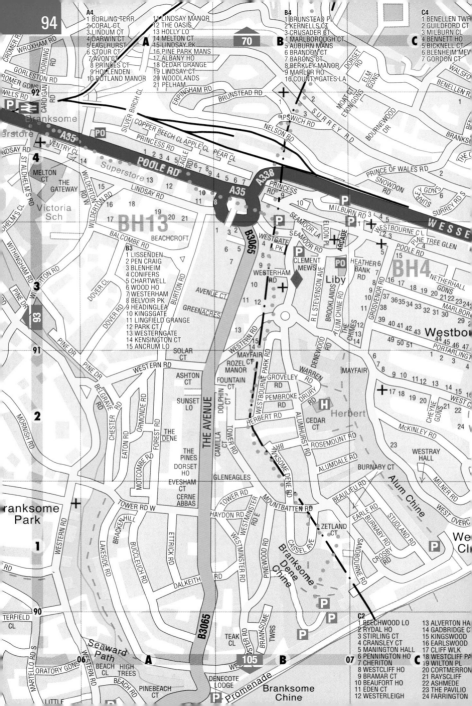

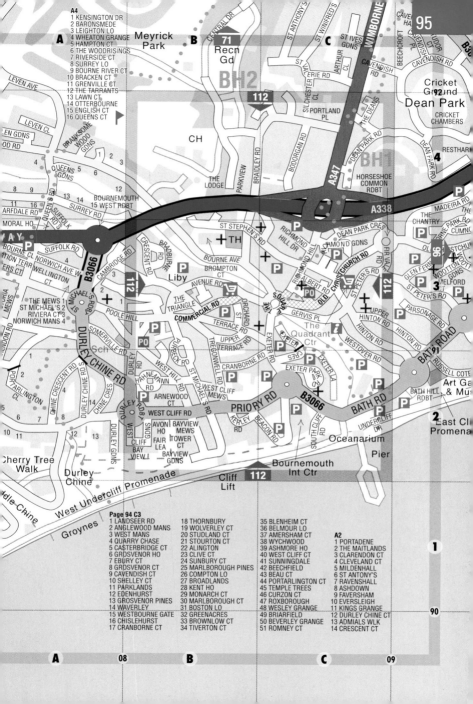

95

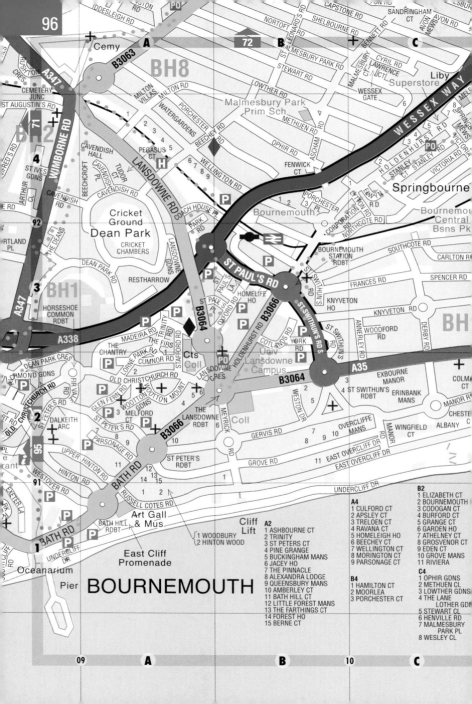

A3
1 WILLOW LO
2 GROSVENOR CT
3 PINE MANS
4 VALE MONS
5 KNOLE CT
6 COURTLEIGH MANOR
7 GORSECLIFF CT

B2
1 ST JAMES'S
2 MARINA CT
3 MERMAID CT
4 SAN REMO TWRS
5 MARINA TWRS

B3
1 DONOUGHMORE RD
2 RANDOLPH RD
3 THE CRESCENT
4 CARNARVON RD
5 Royal Arc
6 Soveriegn Ctr
7 HORACE RD
8 ARGYLL MANS
9 FAIRHAVEN CT

B4
1 ST ANN'S CT
2 ST GEORGE'S CT
3 ST DAVID'S CT
4 ST JOHN'S CT

C2
1 WOLLSTONECRAFT RD
2 CLEASBY GRANGE
3 LAVERSTOCK
4 OCEAN HTS
5 CARLINFORD

C3
1 CLIFTON CT
2 HEATHCOTE CT
3 GRANTLEY RD
4 THESSALY CT
5 ST GEORGES MANS
6 WATKIN RD

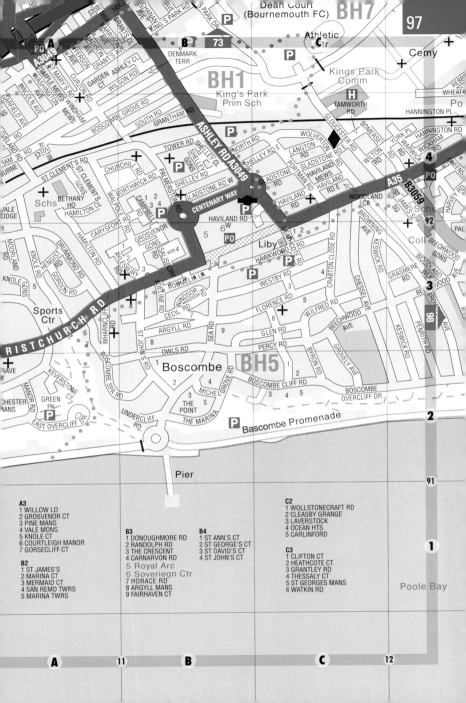

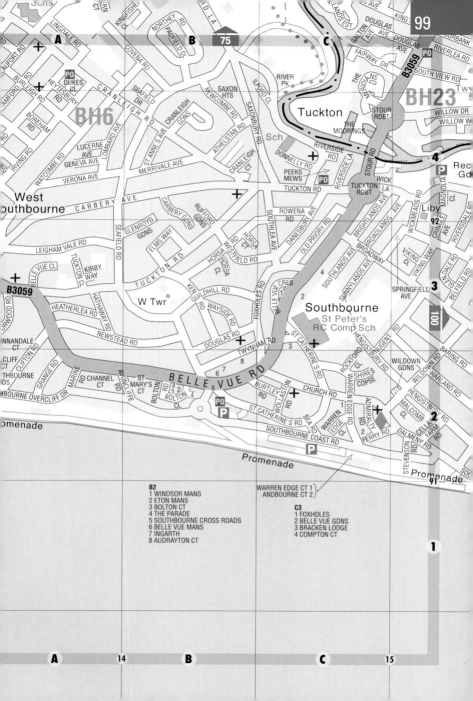

BH23

BH6

Tuckton

West Southbourne

Southbourne
St Peter's RC Comp Sch

B3059

Promenade

Promenade

B2
1 WINDSOR MANS
2 ETON MANS
3 BOLTON CT
4 THE PARADE
5 SOUTHBOURNE CROSS ROADS
6 BELLE VUE MANS
7 INGARTH
8 AUDRAYTON CT

WARREN EDGE CT 1
ANDBOURNE CT 2

C3
1 FOXHOLES
2 BELLE VUE GDNS
3 BRACKEN LODGE
4 COMPTON CT

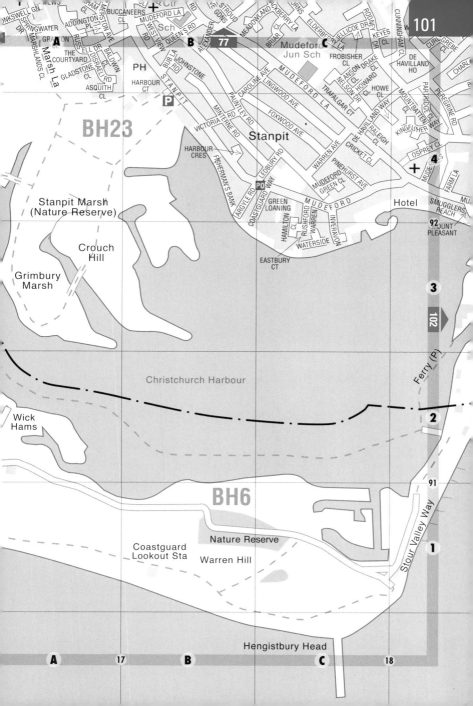

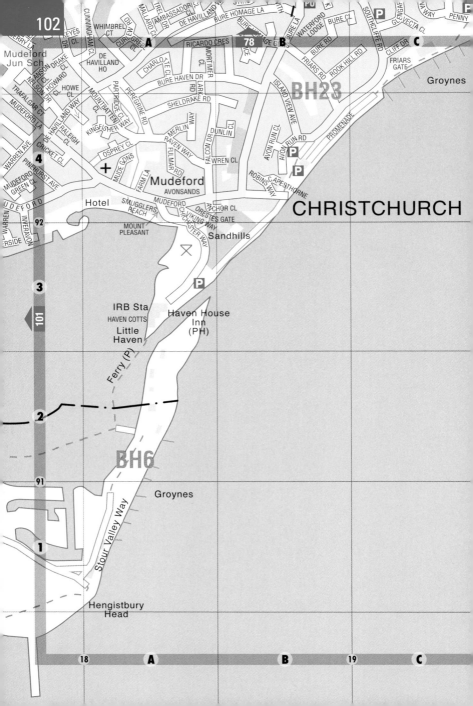

Mudeford
Jun Sch

BH23

Groynes

FRIARS
GATE

CHRISTCHURCH

Mudeford

AVONSANDS

Hotel

Sandhills

MOUNT
PLEASANT

IRB Sta

HAVEN COTTS

Little
Haven

Haven House
Inn
(PH)

Ferry (P)

BH6

Groynes

Stour Valley Way

Hengistbury
Head

CUNNINGHAM CL
WHIMBREL
CT
CURLEW CL
DE
HAVILLAND
HO
MALLARD CL
TREGONWELL
AMBASSADOR CL
DE HAVILLAND
BURE HOMAGE LA
BURE HOMAGE CL
SMITH
PU
K
GLENGA
VA WAY
PENNY
RICARDO CRES
78
WATERFORD
LODGE
BURE RD
BURE CL
SOUTHCLIFFE RD
CLIFF DR
EVECTA CL

CHARLOTTE CL
BURE HAVEN DR
MORTIMER
CL
ARK RD
FRIARS RD
ROOK HILL RD

HOWE
CL
PARTRIDGE CL
PEREGRINE RD
SHELDRAKE RD
ISLAND VIEW AVE

MOUNT BATTEN WAY
MERLIN
WAY
RAVEN WAY
FULMAR RD
DUNLIN
FALCON DR
WREN CL
AVON RUN CL
AVON RUN RD
PROMENADE

KINGFISHER WAY
OSPREY CL
MUDE GDNS
FARM LA
ROBINS
WAY
C APESTHORNE

MUDEFORD LA
RALEIGH
DE HAVILLAND
CRICKET CL
ANCHOR CL
ORESTES GATE
VIKING WAY

WARREN AVE
MUDEFORD
GREEN CL
PINEHURST AVE
SMUGGLERS
REACH
MUDEFORD
CHESTER WAY

UDEFORD
INVERALON
ERSIDE
WARREN

EYES
RANSON
NELSON CL
HOWARD
DRAKE CL
TRAFALGAR CL

PEARCE AV
ELMS AVE
AUSTIN
KE DENE RD
PARTRIDGE DR
CRES
LD DR
HILL AVE

A
B
92
BROWNSEA VIEW RD
C

B3369
ANTHONY'S AVE

Blue Lagoon

90

THE CAPSTANS 1
LAGOON CL 2
SALTERNS CT 3
BROWNSEA CT 4

LAGOON RD
PO
2
4
HURST HILL
DEAN SWIFT CRES
FAIRWAY RD
GREENWOOD AVE
COMPTON AVE
LILLIPUT RD

SALTERNS WAY
Sch
Harbour Prospect
LAGADO CL
4

GARDENS CRES
DORSET LAKE AVE
GARDENS FIRST LA
THE CL PATCHINS
GULLIVER
Lilliput

SALTERNS QUAY
SALTERNS POINT
AVALON
BH14
Luscombe Valle

Pier
P
Marina
SANDBANKS RD
MOUNT RD
BINGHAM AVE

Lifeboat Sta
Landing
WENTWORTH
CRICHEL
MINTERNE RD
3

Stage
COOLHURST
MINTERNE GRANGE
104

WITLEY
HARBOUR WATCH
LITTLE CT
MOUNT GRACE DR
HONEYWOOD
MOUNT RD
BR

DAYTONA
ALINGTON HO
ALINGTON RD
ALINGTON CL
89

Pier
B3369
SHORE RD

2

Poole Harbour

Main Channel

1

Ferry (P)
(April to September)

88

wnsea
sland
BH13
BH13
BANKS RD
B3369

3
A
B
04
106
C

Piers
P

Branksome Park

A **93** B C

HILL AVE
MAIG AVE
LAWRENCE DR
BURY RD
MARTELLO RD
WESTERN AVE

ANTHONY'S AVE
FAIRWAY RD
GREENWOOD AVE
COMPTON AVE
90
Sch
HARBOUR PROSPECT
CHESTERFIELD CL
SPENCER RD
BH13

LILLIPUT RD

illiput **4**
LAGADO CL
MOUNT RD
BINGHAM AVE

BH14

Luscombe Valley

Canford Cliffs

Compton Acres Gdns

CARISBROOKE

CHARTCOMBE
THE GLEN

CANFORD CLIFFS RD
DE MAULEY RD
DE MAULEY CT
MOORFIELDS RD
NEWTON RD
ELMSTEAD RD
RAVINE RD
ORATORY G'
CHAUCER RD
WESTLANDS DR
PO

MARTELLO RD S
LITTLE CT
1 2

WESTERN RD **B30**

MICHEL
MINTERNE RD
MINTERNE GRANGE
TLEY
HARBOUR WATCH
LITTLE CT
3
ALINGTON HO
ALINGTON RD
HONEYWOOD
MOUNT GRACE DR
ALINGTON CL
THE DRIVE
BRUDENELE AVE
DORNIE RD
NAIRN RD
INVERNESS RD
CANFORD CRES

HAVEN RD

MACANDREW RD
BODLEY RD
BEAUMONT RD
BESSBOROUGH RD
CLIFF DR
MAXWELL RD
ESPLANADE
MERIDEN CL
THE CIRCLE
RAVINE CT

KINGSLAND CT
HERITAGE CT
4 5
OWLSHO
MARTELLO TWRS
Canford Cliff

103
B3369

89

SHORE RD
B3369
WATERS EDGE
BRUDENELL RD
HARBOUR CL
B3065

BH13
HAVEN RD

FLAGHEAD RD
ST CLAIR RD
FLAGHEAD CHINE RD
CLIFF DR

Canford Cliff Chine

St Ann's
H
Flag Head Chine
FLAGHEAD

2

HIVE GDNS
VISTA MARINA
CHADDESLEY GLEN
CORFE
LITTLE FOSTERS

Promenade

C4
1 KENILWORTH CT
2 BRACKENS WAY
3 STONELEIGH
4 BRANKSOME CT
5 MARTELLO HO

1

SHORE RD
CHADDESLEY WOOD RD

Poole Head

C3
1 MERROW CHASE
2 CANFORD PL
3 RIVIERA CT
4 IMPERIAL CT
5 RAVINE GDNS
6 KILLOCK
7 FINESHADE
8 SEA POINT
9 TREETOPS
10 PINE LODGE
11 LEYTON CONYERS
12 STANTON LACY
13 BURNAGE CT

1 HARBOUR CT
2 HAVENHURST
3 CHADDESLEY GRANGE
4 CHADDESLEY PINES
5 CANFORD CT

SANTOY

88

BANKS RD **B3369**

106 A 05 B C

P

West Cliff

BH4

BH13

B3065

LAKESIDE RD

BRACK

BUCCLEUCH RD

ETRICK RD

WESTMINSTER RD

WEST

PINEWOOD RD

CASSEL AVE

ZETLAND CT

NABY RD

CROSBY RD

LAND RD

SANDBOURNE RD

DALKEITH RD

THE AVENUE

RD

Branksome Dene Chine

94

BUCCLEUCH RD

LAKESIDE RD

WESTMINSTER RD

BRANKSOME TWRS

TEAK CL

eaward Path

BEACH CL

HIGH TREES

BEACH RD

DENECOTE LODGE

Promenade

PINEBEACH CT

PINECLIFF RD

Branksome Chine

Liby

UTH DGE

A

B

C

90

4

3

89

2

88

A

B

07

C

1

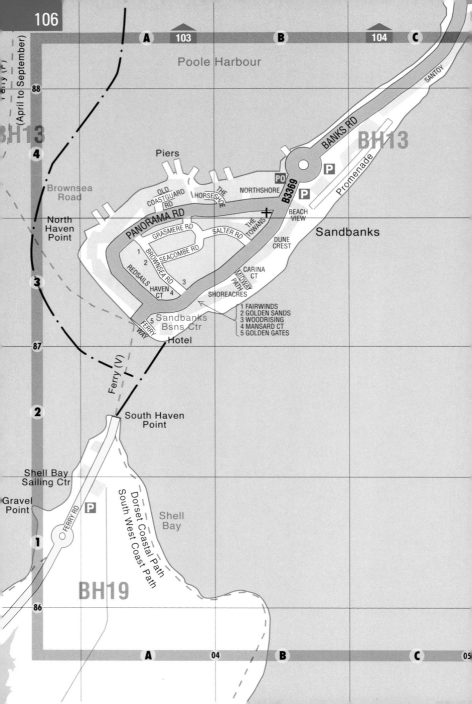

Poole Harbour

Ferry (F) (April to September)

BH13

BH13

Piers

Brownsea Road

OLD COASTGUARD RD
THE HORSESHOE
PANORAMA RD
North Haven Point
GRASMERE RD
BROWNSEA RD
SEACOMBE RD
REDSAILS
HAVEN CT
FERRY WAY
SALTER RD
THE TOWANS
MIDWAY PATH
SHOREACRES
CARINA CT
DUNE CREST
BEACH VIEW

NORTHSHORE
PO
P
P
BANKS RD
B3369
Promenade
SANTOY

Sandbanks

Sandbanks Bsns Ctr
Hotel

1 FAIRWINDS
2 GOLDEN SANDS
3 WOODRISING
4 MANSARD CT
5 GOLDEN GATES

Ferry (V)

South Haven Point

Shell Bay Sailing Ctr

Gravel Point

FERRY RD
P

Dorset Coastal Path
South West Coast Path

Shell Bay

BH19

103

104

A   B   C

88

4

3

87

2

86

1

A   04   B   C   05

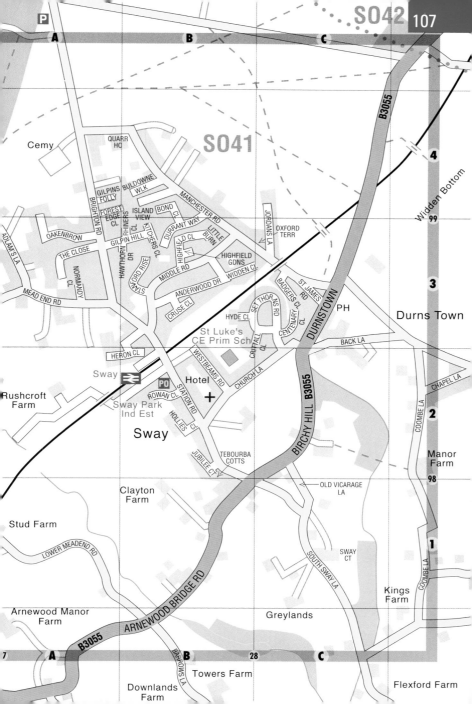

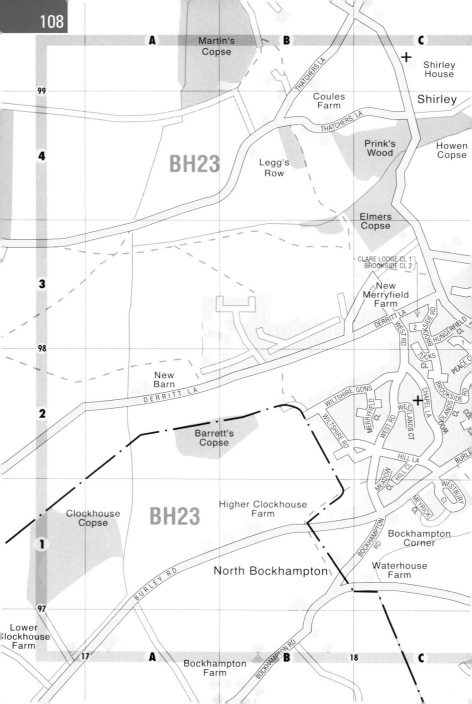

A Martin's Copse **B** **C**

Shirley House

THATCHERS LA

Coules Farm

99

THATCHERS LA

Shirley

4

BH23

Legg's Row

Prink's Wood

Howen Copse

Elmers Copse

CLARE LODGE CL 1
BROOKSIDE CL 2

3

New Merryfield Farm

DERRITT LA

WEST RD

BROOKSIDE RD

HUNGERFIELD CL

98

TUCKS CL

2

1

PEACE C

New Barn

DERRITT LA

WILTSHIRE GDNS

CHAPEL LA

BROOKSIDE RD

WOODLANDS CL

COL

2

WILTSHIRE RD

MERRYFIELD CL

WEST RD

WESTLANDS CT

BURLE

Barrett's Copse

HILL LA

MEADOW CL

HILL CL

WESTBURY CL

Higher Clockhouse Farm

MEVRICK CL

Clockhouse Copse

BH23

BOCKHAMPTON RD

Bockhampton Corner

1

North Bockhampton

Waterhouse Farm

BURLEY RD

97

Lower Clockhouse Farm

17 **A** Bockhampton Farm **B** **18** **C**

BOCKHAMPTON RD

Chordle
Walhampton Sch

Pike Lake

A **B** **C**

MARSH LA

UNDERSHORE

MARRAM CL

Lymington River

WILLIAM RD

WALHAMPTON HILL

B3054

1 SEATON CL
2 FROMOND CL
3 JONATHAN CL

ST CYRES MEMORIAL COTTS

BRICKFIELD

Mon

Walhampton

Lower Buckland

A3
1 LIME TREE HO
2 BARFIELDS CT
3 COURTLANDS
4 CARLTON HO

MONUMENT LA

CLINTON RD

OLD FARMHOUSE MEWS

BUCKLAND CT

TITHE BARN

BUCKLAND VIEW

PRIVATE RD

FAIRLEA RD

Rehabilitation Unit

BROOMFIELD LA

EAST HILL

LC

BRIDGE RD

B3054

WATERLOO RD

1 RIVER CT
2 Riverside Bsns Pk
3 ADELAIDE CT
4 BRITANNIA PL
5 HAMILTON MEWS
6 TRAFALGAR PL

4

96

3

H

HILLCROFT CL

MADRISA CT

BRUNSWICK CT

Libys

GOSPORT ST

STATION ST 4

MILL LA

Lymington Town

ISLAND POINT

UNDERSHORE RD

FERRYPOINT

SOUTH BADDESLEY RD

P

P

P

P

P

P

PARISH CT

EMSWORTH RD

SCHOOL LA

Mus

NEW ST MEWS

CANNON ST

CANNON HO

ANGEL MEWS

EARLEY CT

HAYDENS CT

ELGAR CT

QUAY

ST THOMAS'S ST

QUAY ST

OLD QUAY

CAPTAIN'S ROW

NELSON PL

ADMIRALS CT

Marina

P

Lymington Pier

Ferry Terminal

Country Club

2

Lymington River

P

P

RED HOUSE MEWS

RASHLEY MEWS

PILGRIM PL

SOLENT MEAD

HIGH ST

ASHLEY LA

GROVE

PASTURES

WEST HAYES

GROVE RD

SOUTH ST

BATH RD

QUEEN KATHERINE RD

FLUSHARDS

SOLENT CL

BATH RD

MONMOUTH CT

THOMAS'S ST

RASHLEY MEWS

CHURCH LA

BINGHAM DR

GROVE PL

WATERFORD CL

SOLENT AVE

SPRINGFIELD CL

FAIRFIELD CL

THE CLOISTERS

COURTENAY PL

DANIELL'S WLK

DANIELL'S CL

RIVERS REACH 1
WINTON CL 2

MAYFLOWER

P

P

IRB Sta

95

Yacht Haven

1

KEYS MEAD

LOCKERLEY CL

NEWENHAM RD

DANIELL'S MEAD

PYRFORD MEWS

AMBLESIDE RD

OLD ORCHARDS

BRAMLEY CL

OAKLANDS

MARINERS

BROAD LA

WATERFORD LA

BROOK RD

BURGARD GR

KING'S STANLEY RD

STANLEY RD

SPRING RD

KINGSFIELD

WESTFIELD RD

KING'S SALTERN RD

P0

A1
1 BELMORE HO
2 SALTERNE HO
3 PYRFORD GDNS
4 VICTORIA PL
5 GOLD MEAD CL
6 PEARMAIN DR
7 PEARTREE CT
8 PIPPIN CL
9 CHURCH MEAD
10 WOODSIDE CL

VITRE GDNS

TRANMERE CL

BRACKENS WAY

ALL SAINTS RD

WOODSIDE AVE

WOODSIDE LA

VINEY RD

De La Warr House

NORMANDY LA

COASTGUARD COTTS

B1
1 WORCESTER PL
2 BROADMEAD CL
3 RUSSET CL
4 MONKS CT
5 CONFERENCE PL

Woodside

A **B** **C**

33

Normandy Farm

Waterford

NORMANDY LA

Scale: 7 inches to 1 mile

0 — 110 yards — 220 yards
0 — 125 m — 250 m

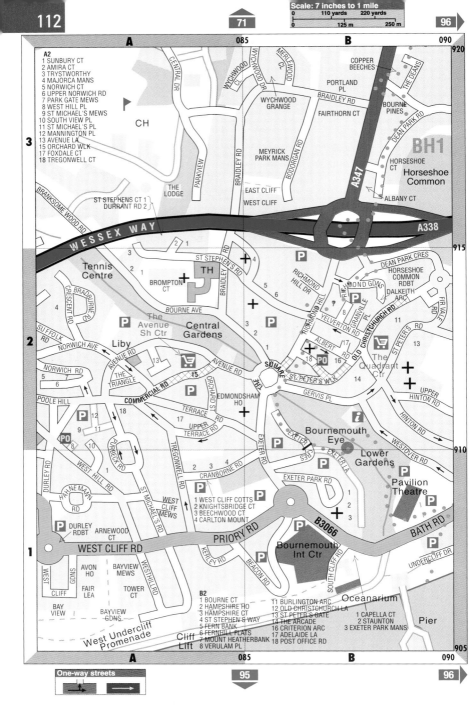

A2
1 SUNBURY CT
2 AMIRA CT
3 TRYSTWORTHY
4 MAJORCA MANS
5 NORWICH CT
6 UPPER NORWICH RD
7 PARK GATE MEWS
8 WEST HILL PL
9 ST MICHAEL'S MEWS
10 SOUTH VIEW PL
11 ST MICHAEL'S PL
12 MANNINGTON PL
13 AVENUE LA
15 ORCHARD WLK
17 FOXDALE CT
18 TREGONWELL CT

B2
1 BOURNE CT
2 HAMPSHIRE HO
3 HAMPSHIRE CT
4 ST STEPHEN'S WAY
5 FERN BANK
6 FERNHILL FLATS
7 MOUNT HEATHERBANK
8 VERULAM PL
11 BURLINGTON ARC
12 OLD CHRISTCHURCH LA
13 ST PETER'S GATE
14 THE ARCADE
15 CRITERION ARC
16 ADELAIDE LA
17 POST OFFICE RD
18 POST OFFICE RD

1 CAPELLA CT
2 STAUNTON
3 EXETER PARK MANS

CH
BH1
Horseshoe Common

COPPER BEECHES
THE DEANS
PORTLAND PL
BRAIDLEY RD
BOURNE PINES
FAIRTHORN CT
DEAN PARK RD
HORSESHOE CT
WYCHWOOD CL
WYCHWOOD DR
MERLEWOOD CL
WYCHWOOD GRANGE
BODORGAN RD
MEYRICK PARK MANS
ALBANY CT
A347
A338

BRANKSOME WOOD RD
PARKVIEW
BRAIDLEY RD
THE LODGE
ST STEPHENS CT 1
DURRANT RD 2
EAST CLIFF
WEST CLIFF

WESSEX WAY

Tennis Centre
BRADBURNE RD
CRESCENT RD
SUFFOLK RD
NORWICH AVE
Liby
NORWICH RD
POOLE HILL
PO
DURLEY RD
HAHNEMANN RD
WEST HILL RD
DURLEY RDBT
ARNEWOOD CT
WEST CLIFF RD
AVON HO
BAYVIEW MEWS
FAIR LEA
TOWER CT
WEST CLIFF GDNS
BAY VIEW
BAYVIEW GDNS

West Undercliff Promenade
Cliff Lift

ST STEPHEN'S RD
BROMPTON CT
TH
BOURNE AVE
The Avenue Sh Ctr
Central Gardens
AVENUE RD
THE TRIANGLE
COMMERCIAL RD
ORCHARD ST
TERRACE RD
UPPER TERRACE RD
EDMONDSHAM HO
PURBECK RD
TREGONWELL RD
WEST CLIFF MEWS
ST MICHAEL'S RD
CRANBORNE RD
EXETER RD
PRIORY RD
KERLEY RD
BEACON RD

THE SQUARE
ST PETER'S WK
GERVIS PL
RICHMOND HILL DR
RICHMOND HILL
YELVERTON RD
GRANVILLE RD
ALBERT RD
PO
DEAN PARK CRES
HORSESHOE COMMON RDBT
DALKEITH ARC
OLD CHRISTCHURCH RD
ST PETER'S RD
FIR VALE RD
The Quadrant Ctr
UPPER HINTON RD
HINTON RD

Bournemouth Eye
Lower Gardens
EXETER LA
EXETER CRES
WESTOVER RD
Pavilion Theatre
EXETER PARK RD
B3066
BATH RD
UNDERCLIFF DR
Bournemouth Int Ctr
SOUTH CLIFF RD
Oceanarium
Pier

1 WEST CLIFF COTTS
2 KNIGHTSBRIDGE CT
3 BEECHWOOD CT
4 CARLTON MOUNT

One-way streets

Index

Street names are listed alphabetically and show the locality, the Postcode district, the page number and a reference to the square in which the name falls on the map page

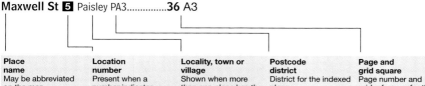

Maxwell St 5 **Paisley PA3**..............**36 A3**

Place name May be abbreviated on the map	**Location number** Present when a number indicates the place's position in a crowded area of mapping	**Locality, town or village** Shown when more than one place has the same name	**Postcode district** District for the indexed place	**Page and grid square** Page number and grid reference for the standard mapping

Towns and villages are listed in CAPITAL LETTERS
Public and commercial buildings are highlighted in magenta. **Places of interest** are highlighted in blue with a star

Abbreviations used in the index

Acad	**Academy**	Ct	**Court**	Hts	**Heights**	Pl	**Place**
App	**Approach**	Ctr	**Centre**	Ind	**Industrial**	Prec	**Precinct**
Arc	**Arcade**	Ctry	**Country**	Inst	**Institute**	Prom	**Promenade**
Ave	**Avenue**	Cty	**County**	Int	**International**	Rd	**Road**
Bglw	**Bungalow**	Dr	**Drive**	Intc	**Interchange**	Recn	**Recreation**
Bldg	**Building**	Dro	**Drove**	Junc	**Junction**	Ret	**Retail**
Bsns, Bus	**Business**	Ed	**Education**	L	**Leisure**	Sh	**Shopping**
Bvd	**Boulevard**	Emb	**Embankment**	La	**Lane**	Sq	**Square**
Cath	**Cathedral**	Est	**Estate**	Liby	**Library**	St	**Street**
Cir	**Circus**	Ex	**Exhibition**	Mdw	**Meadow**	Sta	**Station**
Cl	**Close**	Gd	**Ground**	Meml	**Memorial**	Terr	**Terrace**
Cnr	**Corner**	Gdn	**Garden**	Mkt	**Market**	TH	**Town Hall**
Coll	**College**	Gn	**Green**	Mus	**Museum**	Univ	**University**
Com	**Community**	Gr	**Grove**	Orch	**Orchard**	Wk, Wlk	**Walk**
Comm	**Common**	H	**Hall**	Pal	**Palace**	Wr	**Water**
Cott	**Cottage**	Ho	**House**	Par	**Parade**	Yd	**Yard**
Cres	**Crescent**	Hospl	**Hospital**	Pas	**Passage**		
Cswy	**Causeway**	HQ	**Headquarters**	Pk	**Park**		

Index of towns, villages, streets, hospitals, industrial estates, railway stations, schools, shopping centres, universities and places of interest

A

Aaron Cl BH17........ 67 C3
Abbey Gdns BH21...... 25 A1
Abbey Rd BH22........ 28 A4
Abbotsbury Rd BH18... 37 C1
Abbots Cl BH23........ 79 C2
Abbott Cl BH9........ 72 A3
Abbott Rd BH9........ 72 A3
Abbott St BH21........ 21 A2
Abbotts Way BH22..... 28 A4
Aberdare Rd BH10..... 51 B3
Abingdon Dr BH23.... 80 C3
Abingdon Rd BH17.... 67 A4
Abinger Rd BH7 ...... 74 B1
Abney Rd BH10........ 51 A3
Acacia Ave BH31........ 5 C4
Acacia Rd SO41....... 63 C1
Acland Rd BH9 .... 72 B3
Acorn Ave BH15 ..... 91 A2
Acorn Bsns PkBH12... 68 B4
Acorn Cl
  Christchurch BH23 ... 75 C3
  New Milton BH25 .... 62 C2
  St Leonards BH24 .... 18 C3
Acorn Cotts BH31....... 2 C3
Acorns The
  West Moors BH24 ..... 28 B4
  Wimborne Minster BH21.. 32 A4

Acorn Way BH31........ 3 A2
Acres Rd BH11........ 50 B2
Acton Rd BH10 .... 50 B1
Adamsfield Gdns BH10.. 50 C2
Adastral Rd BH17..... 67 C4
Adastral Sq BH17..... 67 C4
Ad Astro Fst SchBH17.. 47 C1
Addington Ct 1 SO41.. 87 A3
Addington Pl BH23 .... 77 A1
Addiscombe Rd BH23 .. 76 A2
Addison Sq BH24 ..... 13 C3
Adelaide Cl BH23...... 75 C3
Adelaide Ct SO41...... 111 B3
Adelaide La 1 BH11... 112 B2
Adeline Rd BH1, BH5 .... 97 B3
Adlam's La SO41...... 107 A3
Admirals Ct SO41..... 111 B3
Admirals Wlk 13 BH2 .. 95 A2
Admiralty Rd BH6 .... 99 C2
  Aerial PkBH21 .... 25 B2
Agar's La SO41....... 84 B4
Agarton La SO41...... 87 C4
Aggis Farm BH31 .... 2 B2
Airetons Cl BH18 .... 46 C3
  Airfield Ind Est
    Christchurch BH23 .... 77 C1
    Christchurch BH23 .... 78 A2
Airfield Rd BH23...... 77 C1
Airfield Way BH23 .... 77 C2

Airspeed Rd BH23 .... 78 B2
Akeshill Cl BH25...... 62 B3
Alan Ct 10 BH22 ..... 80 B2
Albany BH1 .... 96 C2
Albany Cl BH25....... 81 C4
Albany Ct BH2........ 112 B3
Albany Dr BH21........ 4 B1
Albany Gdns BH15 .... 89 C2
Albany Ho 17 BH13 ... 94 A4
  Albany PkBH17 .... 66 B4
Albemarle Rd BH3 .... 71 C3
Albert Rd
  Bournemouth BH1 .... 112 B2
  Corfe Mullen BH21.... 37 A1
  Ferndown BH22 .... 27 A1
  New Milton BH25 ..... 61 C1
  Poole BH12........... 69 A2
Albion Cl BH17 .... 68 B3
Albion Rd BH23........ 75 C4
Albion Way BH31 ...... 2 A3
Alby Rd BH12......... 69 C1
Alcester Rd BH12..... 69 A2
Aldbury Ct BH25...... 82 A1
Alder Cl BH23 .... 77 A4
Alder Cres BH12...... 69 C3
Alder Hills BH12...... 70 A3
  Alder Hills Ind PkBH12.. 70 A3
  Alder Hills Nature
    Reserve* BH12........ 70 A3

Alder Hts BH12 .... 70 A3
Alderley Rd BH10..... 51 A4
ALDERNEY 48 C1
Alderney Ave BH12 ... 49 A1
  Alderney HosplBH12 .. 48 C2
Alderney Rdbt BH12 .. 49 A2
Alder Rd BH12........ 69 C2
Aldis Gdns BH15...... 89 B2
Aldridge Rd
  Bournemouth BH10 ... 42 C1
  Ferndown BH22 .... 35 B3
Aldridge Way BH22 ... 35 C3
Alexander Cl BH23.... 77 B1
Alexander Ct BH22 ... 35 B3
Alexandra Ct BH22 ... 35 B3
Alexandra Lodge 8
  BH1.................. 96 A2
Alexandra Rd
  Bournemouth BH6 .... 98 C4
  Lymington SO41....... 110 B4
  Poole BH14........... 69 A1
Alford Rd BH3 .... 71 A3
Alington Cl BH14 .... 103 C3
Alington Ho BH14..... 103 C3
Alington Rd
  Bournemouth BH3 .... 72 A1
  Poole BH14........... 103 C3
Alipore Cl BH14....... 93 A3
Alipore Hts BH14 ..... 93 A3

Aar–Alv

  Allenbourn Mid Sch
    BH21................ 22 C1
Allenby Cl BH17 ...... 46 B2
Allenby Rd BH17...... 46 B2
Allen Ct BH21 .... 22 C1
Allen Rd BH21 .... 30 C4
Allens La BH16 .... 65 A1
Allens Rd BH16....... 65 A3
Allenview Rd BH21 ... 22 C1
Allison Ct 6 SO41.... 86 B2
All Saints Rd SO41.... 111 B1
Alma Rd BH9 .... 72 A2
Almer Rd BH15 .... 89 B3
Almond Gr BH12...... 69 A3
Almshouses BH10 .... 50 C1
Alpha Ctr TheBH17.... 66 B3
Alpine Rd BH24....... 20 A2
Alton Rd
  Bournemouth BH10 ... 50 B1
  Poole BH14........... 92 C3
Alton Rd E BH14...... 93 A2
Alum Chine Rd BH4.... 94 B3
Alumdale Rd BH4..... 94 B2
Alumhurst Rd BH4.... 94 A2
Alvandi Gdns 2 BH25... 62 B1
Alverton Ave BH15.... 91 A4

Alverton Hall **13** BH4 . . . . . . 94 C2
Alyth Rd BH3 . . . . 71 A2
Ambassador Cl BH2 . . . . 78 A1
Ambassador Ind Est
  BH23 . . . . 78 A1
Amberley Cl BH23 . . . . 79 C3
Amberley Ct **10** BH1 . . . . . . 96 A2
Amberley Ho BH22 . . . . 27 A3
Amber Rd BH21 . . . . 44 C4
Amberwood
  Ferndown BH22 . . . . 27 B3
  Milford on S SO41 . . . . . . 86 B3
Amberwood Dr BH23 . . . 59 C1
Amberwood Gdns
  BH23 . . . . 60 A1
Amberwood Ho BH23 . . . . . 60 A1
Ambleside BH23 . . . . 55 B2
Ambleside Rd SO41 . . . . . . 111 B2
Ambury La BH23 . . . . 77 C3
Amersham Ct **37** BH4 . . . . 94 C3
Amesbury Rd BH6 . . . . 74 C1
Amethyst Rd BH23 . . . . 77 C2
AMEYSFORD 16 A1
Ameysford Rd BH22 . . . . . . 26 C3
Ameys La BH22 . . . . 27 C3
Amira Ct **2** BH2 . . . . 112 A2
Ampfield Rd BH8 . . . . 53 A2
Amsterdam Sq BH23 . . . . . . 77 A1
Anchorage Way SO41 . . . 110 C2
Anchor Cl
  Bournemouth BH1 . . . . . . 41 C2
  Christchurch BH23 . . . . . 102 A4
Anchor Mews SO41 . . . . . 111 A3
Anchor Rd BH11 . . . . 41 C1
Ancrum Lo **15** BH4 . . . . . . 94 B3
Andbourne Ct BH6 . . . . 99 C2
Anderwood Dr SO41 . . . 107 B3
Andover Rd BH23 . . . . 78 B2
Andre Ct BH23 . . . . 80 B3
Andrew La BH25 . . . . 83 A4
Andrews Cl BH11 . . . . 50 A3
Andrew's Lodge SO41 . . 110 C4
Androse Gdns BH24 . . . . . . 13 A2
Angel Ct SO41 . . . . 111 A3
Angeline Cl BH23 . . . . 79 C3
Angel La
  Barton on S BH25 . . . . . . 83 A2
  Ferndown BH22 . . . . 34 B3
Angel Mews BH15 . . . . 90 B2
Anglewood Mans **2**
  BH4 . . . . 94 C3
Anglo-European Coll of
  Chiropractic BH5 . . . . . . 98 A3
Anjou Cl BH11 . . . . 41 A1
Annandale Ct BH6 . . . . 99 A3
Anne Cl BH23 . . . . 76 A4
Annerley Rd BH1 . . . . 96 C3
Annet Cl BH15 . . . . 89 B2
Anson Cl
  Christchurch BH23 . . . . . . 77 C1
  Ringwood BH24 . . . . 14 A4
Anstey Cl BH11 . . . . 42 A2
Anstey Rd BH11 . . . . 42 A1
Anthony's Ave BH14 . . . . . . 92 C1
Antler Dr BH25 . . . . 61 B3
Anvil Cres BH18 . . . . 37 C1
Apollo Cl BH12 . . . . 69 A3
Apple Cl BH13 . . . . 94 A4
Apple Gr BH23 . . . . 55 B1
Appleslade Way BH25 . . . . 62 B3
Appletree Cl
  Bournemouth BH6 . . . . . . 98 C4
  New Milton BH25 . . . . 82 A3
Apple Tree Gr BH22 . . . . . . 27 B2
Approach Rd BH14 . . . . 92 B3
April Cl BH11 . . . . 50 A4
Apsley Cres BH17 . . . . 46 C1
Apsley Ct **3** BH8 . . . . 96 A4
Aragon Way BH9 . . . . 52 B3
Arcade BH4 . . . . 94 B3
Arcade The **14** BH1 . . . . 112 B2
Arcadia Ave BH6 . . . . 72 B2
Arcadia Rd BH23 . . . . 75 C4
Archdale Cl BH10 . . . . 51 A2
Archgate SO41 . . . . 111 A3
Archway Rd BH14 . . . . 93 B4
Arden Rd BH9 . . . . 51 C3

Arden Wlk BH25 . . . . 82 B4
Ardmore Rd BH14 . . . . 92 B4
Arena Bsns Ctr BH17 . . . . . 66 B4
Argyle Rd BH23 . . . . 101 B4
Argyll Mans **8** BH5 . . . . . 97 B3
Argyll Rd
  Bournemouth BH5 . . . . . . 97 B2
  Poole BH12 . . . . 69 A2
Ariel Cl BH6 . . . . 100 B3
Ariel Dr BH6 . . . . 100 B3
Ark Dr BH22 . . . . 35 C3
Arley Rd BH14 . . . . 92 A2
Arlington Ct BH25 . . . . 82 B2
Arne Ave BH12 . . . . 69 B3
Arne Cres BH12 . . . . 69 C3
Arnewood Bridge Rd
  SO41 . . . . 107 B1
Arnewood Ct BH2 . . . . 112 A1
Arnewood Ho SO41 . . . . . . 84 C2
Arnewood Rd BH6 . . . . 99 A4
Arnewood Sch The
  BH25 . . . . 61 C1
Arnold Cl BH22 . . . . 16 C3
Arnold Rd BH22 . . . . 16 C3
Arnolds Cl BH25 . . . . 81 C3
Arran Way BH23 . . . . 80 B4
Arrowsmith Ct BH18 . . . . . . 46 A4
Arrowsmith La BH21 . . . . . . 39 B3
Arrowsmith Rd BH21 . . . . . 39 B3
Arthur Cl BH2 . . . . 71 C1
Arthur La **3** BH23 . . . . . . 76 A2
Arthur Rd BH23 . . . . 76 A2
Arts Inst of Bournemouth
  The BH12 . . . . 70 C4
Arundel Cl BH25 . . . . 61 B2
Arundel Way BH23 . . . . 79 C2
Ascham Rd BH8 . . . . 96 B4
Ascot Rd BH18 . . . . 46 A4
Ashbourne Cl **1** BH1 . . . 96 A2
Ashbourne Rd BH5 . . . . 98 B4
Ashburn Garth BH24 . . . . . 14 B2
Ashburton Gdns BH10 . . . . 51 A1
Ash Cl BH16 . . . . 64 B4
Ashdene Cl BH21 . . . . 23 A1
Ashdown **8** BH2 . . . . 95 A2
Ashdown Cl BH17 . . . . 47 C1
Ashdown Tech Coll
  BH17 . . . . 47 B1
Ashdown Wlk BH25 . . . . . . 82 C4
Ashford Rd BH6 . . . . 75 A2
Ash Gr Hordle SO41 . . . . . . 85 B2
  Ringwood BH24 . . . . 14 A2
ASHINGTON 30 A1
Ashington Gdns BH21 . . . . 37 C4
Ashington La BH21 . . . . 30 A1
Ashington Pk BH25 . . . . 82 B3
Ashleigh Rise BH10 . . . . . . 51 A2
Ashlet Gdns BH25 . . . . 63 A2
ASHLEY New Milton 63 A1
  St Leonards 11 C2
Ashley Arnewood Ct **5**
  BH25 . . . . 82 B4
Ashley Cl
  Bournemouth BH1 . . . . . . 73 B2
  Ringwood BH24 . . . . 14 B2
Ashley Common Rd
  BH25 . . . . 62 C2
Ashley Cross BH14 . . . . 92 A4
Ashley Ct BH22 . . . . 28 A4
Ashley Drive N BH24 . . . . . 11 A1
Ashley Drive S BH24 . . . . . 11 A1
Ashley Drive W BH24 . . . . . 11 A1
ASHLEY HEATH 10 C2
Ashley Heath Cvn Pk
  BH24 . . . . 10 B2
Ashley Heath Ind Est
  BH21 . . . . 9 C3
Ashley Inf Sch BH25 . . . . . . 63 A1
Ashley Jun Sch BH25 . . . . . 62 C1
Ashley La
  Hordle BH25, SO41 . . . . . 63 B2
  Lymington SO41 . . . . . . 111 A2
Ashley Meads BH25 . . . . . . 63 A2
Ashley Pk BH24 . . . . 11 B2
Ashley Rd
  Bournemouth BH1 . . . . . . 97 B4
  New Milton BH25 . . . . 62 C1
  Poole BH14 . . . . 68 C1
Ashling Cl BH8 . . . . 72 C3
Ashling Cres BH8 . . . . 72 B3

Ashmead **22** BH4 . . . . . . 94 C2
Ashmeads Cl BH21 . . . . 24 A2
Ashmeads Way BH21 . . . . . 24 A2
Ashmore Ave BH11 . . . . 31 A4
Ashmore Ave
  Barton on S BH25 . . . . . . 82 B2
  Hamworthy BH15 . . . . 89 C1
Ashmore Cres BH15 . . . . . . 89 C1
Ashmore Gr BH23 . . . . 79 B4
Ashmore Ho **30** BH4 . . . . 94 C3
Ashridge Ave **1** BH10 . . . 43 A1
Ashridge Gdns BH10 . . . . . 43 A1
Ashridge Par **2** BH10 . . . 43 A1
Ashstead Gdns BH8 . . . . . . 52 C2
Ashton Ct
  3 New Milton BH25 . . . 62 B1
  Poole BH13 . . . . 94 A2
Ashton Rd BH9 . . . . 51 C2
Ashtree Cl BH25 . . . . 83 A4
Ashurst Rd
  Bournemouth BH8 . . . . . . 53 A2
  West Moors BH22 . . . . . . 16 C3
Ashwell Ct BH23 . . . . 75 C4
Ashwood Dr BH18 . . . . 46 C4
Aspen Dr BH31 . . . . 3 B1
Aspen Gdns BH12 . . . . 69 C3
Aspen Pl BH25 . . . . 82 B3
Aspen Rd BH12 . . . . 69 C3
Aspen Way BH12 . . . . 69 C3
Asquith Cl BH23 . . . . 77 A1
Astbury Ave BH12 . . . . 70 A4
Aston Mead BH23 . . . . 55 B3
Athelney Ct **7** BH1 . . . . . 96 B2
Athelstan Rd BH6 . . . . 99 B4
Athelston Ct SO41 . . . . . . 110 C2
Atkinson Cl BH25 . . . . 82 B2
Atrium The BH22 . . . . 27 B3
Aubrey Cl SO41 . . . . 87 C2
Auburn Mans **5** BH23 . . . 94 B4
Auckland Rd BH23 . . . . 78 C2
Audemer Ct BH24 . . . . 14 A4
Audrayton Ct **8** BH6 . . . . 99 B2
Austen Ave BH10 . . . . 43 B2
Auster Cl BH23 . . . . 78 B2
Austin Ave BH14 . . . . 92 B1
Austin Cl BH1 . . . . 97 A4
Autumn Cl BH22 . . . . 26 B3
Autumn Copse BH25 . . . . . 83 A4
Autumn Rd BH11 . . . . 49 A3
Avalon BH14 . . . . 103 C4
Avebury Ave BH10 . . . . 43 B2
Avenue Ct BH13 . . . . 94 B3
Avenue La **13** BH2 . . . . . 112 A2
Avenue Rd
  Bournemouth BH2 . . . . . 112 A2
  Christchurch BH23 . . . . . . 75 C2
  Lymington SO41 . . . . . . 111 A3
  New Milton BH25 . . . . 62 A1
  Walkford BH23 . . . . 60 C1
  Wimborne Minster BH21 . 31 A4
Avenue Sh Ctr The
  BH2 . . . . 112 A2
Avenue The
  Bournemouth BH9 . . . . . . 51 C3
  Poole BH13 . . . . 94 A2
  West Moors BH22 . . . . . . 16 C3
  West Moors BH24 . . . . . . 28 B4
Avon Ave BH24 . . . . 20 B3
Avon Bldgs BH23 . . . . 76 B2
Avonbourne Sch BH7 . . . . . 74 A2
AVON CASTLE 20 B3
Avon Castle Dr BH24 . . . . . 20 B3
Avon Cl
  Bournemouth BH8 . . . . . . 73 A1
  Lymington SO41 . . . . . . 110 B2
Avoncliffe Rd BH6 . . . . 99 B2
Avon Cotts BH23 . . . . 56 C4
Avon Ct
  Christchurch BH23 . . . . . . 76 C1
  7 Poole BH13 . . . . 94 A4
Avon Gdns BH23 . . . . 109 A3
Avon Heath Ctry Park
  Visitor Ctr* BH24 . . . . . 19 B2
Avon Heath Ctry Pk
  (North Pk)* BH24 . . . . . 19 C3
Avon Ho BH2 . . . . 112 A1
Avon Mews BH8 . . . . 72 C1
Avon Pk BH24 . . . . 12 B2

Avon Rd
  Bournemouth BH8 . . . . . . 72 C1
  West Moors BH22 . . . . . . 16 C2
Avon Road E BH23 . . . . 76 A3
Avon Road W BH23 . . . . . . 75 C3
Avon Run Cl BH23 . . . . 102 B4
Avon Run Rd BH23 . . . . . . 102 B4
Avonsands BH23 . . . . 102 A4
Avon View Par BH23 . . . . . . 56 C2
Avon View Rd BH23 . . . . . . 56 C2
Avon Wharf BH23 . . . . 100 C4
Award Rd
  Ferndown BH21 . . . . 25 C1
  Wimborne Minster BH21 . 26 A2
Axford Cl BH8 . . . . 53 A2
Aylesbury Rd BH1 . . . . 97 B3
Aysha Cl BH25 . . . . 82 B3
Azalea Cl BH24 . . . . 11 B1
Aztec Ctr BH17 . . . . 67 A4
Azura Cl BH21 . . . . 9 C2

B

Back La SO41 . . . . 107 C3
Badbury Cl BH18 . . . . 46 C3
Badbury Ct BH22 . . . . 27 C3
Badbury View BH21 . . . . . . 23 A1
Badbury View Rd BH21 . . . 37 A4
Baden Cl BH25 . . . . 82 B3
Baden-Powell & St
  Peter's CE Mid Sch
  BH14 . . . . 92 B3
Bader Rd BH17 . . . . 67 B4
Badgers Cl
  St Leonards BH24 . . . . . . 11 A1
  Sway SO41 . . . . 107 C3
Badgers Copse BH25 . . . . . 62 C4
Badgers Wlk BH22 . . . . 27 B3
Badger Way BH31 . . . . 2 C1
Bailey Cl BH25 . . . . 63 A2
Bailey Cres BH15 . . . . 66 C3
Bailey Dr BH23 . . . . 75 C2
Bailey Hall BH23 . . . . 75 C2
Baiter Gdns BH15 . . . . 90 C1
Baker Rd BH11 . . . . 42 A1
Bakers Farm Rd BH31 . . . . . 2 B3
Bakers View BH21 . . . . 37 A4
Balcombe Rd BH13 . . . . 94 A3
Baldwin Cl BH21 . . . . 77 A1
Balena Cl BH17 . . . . 66 A4
Balfour Cl BH23 . . . . 79 A3
Balfour Rd BH9 . . . . 51 C1
Ballam Cl BH16 . . . . 64 C3
Ballard Cl
  New Milton BH25 . . . . 62 B2
  Poole BH15 . . . . 91 A1
Ballard Coll BH25 . . . . 62 A2
Ballard Rd BH15 . . . . 91 A1
Ballard Sch BH25 . . . . 62 A2
Balmoral Ave BH8 . . . . 73 B4
Balmoral Ct **3** BH23 . . . . 80 B2
Balmoral Ho BH2 . . . . 95 A3
Balmoral Rd BH14 . . . . 92 C3
Balmoral Wlk BH25 . . . . 61 C2
Balston Rd BH14 . . . . 68 A2
Balston Terr BH15 . . . . 90 B2
Banbury Rd BH17 . . . . 66 C3
Bancroft Ct **11** BH15 . . . 91 A1
Bank Chambers BH14 . . . . . 93 B3
Bank Cl BH23 . . . . 76 B1
Bankhill Dr SO41 . . . . 110 C4
Bankside Rd BH9 . . . . 52 A2
Banks Rd BH13 . . . . 106 B4
Banstead Rd BH18 . . . . 38 A1
Barberry Way BH31 . . . . 3 C1
Barbers Gate **9** BH15 . . . 90 B1
Barbers Piles **1** BH15 . . . 90 B1
Barbers Wharf **8** BH15 . . 90 B1
Barclay Mans BH2 . . . . 71 C1
Barfields SO41 . . . . 111 A3
Barfields Ct **2** SO41 . . . 111 A3
Bargates BH23 . . . . 76 B2
Baring Rd BH6 . . . . 100 A2
Barlands Cl BH23 . . . . 56 C1
Barn Cl BH16 . . . . 64 A3
Barnes Cl BH10 . . . . 51 A3
Barnes Cres
  Bournemouth BH10 . . . . . 51 A3
  Wimborne Minster BH21 . 31 B4
Barnes La SO41 . . . . 86 C4

Barnes Rd BH10 . . . . 51 A3
Barnfield BH23 . . . . 79 A3
Barn Rd BH18 . . . . 46 B3
Barnsfield Rd BH24 . . . . 19 C2
Barns Rd BH22 . . . . 28 A2
Barons Ct **7** BH12 . . . . . . 94 B4
Baronsmede **2** BH2 . . . . . 95 A4
Barons Rd BH11 . . . . 41 A2
Barrack Rd BH23 . . . . 75 B3
Barrie Rd BH9 . . . . 51 C3
Barrow Dr BH8 . . . . 53 C1
Barrowgate Rd BH8 . . . . . . 53 A2
Barrowgate Way BH8 . . . . . 53 A2
Barrow Rd BH8 . . . . 53 C1
Barrow View BH22 . . . . 26 B2
Barrow Way BH8 . . . . 53 C1
Barrs Ave BH25 . . . . 62 B2
Barrs Wood Dr BH25 . . . . . 62 B2
Barrs Wood Rd BH25 . . . . . 62 B2
Barry Gdns BH18 . . . . 37 C1
Barter Rd BH12 . . . . 70 A3
Barters La BH18 . . . . 45 C3
Bartlett Dr BH7 . . . . 74 B3
Bartley Ct **2** BH21 . . . . . . 22 B1
Barton Chase BH25 . . . . 81 C2
Barton Common La
  BH25 . . . . 82 B2
Barton Common Rd
  BH25 . . . . 82 B1
Barton Court Ave BH25 . . . . 82 A2
Barton Court Rd BH25 . . . . 82 A3
Barton Croft BH25 . . . . 82 A1
Barton Dr BH25 . . . . 81 C3
Barton Ho BH25 . . . . 81 B2
Barton La BH25 . . . . 81 B3
Barton Lo BH12 . . . . 68 B1
BARTON ON SEA 81 C1
Bartonside Rd BH25 . . . . . . 80 C2
Barton Way BH25 . . . . 81 C3
Barton Wood Rd BH25 . . . . 81 B2
Bascott Cl BH11 . . . . 50 A1
Bascott Rd BH11 . . . . 50 A1
Bashley Cross Rd BH25 . . . 61 B4
Bashley Dr BH25 . . . . 62 B4
Bashley Rd BH25 . . . . 62 A4
Bassett Rd BH12 . . . . 68 B2
Batchelor Cres BH11 . . . . . 49 C3
Batchelor Rd BH11 . . . . 50 A3
Batcombe Cl BH11 . . . . 49 B3
Bath Hill Ct **11** BH1 . . . . 96 A2
Bath Hill Rdbt BH1 . . . . 96 A1
Bath Rd
  Bournemouth BH1 . . . . . . 96 A2
  Lymington SO41 . . . . . . 111 C2
Batstone Way BH22 . . . . . . 26 B2
Batten Cl BH23 . . . . 77 A2
Baverstock Rd BH12 . . . . . . 70 B4
Bay Cl
  Three Legged Cross
  BH21 . . . . 8 C4
  Upton BH16 . . . . 64 B2
Bay Hog La BH15 . . . . 90 B2
Baynton Ho SO41 . . . . . . 110 C3
Bays Ct SO41 . . . . 110 B3
Bays Rd SO41 . . . . 110 B2
Bay Tree Way BH23 . . . . 79 A4
Bay View BH2 . . . . 112 A1
Bayview Gdns BH2 . . . . . . 112 A1
Bayview Mews BH2 . . . . . . 112 A1
Beach Ave BH25 . . . . 81 C2
Beach Cl BH13 . . . . 105 A4
Beachcroft BH13 . . . . 94 A3
Beach Rd Poole BH13 . . . . 105 A4
  Upton BH16 . . . . 64 A2
Beach View BH13 . . . . 106 B4
Beacon Cl SO41 . . . . 85 B3
Beacon Ct BH23 . . . . 79 C2
Beacon Dr BH23 . . . . 79 C2
Beacon Gdns BH18 . . . . . . 45 B3
BEACON HILL 44 A2
Beacon Hill La BH21 . . . . . 44 B3
Beacon Park Cres
  BH16 . . . . 64 A4
Beacon Park Rd BH16 . . . . 64 A4
Beacon Rd
  Bournemouth BH2 . . . . . 112 C1
  Broadstone BH18 . . . . . . 45 B3
  Upton BH16 . . . . 64 B3
Beaconsfield Rd
  Christchurch BH23 . . . . . . 76 B2

Beaconsfield Rd continued
Poole BH12. . . . . **69** A2
Beacon Way BH11 and 18 . . . . **45** B3
Beamish Rd BH17. . . . . **67** C4
BEAR CROSS **41** C1
Bear Cross Ave BH11. . . . **41** C2
Bear Cross Rdbt BH11 . . **41** C2
BEARWOOD **41** B2
Bearwood Prim Sch
BH11. . . . . **40** C2
Beatrice Ct 5 SO41. . . . . **86** B2
Beatty Cl BH24 . . . . **14** A4
Beatty Rd BH9. . . . . **72** B4
Beauchamp Pl BH23 . . . . **76** A2
Beauchamps Gdns BH7 . . **74** A3
Beaucroft La BH21. . . . . . . **23** B1
Beaucroft Rd BH21 . . . . . . **23** B2
Beaucroft Sch BH21 . . . . . **23** B2
Beau Ct
43 Bournemouth BH4 . . . **94** C3
9 New Milton BH25 . . . . **62** A1
Beaufort Cl BH23 . . . . **78** B2
Beaufort Dr BH21. . . . . **22** C1
Beaufort Ho 10 BH4. . . . . . **94** C3
Beaufort Mews BH21 . . . . **30** B4
Beaufort Rd BH6. . . . . **75** A1
Beaufoys Ave BH22 . . . . . **27** A3
Beaufoys Cl BH22. . . . . **26** C3
Beaufoys Ct BH22. . . . . **26** C2
Beaulieu Ave BH23 . . . . . **75** B2
Beaulieu Cl BH25 . . . . **61** B2
Beaulieu Rd
Bournemouth BH4 . . . . . . **94** B1
Christchurch BH23 . . . . . . **75** B2
Beaumont Rd BH13 . . . . **104** C3
Beaver Ind Est BH23 . . . . **78** A2
Beccles Cl BH15 . . . . **89** C2
Becher Rd BH14 . . . . **93** B4
Beckhampton Rd BH15 . . **89** B3
BECKLEY **60** C4
Beckley Copse BH23. . . . . **60** A1
Becton La BH25 . . . . **82** B3
Becton Mead BH25 . . . . . **82** B3
Bedale Way BH15. . . . . **67** C1
Bedford Cres BH7 . . . . **74** C2
Bedford Rd N BH12 . . . . . **48** C2
Bedford Rd S BH12 . . . . . **48** C2
Beech Ave
Bournemouth BH6 . . . . . . **98** C3
Christchurch BH23 . . . . . . **75** A3
Beechbank Ave BH17 . . . **45** C1
Beech Cl
Broadstone BH18. . . . . **45** B4
Hordle SO41. . . . . **85** B2
Verwood BH31 . . . . **2** B1
Beechcroft BH1. . . . . **96** A4
Beechcroft La BH24. . . . . **13** C4
Beechcroft Mews 1
BH24. . . . . **13** C4
Beech Ct BH21 . . . . **31** B4
Beeches The BH7 . . . . **74** A3
Beechey Ct 6 BH8 . . . . . . **96** A4
Beechey Rd BH8. . . . . **96** A4
Beechfield 42 BH4 . . . . . . **94** C3
Beech La BH22 . . . . **18** C2
Beechwood Ave
Bournemouth BH5 . . . . . . **98** A3
New Milton BH25 . . . . **61** C3
Beech Wood Cl BH18 . . . **46** A3
Beechwood Ct BH7 . . . . **112** A1
Beechwood Gdns BH5 . . **98** A3
Beechwood Lo 1 BH4. . **94** C2
Beechwood Rd BH22. . . . **17** A1
Belben Cl BH12. . . . . **49** A2
Belben Rd BH12 . . . . **48** C2
Belfield Rd BH6 . . . . **100** A3
Belgrave Ct BH1. . . . . **97** A2
Belgrave Rd BH13 . . . . . . **94** A2
Belle Vue Cl BH6. . . . . **99** A3
Belle Vue Cres BH6 . . . . . **99** C3
Belle Vue Gdns 2 BH6 . . **99** C3
Belle Vue Gr BH22 . . . . . . **17** A2
Belle Vue Mans 6 BH6. . **99** B2
Belle Vue Rd
Bournemouth BH6 . . . . . . **99** A3
Poole BH14. . . . . **92** C3
Belle Vue Wlk BH22 . . . . **35** B2
Bellflower Cl BH23. . . . . . **78** B3
Bell Heather Cl BH16 . . . **64** B4
Bells Ho BH21 . . . . **23** A2

Belmont Ave BH8 . . . . **52** C1
Belmont Cl BH31 . . . . **3** A1
Belmont Rd
New Milton BH25 . . . . **62** C2
Poole BH14. . . . . **68** C1
Belmore Ct SO41 . . . . . . **110** C2
Belmore Ho 1 SO41. . . **111** A1
Belmore La SO41. . . . . . **111** A2
Belmore Rd SO41. . . . . . **110** C2
Belmour Lo 32 BH4 . . . . **94** C3
Belvedere Rd
Bournemouth BH3 . . . . . . **72** A1
Christchurch BH23 . . . . . . **76** A2
Belvoir Pk 3 BH13 . . . . . **94** B3
Bemister Rd BH9 . . . . **72** A3
Benbow Cres BH12 . . . . . **49** B1
Benbridge Ave BH11 . . . . **41** C1
Bendigo Rd BH23 . . . . **75** B3
Benellen Ave BH4 . . . . **94** C4
Benellen Gdns BH4 . . . . . **95** A4
Benellen Rd BH4 . . . . **70** C1
Benellen Twrs 1 BH4. . . **94** C4
Bengal Rd BH9 . . . . **71** B4
Benjamin Ct BH23 . . . . . . **75** C2
Benjamin Rd BH15. . . . . . **89** A2
Benmoor Rd BH17. . . . . . **66** A4
Benmore Cl BH25. . . . . . . **82** C4
Benmore Rd BH9 . . . . **72** A4
Bennett Ho 4 BH4 . . . . . **94** C4
Bennett Rd BH8 . . . . **72** C1
Bennion Rd BH10. . . . . . . **50** C3
Benridge Bsns Pk BH17 . . **66** B4
Benridge Cl BH18. . . . . . . **46** A3
Benson Cl BH23 . . . . **109** A3
Benson Rd BH17. . . . . **67** A3
Bentley Rd BH9. . . . . **51** C3
Bere Cl BH17 . . . . **47** A2
Beresford Cl BH12 . . . . . . **69** A2
Beresford Gdns BH23 . . . **77** B1
Beresford Rd
Bournemouth BH5 . . . . . . **98** B3
Lymington SO41 . . . . **110** B3
Poole BH12. . . . . **69** A2
Berkeley Ave BH12. . . . . . **69** A4
Berkeley Cl BH31 . . . .**2** B3
Berkeley Rd BH3. . . . . **71** B3
Berkley Ave BH22 . . . . **35** A2
Berkley Manor 8 BH13 . . **94** B4
Bermuda Ct 5 BH25 . . . . **80** A2
Bernards Ct BH23 . . . . **75** B3
Berne Ct 15 BH1. . . . . **96** A2
Beron Ct BH15. . . . . **91** B4
Berrans Ave BH11 . . . . **42** B2
Berrans Ct BH11 . . . . **42** A2
Berryfield Rd SO41. . . . . . **84** A1
Bertram Rd BH25 . . . . **62** C2
Berwick Rd BH14 . . . . **71** B2
Bessborough Rd BH13 . **104** B3
Bessemer Cl BH31 . . . . **5** C1
Beswick Ave BH10 . . . . . . **51** A2
Bethany Cl BH12. . . . . **70** A3
Bethany Ho BH11. . . . . . . **97** A4
Bethany Jun CE Sch
BH1. . . . . **97** A4
Bethia Cl BH8. . . . . **73** A1
Bethia Rd BH8. . . . . **73** A1
Betsy Cl BH23 . . . . **109** A3
Betsy La BH23 . . . . **109** A3
Bettiscombe Cl BH17 . . . **47** B2
Beverley Gdns BH10 . . . . **51** A3
Beverley Grange 50
BH4. . . . . **94** C3
Bexington Cl BH11. . . . . . **49** B3
Bickerley Gdns BH24. . . . **13** A2
Bickerley Rd BH24 . . . . . . **13** A2
Bickerley Terr BH24. . . . . **13** A3
Bicknell Ct 5 BH4. . . . . . **94** C4
Bicknell Sch BH7. . . . . **74** A2
Bicton Rd BH11. . . . . **50** B3
Billington Pl SO41. . . . . . **110** C1
Bindon Cl BH12. . . . . **69** B3
Bingham Ave BH14 . . . . **104** A4
Bingham Cl
Christchurch BH23 . . . . . . **77** B2
Verwood BH31 . . . . **5** B4
Bingham Dr
Lymington SO41 . . . . **111** A2
Verwood BH31 . . . . **5** A4
Bingham Rd
Bournemouth BH9 . . . . . . **72** A2

Bingham Rd continued
Christchurch BH23 . . . . . . **77** B2
Verwood BH31 . . . . **5** A4
Binnie Rd BH12. . . . . **69** B1
Birch Ave Beckley BH25 . . **61** A4
Burton BH23. . . . . **56** C2
Ferndown BH22 . . . . **35** C1
Birch Cl
Corfe Mullen BH21. . . . . . **37** A2
Poole BH14. . . . . **93** B3
St Leonards BH24 . . . . **18** B3
Birch Copse BH17 . . . . . . **66** A4
Birch Ct SO41 . . . . **110** A1
Birchdale Rd BH21. . . . . . **23** A1
Birch Dr BH8 . . . . **54** A1
Birch Gr Old Milton BH25 . . **82** A3
West Moors BH22 . . . . **9** C3
Birch Rd BH24. . . . . **19** C4
Birch Wlk BH22. . . . . **35** C3
Birchwood Cl BH23 . . . . . **79** B3
Birchwood Mews BH14 . . **93** A3
Birchwood Rd
Poole BH14. . . . . **93** A3
Upton BH16 . . . . **64** B2
Birchy Hill SO41 . . . . **107** C2
Birds Hill Gdns 1
BH15. . . . . **91** B3
Bird's Hill Rd BH15 . . . . . **91** B3
Birkdale Cl BH18 . . . . **38** A1
Birkdale Rd BH18. . . . . . . **38** A1
Bishop Cl BH12. . . . . **70** C3
Bishop Ct BH24 . . . . **13** B4
Bishop of Winchester
Comp Sch The BH8 . . . . **73** A4
Bishop Rd BH9 . . . . **72** A3
Bishops Cl BH17 . . . . **73** C2
Bishops Ct BH18. . . . . **46** A3
Bitterne Way
Lymington SO41. . . . . . . **110** C1
Verwood BH31 . . . . **3** A1
Blackberry La BH23. . . . . **77** C1
Blackbird Cl BH17 . . . . . . **65** B4
Blackbird Way BH23 . . . **109** B2
Blackburn Rd BH12 . . . . . **68** B2
Blackbush Rd SO41. . . . . **86** B3
Blackfield La BH22. . . . . . **16** C3
Blackfield Rd BH8 . . . . . . **53** A2
Black Hill BH31. . . . . **3** A2
Black Moor Rd BH31. . . . . **5** C4
Blacksmith Cl BH21. . . . . **37** A1
Blackthorn Cl SO41. . . . **110** A1
Blackthorn Way
New Milton BH25 . . . . **63** A2
Verwood BH31 . . . . **3** B1
BLACKWATER **55** A3
Blackwater Cl BH23 . . . . . **55** A3
Blackwater Dr BH21 . . . . **39** A3
Blair Ave BH14 . . . . **92** C4
Blair Cl BH25 . . . . **61** B2
Blake Dene Rd BH14 . . . . **92** B1
Blake Hill Ave BH14. . . . . **93** A1
Blake Hill Cres BH14 . . . . **92** C1
Blandford Cl BH15. . . . . . **89** C2
Blandford Ct 2 SO41 . . . **87** A3
Blandford Rd
Corfe Mullen BH21. . . . . . **37** A4
Hamworthy BH16. . . . . . . **89** A4
Pamphill BH21. . . . . **21** A3
Blandford Rd N
Upton BH16 . . . . **64** B3
Upton BH16 . . . . **64** B4
Blaney Way BH21 . . . . **36** C2
BLASHFORD. **6** B3
Blashford Lakes Study Ctr
BH24. . . . . **7** A2
Blenheim 3 BH13 . . . . . . **94** B3
Blenheim Cres SO41. . . . **63** C2
Blenheim Ct
55 Bournemouth BH4 . . **94** C3
Christchurch BH23 . . . . . . **76** A3
Blenheim Dr BH21 . . . . . . **78** B1
Blenheim Mews 6
BH4. . . . . **94** C4
Blind La BH21 . . . . **22** B1
Bloomfield Ave BH9 . . . . **51** C2
Bloomfield Pl BH9 . . . . . . **51** C2
Bloxworth Rd BH12 . . . . . **69** C4
Bluebell Cl BH23. . . . . **78** B3
Bluebell La BH17 . . . . **45** C1
Bluff The BH10 . . . . **51** C4

Blyth Cl BH23. . . . . **55** A3
Blythe Rd BH21. . . . . **37** A2
Blythswood Ct BH25 . . . . **81** C2
Bob Hann Cl BH12 . . . . . . **69** A1
Bodley Rd BH13 . . . . **104** C3
Bodorgan Rd BH2 . . . . . **112** B3
Bodowen Cl BH23 . . . . . . **57** A1
Bodowen Rd BH23 . . . . . . **77** A4
Bognor Rd BH18. . . . . **45** C4
Boldre Cl
Barton on S BH25. . . . . . . **81** A3
Poole BH12. . . . . **69** A3
Boleyn Cres BH9. . . . . **52** C3
Bolton Cl BH6 . . . . **99** B2
Bolton Cres BH22. . . . . . . **28** A2
Bolton Ct 3 BH6. . . . . **99** B2
Bolton Rd BH6. . . . . **99** B2
Boltons The SO41. . . . . . . **87** A2
Bond Ave BH22 . . . . **16** B4
Bond Cl SO41. . . . . **107** B4
Bond Rd BH15 . . . . **67** C1
Bonham Rd BH9 . . . . **71** C3
Bonington Cl BH23 . . . . . **77** B3
Border Dr BH16. . . . . **64** C1
Border Rd BH16 . . . . **64** C1
Boreham Rd BH6 . . . . **99** A4
Borthwick Rd BH1. . . . . . **97** B4
BOSCOMBE **97** B4
Boscombe Cliff Rd BH5 . **97** C2
Boscombe Grove Rd
BH1. . . . . **97** A4
Boscombe Overcliff Dr
BH5. . . . . **98** A2
Boscombe Spa Rd BH5 . **97** A2
Bosley Cl BH23 . . . . **55** B1
Bosley Way BH23 . . . . **55** B1
Boston Lo 51 BH4. . . . . . **94** C3
Bosworth Mews BH9. . . . **52** B3
Boulnois Ave BH14. . . . . . **93** B3
Boundary Dr BH21. . . . . . **23** A2
Boundary La BH24 . . . . . . **18** C1
Boundary Rd BH10. . . . . . **51** B1
Boundary Rdbt BH3,
BH10. . . . . **71** A4
Bountys La BH12 . . . . **69** B1
Bourne Ave BH2 . . . . **112** A2
Bourne Cl BH2 . . . . **95** A3
Bourne Ct
1 Bournemouth
BH2. . . . . **112** B2
Wimborne Minster BH21. . **23** A1
BOURNEMOUTH **96** A1
Bournemouth Central
Bsns Pk BH1 . . . . **96** C4
Bournemouth Eye * **112** B2
Bournemouth Ho 2
BH1. . . . . **96** B2
Bournemouth Int Ctr *
BH2. . . . . **112** B1
Bournemouth Learning
Support Centre PRU
BH10. . . . . **51** A1
Bournemouth Memorial
Homes BH8 . . . . **73** C4
Bournemouth Nuffield
Derwent Suite BH7 . . . . **74** B4
Bournemouth Nuffield
Hospl The BH8 . . . . **96** A4
Bournemouth & Poole
Coll Annexe The BH1. . **96** A2
Bournemouth & Poole
Coll (Constitution Hill
Campus) The BH14 . . . . **67** C1
Bournemouth & Poole
Coll (North Road
Campus) The BH11 . . . . **91** C4
Bournemouth & Poole
Coll The BH1 . . . . **96** B2
Bournemouth Rd BH14 . **93** A4
Bournemouth Sch BH8 . **72** C4
Bournemouth Sch for
Girls BH8. . . . . **96** B3
Bournemouth Sta BH8. . **96** B3
Bournemouth Station
Rdbt BH8. . . . . **96** B3
Bournemouth Univ
(Lansdowne Campus)
BH1. . . . . **96** B2

Bournemouth Univ
(Talbot Campus)
BH12. . . . . **70** C4
Bournemouth West Rdbt
BH2. . . . . **95** B3
Bourne Pines BH2 . . . . . **112** B3
Bourne River Ct 9
BH4. . . . . **95** A4
BOURNE VALLEY **70** B2
Bourne Valley Bsns Pk
BH12. . . . . **70** A1
Bourne Valley Rd BH12. . **70** A1
Bournewood Dr BH4. . . . **94** C4
Bourton Gdns BH7. . . . . . **74** B3
Bouverie Cl 7 BH25 . . . . **82** A3
Boveridge Gdns BH9. . . . **52** B3
Bovington Cl BH17. . . . . . **47** C1
Bowden Rd BH12 . . . . **48** C2
Bower Rd BH8. . . . . **73** A3
Bowland Rise BH25 . . . . . **82** C4
Box Cl BH17 . . . . **66** B3
Boyd Rd BH12 . . . . **69** C2
Brabazon Dr BH23 . . . . . . **78** B2
Brabazon Rd BH21 . . . . . . **31** C1
Brabourne Ave BH22. . . . **34** C4
Bracken Cl BH24. . . . . **18** B4
Bracken Ct 10 BH4. . . . . . **95** A4
Brackendale Ct BH21 . . . . **8** C4
Brackendale Rd BH8. . . . . **73** A3
Bracken Glen BH15 . . . . . **67** B1
Brackenhill BH13 . . . . **94** A1
Brackenhill Rd BH21. . . . **24** A3
Bracken Lodge 3 BH6. . **99** C3
Bracken Rd
Bournemouth BH6 . . . . . . **98** C3
Ferndown BH22 . . . . **26** B3
Brackens Way
Lymington SO41 . . . . **111** B1
2 Poole BH13. . . . . **104** C4
Bracken Way BH23. . . . . . **80** B4
Bracklesham Pl BH25 . . . **81** C2
Bradburne Rd BH2. . . . . **112** A2
Bradbury Ho BH22 . . . . . . **27** A3
Bradford Rd BH9 . . . . **52** C3
Bradpole Rd BH8 . . . . **73** B4
Bradstock Cl BH12. . . . . . **69** C4
Braemar Ave BH6. . . . . . **100** A3
Braemar Cl BH6 . . . . **100** A3
Braemar Dr BH23 . . . . **79** C4
Braeside Bsns Pk BH15 . **90** B4
Braeside Rd
St Leonards BH24 . . . . **18** C3
West Moors BH22 . . . . **17** A3
Braidley Rd BH2 . . . . **112** A3
Brailswood Rd BH15 . . . . **91** B4
Braishfield Gdns BH8 . . . **53** A1
Bramar Ct 9 BH4 . . . . . . **94** C2
Bramble Cl BH22 . . . . **16** C2
Bramble La BH23 . . . . **80** B4
Bramble Way BH23 . . . . **109** A3
Bramble Wlk SO41. . . . . **110** B3
Bramley Cl SO41. . . . . . . **111** A1
Bramley Ct BH22 . . . . **26** C2
Bramley Rd
Bournemouth BH10 . . . . . **42** C1
Ferndown BH22 . . . . **27** A2
Brampton Rd BH15 . . . . . **67** A2
Bramshaw Gdns BH8 . . . **53** A2
Bramshaw Way BH25 . . . **81** A3
Branders Cl BH6. . . . . . . **100** A3
Branders La BH6 . . . . **100** B4
Brandon Ct 8 BH12 . . . . . **94** B4
Brandwood Ct 4 BH14 . . **92** A3
Branksea Ave BH15 . . . . . **89** B1
Branksea Cl BH15 . . . . **89** B1
BRANKSOME **69** C1
Branksome Ct BH25. . . . . **82** B4
Branksome Ct 4
BH13. . . . . **104** C4
Branksome Dene Rd
BH4. . . . . **94** B2
Branksome Heath Mid
Sch BH12 . . . . **68** C2
Branksome Hill Rd BH4 . **70** B1
BRANKSOME PARK **93** C1
Branksome Sta BH12 . . . **93** C4

Branksome Twrs
BH13 . . . . **105** B4
Branksome Wood Gdns
BH2 . . . . **95** A4
Branksome Wood Rd BH2,
BH4 . . . . **94** C4
BRANSGORE **109** A2
Bransgore CE Prim Sch
BH23 . . . . **109** B2
Bransgore Gdns BH23 . **109** B3
Branwell CI BH23 . . . . **76** A4
Branwood CI SO41 . . . . . . **85** C3
Brassey CI BH9 . . . . **72** A4
Brassey Rd BH9 . . . . **72** A4
Brassey Terr BH9 . . . . **51** C1
Braxton Ctyd SO41 . . . . . . **85** C1
Breamore CI BH23 . . . . . . **61** B2
Brearley CI BH23 . . . . . . **80** B3
Brecon CI
  Bournemouth BH10 . . . . . . **43** B2
  New Milton BH25 . . . . . . **82** C4
Bredy CI BH17 . . . . **47** A1
Bremble CI BH12 . . . . **48** C2
Briar CI
  Christchurch BH23 . . . . . . **77** C1
  Poole BH15 . . . . **67** B1
Briarfield 46 BH4 . . . . . . **94** C3
Briarswood Rd BH16 . . . . **64** C3
Briar Way BH21 . . . . **24** B1
Brickfield La SO41 . . . . . **111** B4
Brickyard La
  Ferndown BH22 . . . . **26** A2
  Verwood BH31 . . . . **2** A3
Bridge App BH15 . . . . . . **90** B1
Bridge PI BH10 . . . . **43** A3
Bridge Rd SO41 . . . . **111** B4
Bridges CI BH22 . . . . **17** A3
Bridge St BH23 . . . . **76** C1
Bridges The BH24 . . . . . . **12** C3
Bridgewater Rd BH12 . . . . **69** A2
Bridle CI BH16 . . . . **65** A3
Bridle Cres BH7 . . . . **75** A2
Bridle Way BH21 . . . . **24** C2
Bridleways BH31 . . . . **2** C2
Bridport Rd Poole BH12 . . **69** C4
  Verwood BH31 . . . . **2** C2
Brierley Ave BH22 . . . . . . **35** B1
Brierley CI BH10 . . . . **43** B1
Brierley Rd BH10 . . . . . . **51** B4
Brightlands Ave BH6 . . . . **99** C4
Brighton Rd SO41 . . . . . **107** A4
Bright Rd BH15 . . . . **67** B2
Brinsons CI BH23 . . . . . . **56** C2
Brisbane Rd BH23 . . . . . . **75** B4
Britannia Ct BH12 . . . . . . **68** B3
Britannia PI SO41 . . . . . **111** B3
Britannia Rd BH14 . . . . . . **92** A3
Britannia Way BH22 . . . . . **78** B2
Brixey CI BH12 . . . . **68** C3
Brixey Rd BH12 . . . . **68** C3
Broad Ave BH8 . . . . **73** A3
Broadfields CI SO41 . . . . . **87** A3
Broadhurst Ave BH10 . . . . **51** B4
Broad La SO41 . . . . **111** B1
Broadlands 27 BH4 . . . . . **94** C3
Broadlands Ave BH6 . . . . . **99** C3
Broadlands CI
  Bournemouth BH8 . . . . **53** A2
  Walkford BH23 . . . . **60** B1
Broadly CI SO41 . . . . . . **110** A1
Broadmayne Rd BH12 . . . . **70** A4
Broadmead CI 2
  SO41 . . . . **111** B1
Broad Mead Rd BH21 . . . . . **4** C1
Broadmoor Rd BH21 . . . . . **36** C3
Broadshard La BH24 . . . . . **13** B4
Broads The BH21 . . . . **21** C2
BROADSTONE **46** B3
Broadstone Fst Sch
BH18 . . . . **46** B4
Broadstone Mid Sch
BH18 . . . . **38** C1
Broadstone Way
  Broadstone BH17 . . . . **45** C1
  Poole BH17 . . . . **66** B3
Broadwater Ave BH14 . . . . **92** C2
Broadway BH6 . . . . **100** B2

Broadway Ct BH12 . . . . . . **70** A1
Broadway Gables BH14 . **93** B4
Broadway Gdns 6
  BH21 . . . . **30** C4
Broadway Ho BH18 . . . . . . **46** B4
Broadway La BH8 . . . . **52** C3
Broadway Mews BH14 . . . **91** C3
Broadway Pk BH15 . . . . . . **30** C4
Broadway The BH10 . . . . . . **4** A3
Brockenhurst Rd BH9 . . . . **52** B1
Brockhills La BH25 . . . . . . **62** C4
Brockley Rd BH10 . . . . . . **51** B4
Brocks Pine BH24 . . . . . . **19** A3
Brock Way BH31 . . . . **2** A3
Brockwood BH24 . . . . **18** B2
Brombys The 11 BH15 . . . **90** C2
Bromley Ho BH12 . . . . **70** B1
Brompton Ct BH2 . . . . . . **112** A2
Bronte Ave BH23 . . . . **76** A4
Brook Ave BH5 . . . . **62** B2
Brook Ave N BH25 . . . . . . **62** B2
Brook CI BH10 . . . . **50** C4
Brookdale CI BH18 . . . . . . **46** A4
Brookdale Farm BH18 . . . **46** A4
Brook Dr BH31 . . . . **25** B4
Brook Ho BH25 . . . . **81** B2
Brook La
  Bransgore BH23 . . . . **109** A1
  Corfe Mullen BH21 . . . . . . **36** C2
Brookland CI SO41 . . . . . **110** B2
Brooklands BH4 . . . . **94** B3
Brooklyn Ct BH25 . . . . . . **61** C2
Brook Rd
  Bournemouth BH10 . . . . . . **50** C4
  Lymington SO41 . . . . **111** B1
  Poole BH12 . . . . **68** C1
  Wimborne Minster BH21 . . **31** B4
Brook Road Depot
  BH21 . . . . **31** B3
Brooks CI BH24 . . . . **13** C2
Brookside CI BH23 . . . . . **108** C2
Brookside Park Homes
  BH21 . . . . **44** B4
Brookside Rd
  Bransgore BH23 . . . . **108** C2
  Wimborne Minster BH21 . . **31** C4
Brookside Way BH23 . . . . **79** B4
Brook Way BH12 . . . . **78** C2
Broomfield CI BH21 . . . . . . **51** B3
Broomfield La SO41 . . . . . **111** A3
Broomhill CI SO41 . . . . . **110** A1
Broom La BH6 . . . . **98** B3
Broom Rd BH12 . . . . **48** C1
Broom Road Bsns Pk
  BH12 . . . . **108** A3
Broughton Ave BH10 . . . . **51** B3
Broughton CI BH10 . . . . . **51** B3
Brownen Rd BH9 . . . . **72** B3
Browning Ave BH5 . . . . . . **98** A3
Browning Rd BH12 . . . . . . **64** B2
Brownlow Ct 33 BH4 . . . **94** C3
Brownsea Ave BH21 . . . . . **37** A2
Brownsea CI BH25 . . . . . . **61** B2
Brownsea Ct BH14 . . . . . **103** B4
Brownsea Rd BH13 . . . . . **106** A3
Brownsea View Ave
  BH14 . . . . **92** C1
Brownsea View CI
  BH14 . . . . **92** C1
Brudenell Ave BH13 . . . . **104** A2
Brudenell Rd BH13 . . . . . **104** A2
Brunel CI BH31 . . . . **5** C4
Brune Way BH22 . . . . **35** A3
Brunstead PI 1 BH12 . . . **94** B4
Brunstead Rd BH12 . . . . . **94** B4
Brunswick PI SO41 . . . . . **111** A3
Bryanstone Rd BH3 . . . . . **71** B3
Bryant Rd BH12 . . . . **70** A4
Bryony CI BH18 . . . . **45** C3
Bub La BH23 . . . . **77** B1
Buccaneers CI BH24 . . . . . **77** B1
Buccleuch Rd BH13 . . . . . **94** A1
Bucehayes CI BH23 . . . . . **80** A4
Buchanan Ave BH7 . . . . . **73** B1
Buckingham Ct
  1 Christchurch BH23 . . . **80** A2
  Poole BH15 . . . . **91** A3
Buckingham Mans 5
  BH1 . . . . **96** A2
Buckingham Rd BH9 . . . . **69** A3

Buckingham Wlk BH25 . . **61** B2
BUCKLAND **110** C4
Buckland Ct SO41 . . . . . **111** A4
Buckland Dene SO41 . . . **110** C4
Buckland Gr BH23 . . . . . . **59** B1
Buckland Rd BH12 . . . . . . **68** C1
Buckland Terr BH12 . . . . . **68** C1
Buckland View SO41 . . . **111** A4
Bucklers CI SO41 . . . . . **110** C2
Bucklers Mews SO41 . . . **110** C2
Bucklers The SO41 . . . . . **86** A3
Bucklers Way BH8 . . . . . . **53** A2
Buckstone CI SO41 . . . . . . **85** C3
Buckthorn CI BH17 . . . . . **45** C1
Buddens Mdw BH21 . . . . . **44** C4
Buffalo Mews BH15 . . . . . **90** B2
Bugdens La BH31 . . . . **3** A2
Buldowne Wlk SO41 . . . **107** B4
Bullfinch CI BH17 . . . . . . **45** C1
Bunting Rd BH22 . . . . **26** B4
Burbidge CI BH17 . . . . . . **67** B4
Burcombe Rd BH10 . . . . . **42** C1
Burdock CI BH23 . . . . **78** B4
Bure CI BH23 . . . . **78** B1
Bure Haven Dr BH23 . . . . **78** A1
Bure Homage Gdns
  BH23 . . . . **78** B1
Bure Homage La BH23 . . . **78** B1
Bure La BH23 . . . . **78** B1
Bure Pk BH23 . . . . **78** B1
Bure Rd BH23 . . . . **78** B1
Burford CI BH23 . . . . **75** A4
Burford 4 BH1 . . . . **96** B2
Burgess CI BH11 . . . . **49** C4
Burleigh Rd BH6 . . . . **99** A4
Burley CI
  Barton on S BH25 . . . . . . **81** A3
  Verwood BH31 . . . . **2** B1
Burley Rd
  Bransgore BH23 . . . . **108** C2
  Poole BH12 . . . . **68** C2
Burling Terr 1 BH13 . . . **94** A4
Burlington Arc 11
  BH1 . . . . **112** B2
Burnaby Ct BH4 . . . . **94** C1
Burnaby Rd BH4 . . . . **94** C1
Burnage Ct 13 BH13 . . **104** C3
Burnbake Rd BH31 . . . . . . **3** A1
Burnbrae Rd BH22 . . . . . . **35** A1
Burn CI BH31 . . . . **5** B4
Burnett Ave BH23 . . . . . . **75** B3
Burnett Rd BH23 . . . . **75** C2
Burngate Rd BH15 . . . . . . **89** B2
Burnham Dr BH8 . . . . **72** C2
Burnham Rd BH23 . . . . . . **56** C1
Burnleigh Gdns BH25 . . . **62** C2
Burnside BH23 . . . . **79** A3
Burns Rd BH6 . . . . **75** A2
Burnt House La BH23 . . . **109** A3
Burrard Gr SO41 . . . . . . **111** B1
Burrows La BH31 . . . . **2** C4
Bursledon Ho 4 BH25 . . **82** A4
Burtley Rd BH6 . . . . **99** C2
BURTON **57** A1
Burton CE Prim Sch
  BH23 . . . . **56** C2
Burton CI Burton BH23 . . **76** C4
  St Leonards BH24 . . . . . . **10** C1
Burtoncroft BH23 . . . . . . **56** C2
Burton Hall BH23 . . . . . . **56** C2
Burton Hall PI BH23 . . . . **57** A2
Burton Ho BH23 . . . . **77** A4
Burton Rd
  Christchurch BH23 . . . . . . **77** B2
  Poole BH13 . . . . **94** A3
Burt's Hill BH21 . . . . **23** A3
Bury Rd Poole BH13 . . . . . **93** C1
  BH13 . . . . **93** C2
Bushell Rd BH15 . . . . **66** C3
Bushey Rd BH8 . . . . **72** C4
Bushmead Dr BH24 . . . . . **10** C1
Bute Dr BH23 . . . . **80** B3
Butlers La BH24 . . . . **7** A1
Buttercup Dr BH23 . . . . . **78** B4
Buttery The BH22 . . . . . . **77** A2
Byron CI BH22 . . . . **27** A1
Byron Ho 10 BH25 . . . . **82** A4
Byron Rd
  Barton on S BH25 . . . . . . **81** B3
  Bournemouth BH5 . . . . . . **97** C2

Byron Rd continued
  Wimborne Minster BH21 . . **22** C2

C

Cabot Bsns Village
  BH17 . . . . **66** A3
Cabot La BH17 . . . . **66** B4
Cabot Way BH25 . . . . **61** C2
Cadhay CI BH25 . . . . **61** B2
Cadnam Way BH8 . . . . . . **53** A2
Cadogan Rd BH24 . . . . . . **13** C3
Caesar's Way BH15 . . . . . . **45** B4
Caird Ave BH25 . . . . **82** C4
Cairns CI BH23 . . . . **75** C3
Caister CI BH23 . . . . **26** C2
Calder Rd BH17 . . . . **67** C4
Caledonian CI BH23 . . . . . **78** B2
Caledon Rd BH14 . . . . . . **93** B3
Calkin CI BH23 . . . . **76** A4
Calluna Rd BH12 . . . . **68** B4
Calmore CI BH8 . . . . **53** A2
Calvin Rd BH9 . . . . **71** C4
Cambridge Gdns BH23 . . . **55** C1
Cambridge Rd BH2 . . . . . . **95** A3
Camden CI BH9 . . . . **72** B4
Camden Hurst 1 SO41 . . **86** B2
Camellia CI BH21 . . . . **44** B3
Camellia Gdns BH25 . . . . **82** B4
Cameron Rd BH23 . . . . . . **77** A2
Camilla Ct BH13 . . . . **94** B2
Cammel Rd BH22 . . . . **35** A2
Campbell Rd
  Bournemouth BH1 . . . . **97** B4
  Burton BH23 . . . . **56** C2
Campion Gr BH23 . . . . . . **77** C1
Campion Way SO41 . . . . **111** A4
Canberra Rd BH23 . . . . . . **75** B4
Candys CI BH21 . . . . **29** B2
Candys La BH21 . . . . **29** B2
Canford Ave BH11 . . . . . . **50** B2
Canford Bottom BH21 . . . **24** C2
Canford Bottom Rdbt
  BH21 . . . . **24** C1
CANFORD CLIFFS **104** B4
Canford Cliffs Ave
  BH14 . . . . **93** B2
Canford Cliffs Rd BH13 . . **93** B2
Canford Cres BH13 . . . . **104** B3
Canford Ct BH13 . . . . . **104** B2
Canford Gdns BH11 . . . . . **50** A1
CANFORD HEATH **47** B1
Canford Heath Fst & Mid
  Schs BH17 . . . . **67** A3
Canford Heath Nature
  Reserve* BH11 . . . . **48** B4
Canford Heath Rd
  BH17 . . . . **47** B1
CANFORD MAGNA **32** A1
Canford Magna BH21 . . . **32** A1
Canford Park Events
  Arena & Sports Gd*
  BH21 . . . . **40** B3
Canford PI 2 BH13 . . . **104** C3
Canford Rd
  Bournemouth BH11 . . . . . **50** A1
  Poole BH15 . . . . **91** A4
Canford Sch BH21 . . . . . . **32** B2
Canford View Dr BH21 . . . **24** B2
Canford Way BH12 . . . . . . **48** C2
Cannon CI BH18 . . . . **46** A1
Cannon Hill Gdns BH21 . . **24** B3
Cannon Hill Rd BH21 . . . . **24** A3
Cannon Ho SO41 . . . . . . **111** A3
Cannon St SO41 . . . . . . **111** A3
Canons Wlk SO41 . . . . . . **87** A3
Canterbury Ct BH22 . . . . . **17** A1
Canute Dr BH23 . . . . **109** A3
Capella Ct BH21 . . . . **112** B1
Capesthorne BH23 . . . . . **102** B4
Capstans The BH14 . . . . **103** B4
Capstone PI BH8 . . . . **73** A1
Capstone Rd BH8 . . . . . . **72** B4
Captains Cove BH15 . . . . **89** B3
Captain's Row SO41 . . . **111** B3
Caradon PI BH31 . . . . **2** C2
Carbery Ave BH6 . . . . **99** A4
Carbery Gdns BH6 . . . . . . **99** B4
Carbery La 3 BH6 . . . . . **98** C3
Carbery Row 2 BH6 . . . **98** C3

Cardigan Rd
  Bournemouth BH9 . . . . **71** C3
  Poole BH12 . . . . **93** C4
Carey Rd BH9 . . . . **51** C3
Careys Rd BH8 . . . . **53** A3
Carina Ct BH13 . . . . **106** B3
Carisbrooke BH13 . . . . . **104** B3
Carisbrooke Cres BH15 . **89** A3
Carisbrooke Ct
  1 Christchurch BH23 . . . **80** B2
  New Milton BH25 . . . . . . **61** C2
Carisbrooke Way BH23 . . **79** B4
Carlinford 5 BH5 . . . . . . **97** C2
Carlton Ave BH25 . . . . . . **81** A3
Carlton Ho 4 SO41 . . . **111** A3
Carlton Mount BH2 . . . . **112** A1
Carlton Rd BH1 . . . . **96** C3
Carlyle Rd BH6 . . . . **75** A1
Carmel CI BH15 . . . . **89** A2
Carnarvon Rd 4 BH1 . . . **97** B3
Carnegie CI BH22 . . . . . . **69** A1
Caroline Ave BH23 . . . . . . **77** C1
Caroline Rd BH11 . . . . . . **50** B2
Carpenter CI SO41 . . . . . **110** C4
Carradale BH23 . . . . **78** B3
Carrbridge CI BH3 . . . . . . **71** A3
Carrbridge Gdns BH3 . . . **71** A3
Carrbridge Rd BH3 . . . . . **71** A3
Carrick Way BH25 . . . . . . **82** C4
Carrington CI SO41 . . . . . **87** B3
Carrington Cvn Pk
  SO41 . . . . **87** C1
Carrington La SO41 . . . . . **87** B2
Carroll Ave BH22 . . . . **27** B1
Carroll CI BH12 . . . . **70** A2
Carsworth Way BH17 . . . **48** A2
Carter Com Sch BH15 . . . **89** C2
Carters Ave BH15 . . . . . . **89** A4
Carter's La 9 BH15 . . . **90** C2
Cartref CI BH31 . . . . **2** C2
Cartwright CI BH10 . . . . . **50** C4
Carvers Ind Est BH24 . . . **13** B3
Carvers La BH24 . . . . **13** B3
Carysfort Rd BH1 . . . . . . **97** A3
Cashmoor CI 4 BH12 . . **69** C3
Caslake CI BH25 . . . . **81** C4
Cassel Ave BH13 . . . . **94** B1
Casselles Ct 6 BH25 . . **82** A4
Casterbridge 5
  BH4 . . . . **94** C3
Casterbridge Rd BH22 . . . **34** C3
Castle Ave BH23 . . . . **79** B3
Castle CI SO41 . . . . **87** B1
Castle Court Prep Sch
  BH21 . . . . **36** B3
Castle Ct 2 BH23 . . . . **80** A2
Castledene Cres BH14 . . **92** A2
Castle Gate CI BH8 . . . . . **52** C1
Castle Hill BH14 . . . . **92** B4
Castle Lane E BH7 . . . . . . **74** C3
Castle La W BH9 . . . . **52** C1
Castlemain Ave BH6 . . . . **98** C4
Castleman Ct BH22 . . . . . **16** B3
Castleman Way BH24 . . . **13** B2
Castlemews BH24 . . . . . . **12** A1
Castle Par BH7 . . . . **75** A2
Castlepoint BH8 . . . . **53** B1
Castle Rd BH9 . . . . **72** A4
Castle St
  Christchurch BH23 . . . . . . **76** B1
  Poole BH15 . . . . **90** C1
Castleton Ave BH10 . . . . **43** A2
Castlewood BH24 . . . . . . **12** B1
Catalina CI BH23 . . . . . . **78** A1
Catalina Dr BH15 . . . . . . **91** B1
Catherine Wheel Gdns
  BH23 . . . . **55** B2
Caton CI BH12 . . . . **70** B4
Cattistock Rd BH8 . . . . . **53** B1
Cavan Cres BH17 . . . . . . **48** A2
Cavendish Corner Mobile
  Home Pk 8 BH23 . . . . **13** C4
Cavendish Ct 9 BH4 . . . **94** C3
Cavendish Hall BH1 . . . . . **96** A4
Cavendish Rd BH1 . . . . . . **96** A4
Cavendish Rd BH1 . . . . . . **96** A4
Caversham CI BH15 . . . . **89** B3
Cawdor Rd BH3 . . . . **71** A3
Caxton CI BH23 . . . . **78** A2

Cecil Ave BH8 . . . . 72 C3
Cecil Cl BH21. . . . . 37 B2
Cecil Ct BH8 . . . . 72 B3
Cecil Hill BH8 . . . . 72 B3
Cecil Rd
Bournemouth BH5 . . . . . . 97 B3
Poole BH12. . . . . 69 A2
Cedar Ave
Bournemouth BH10 . . . . . 43 A2
Christchurch BH23. . . . . . 75 A3
St Leonards BH24 . . . . . . 18 C3
Cedar Cl BH16. . . . . 64 B4
Cedar Ct BH4. . . . . 94 B2
Cedar Dr Hordle SO41. . . . 85 B2
Wimborne Minster BH21 . . 24 A1
Cedar Gdns BH25. . . . . 81 C4
Cedar Grange **18** BH13. . 94 A4
Cedar Manor BH4. . . . . 94 C3
Cedars The BH4 . . . . 94 C2
Cedar Trad Pk BH21 . . . . . 25 C2
Cedar Way BH22. . . . . 26 C4
Celandine Cl BH23. . . . . . . 78 B3
Cellars Farm Rd BH6. . . . . 67 C2
Cemetery Ave BH15. . . . . . 67 C2
Cemetery Junc BH2 . . . . . . 71 C1
Cemetery Rd BH21. . . . . . . 22 B1
Centenary Cl SO41. . . . . . 107 C3
Centenary Ho BH23. . . . . . 76 B2
Centenary Way BH1 . . . . . . 97 B4
Central Ave
Corfe Mullen BH21. . . . . . 37 A3
Poole BH12. . . . . 69 B2
Central Dr
Bournemouth BH2 . . . . . . 71 B1
West Moors BH24 . . . . . . 28 B4
Centre La SO41. . . . . 85 C3
Centre Pl BH24 . . . . 13 A3
Cerne Abbas BH13. . . . . . . 94 A1
Cerne Cl BH9. . . . . 52 B3
Chaddesley Glen
BH13. . . . . 104 B2
Chaddesley Grange
BH13. . . . . 104 B2
Chaddesley Pines
BH13. . . . . 104 B1
Chaddesley Wood Rd
BH13. . . . . 104 B1
Chaffey Cl BH24 . . . . 14 A4
Chaffinch Cl
Broadstone BH17. . . . . . . 45 C2
New Milton BH25 . . . . . . 61 C1
Chalbury Cl BH17. . . . . 48 A2
Chalbury Ct **2** BH14. . . . 92 B4
Chaldecott Gdns BH10. . 50 C4
Chaldon Rd BH17. . . . . 47 C2
Chalfont Ave BH23. . . . . . . 55 A2
Chalice Cl BH14 . . . . 92 A4
Chalwyn Ind Est BH15,
BH12. . . . . 68 A3
Champion Cl SO41. . . . . . . 87 C2
Chander Cl BH27 . . . . 35 B4
Chandlers Cl BH7. . . . . 74 B3
Chandos Ave BH12. . . . . . . 70 A4
Channel Ct
Barton on S BH25. . . . . . 81 B2
Bournemouth BH6 . . . . . . 99 A2
Chant Cl BH23 . . . . 77 A2
Chantry Cl BH23 . . . . 79 C4
Chantry The BH1. . . . . 96 A3
Chapel Cl BH21. . . . . 36 C2
Chapel La
Bransgore BH23. . . . . . . 108 C2
Corfe Mullen BH21. . . . . . 36 C1
Poole BH15. . . . . 90 C2
Wimborne Minster BH21 . . 22 B1
Chapel Rd BH14 . . . . 92 A4
Chapel Rise BH24. . . . . 20 B2
Charborough Rd BH18 . . 46 B3
Charing Cl BH24 . . . . 13 B2
Charles Cres BH25 . . . . 62 B3
Charles Gdns BH10 . . . . . 51 A2
Charles Keightley Ct
BH21. . . . . 31 A4
Charles Rd
Christchurch BH23. . . . . . 77 C3
Poole BH15. . . . . 91 A3
Charlotte Cl
Christchurch BH23. . . . . . 78 A1
3 New Milton BH25 . . . . 82 A4

Charlotte Cl continued
Poole BH12. . . . . 70 C3
Charlton Cl
Bournemouth BH9 . . . . . . 52 C3
Hordle SO41. . . . . 63 C1
Charltons The BH2. . . . . . . 71 C1
CHARMINSTER 52 B1
Charminster Ave BH9 . . . 72 B4
Charminster Cl BH8 . . . . . 52 B1
Charminster Pl BH8 . . . . . 52 C1
Charminster Rd BH8 . . . . 72 B2
Charmouth Gr BH14 . . . . 92 A4
Charnock Cl SO41 . . . . . . 63 C1
Charnwood Ave BH9. . . . . 52 B2
Charnwood Cl BH22 . . . . . 16 C2
Chartcombe BH13 . . . . . 104 B4
Charter Rd BH11. . . . . 41 A2
Chartwell **5** BH13 . . . . . 94 B3
Chaseside BH7 . . . . 74 A3
Chase The
St Leonards BH24 . . . . . . 12 B1
Verwood BH31 . . . . 3 C1
Chatsworth Rd
Bournemouth BH8 . . . . . . 72 C1
Poole BH14. . . . . 68 B1
Chatsworth Way BH15 . . . 61 C2
Chaucer Cl BH21 . . . . 22 C2
Chaucer Dr SO41. . . . . 87 A3
Chaucer Rd BH13. . . . . . 104 C4
Cheam Rd BH18 . . . . 45 C4
Cheddington Rd BH9 . . . . 52 A3
Chedington Cl BH17 . . . . . 47 B2
Chelmsford Rd BH16. . . . . 64 A3
Cheltenham Rd BH12 . . . . 68 C1
Chene Rd BH21. . . . . 31 A4
Chequers Cl SO41 . . . . . . 110 A2
Cherford Rd BH11 . . . . . . 50 B2
Cherita Ct BH15 . . . . 67 C2
Cheriton **7** BH4 . . . . 94 C2
Cheriton Ave BH7. . . . . 74 C3
Cheriton Way BH21 . . . . . 22 C2
Cherrett Cl BH11 . . . . 49 C4
Cherries Dr BH9. . . . . 51 B2
Cherry Cl BH14 . . . . 92 B4
Cherry Ct BH8 . . . . 68 B1
Cherry Gr BH22. . . . . 26 C2
Cherry Hill Gdns BH16 . . 64 B2
Cherry Hill Gr BH16. . . . . 64 B2
Cherry Tree Cl
Hordle SO41. . . . . 85 B2
St Leonards BH24 . . . . . . 18 B3
Cherry Tree Ct **4** BH25. . 82 B3
Cherry Tree Dr BH25. . . . . 61 B4
Cheshire Dr BH8. . . . . 54 A1
Chesilbourne Gr BH8 . . . . 53 A2
Chesildene Ave BH8 . . . . . 53 A2
Chesildene Dr BH8 . . . . . . 53 A2
Chesil Gdns BH12. . . . . . . 68 B4
Chessel Ave BH5. . . . . 97 C3
Chesterfield Cl BH13. . . . 104 C4
Chesterfield Ct BH1. . . . . . 96 C2
Chester Rd BH13 . . . . 94 A2
Chestnut Ave
Barton on S BH25. . . . . . 82 A2
Bournemouth BH6 . . . . . . 98 C3
Christchurch BH23. . . . . . 75 A3
Chestnut Gr BH21 . . . . . . 25 B2
Chestnut Way BH23. . . . . 56 C2
Chetnole Cl BH17 . . . . 48 A1
Chetwode Way BH17. . . . . 46 B2
Cheviot Court Flats
BH23. . . . . 77 C3
Cheviots The BH14 . . . . . . 92 C3
Cheviot Way BH31 . . . . . . 2 C1
Chewton Common Rd
BH23. . . . . 80 B3
Chewton Farm Rd
BH23. . . . . 80 C4
Chewton Lodge BH23 . . . 80 B3
Chewton Mews BH23 . . . . 60 A1
Chewton Way BH23. . . . . . 80 B4
Cheyne Gdns BH4 . . . . . . 94 C2
Chichester Rd BH24 . . . . . 7 A1
Chichester Way BH23 . . 102 A4
Chichester Wlk BH21 . . . . 31 B1
Chickerell Cl BH9. . . . . 52 B2
Chideock Cl BH12 . . . . . . 69 B2
Chigwell Rd BH8 . . . . 72 B4
CHILBRIDGE 21 B3

Chilcombe Rd BH6 . . . . . . 98 B4
Chilfrome Cl BH17. . . . . . . 46 C1
Chiltern Cl
Old Milton BH25 . . . . . . 81 C4
Poole BH4. . . . . 70 B1
Chiltern Ct **5** BH23. . . . . 77 C3
Chiltern Dr
Barton on S BH25. . . . . . 81 B3
Verwood BH31. . . . . 2 C1
Chimes The BH4. . . . . 94 B3
Chine Cres BH2. . . . . 95 A2
Chine Crescent Rd BH2 . . 95 A2
Chine Wlk BH22 . . . . 35 B1
Chislehurst **16** BH4 . . . . 94 C3
Chiswell Rd BH17. . . . . 47 A1
Chloe Gdns BH12 . . . . 69 A3
Chorley Cl BH15 . . . . 66 C2
Chris Cres BH16 . . . . 64 C3
CHRISTCHURCH 101 A4
Christchurch Bay Rd
BH25. . . . . 81 C2
Christchurch By-Pass
BH23. . . . . 77 A3
Christchurch Castle★
BH23. . . . . 76 B1
Christchurch Hospl
BH23. . . . . 75 C3
Christchurch Jun Sch
BH23. . . . . 76 A2
Christchurch Prim Sch
BH23. . . . . 76 A2
Christchurch Priory★
BH23. . . . . 76 C1
Christchurch Rd
Barton on S BH25. . . . . . 81 A3
Bournemouth, Boscombe
BH1, BH7 . . . . 97 A3
Bournemouth, Iford BH7 . . 74 B1
Ferndown BH22 . . . . 34 C1
Hordle SO41. . . . . 85 A2
Hurn BH23 . . . . 54 C4
Ringwood BH24 . . . . 13 A3
Christchurch Sta BH23. . 76 A2
Christopher Cres BH15. . 66 C2
Christ the King RC Prim
Sch BH11 . . . . 42 A1
Churchfield Cres BH15. . 91 A4
Churchfield Ct **2** BH15. . 91 B3
Churchfield Rd BH15. . . . 91 B3
Church Hill
Milford on S SO41 . . . . . 87 B2
Verwood BH31 . . . . 2 B2
Churchill Cres BH12 . . . . . 68 C2
Churchill Ct BH25. . . . . . . 61 C1
Churchill Gdns BH12. . . . 68 C1
Churchill Rd
Bournemouth BH1 . . . . . . 97 B4
Poole BH12. . . . . 69 A2
Wimborne Minster BH21. . 31 B3
Church La
Christchurch BH23. . . . . . 76 B1
Ferndown BH22 . . . . 43 C3
Lymington SO41 . . . . . . 111 A2
Old Milton BH25. . . . . . . 81 C4
Sway SO41. . . . . 107 B2
Church Mead **9** SO41 . . 111 A1
Churchmoor Rd BH21. . . . 24 A1
Church Rd
Bournemouth BH6 . . . . . . 99 C2
Ferndown BH22 . . . . 26 C1
Poole BH14. . . . . 92 A4
Three Legged Cross BH21 . . 4 B1
Church St
Christchurch BH23. . . . . . 76 C1
Poole BH15. . . . . 90 B1
6 Wimborne Minster
BH21. . . . . 22 B1
Cinnamon La **7** BH15. . . 90 B1
Circle The
3 Bournemouth BH9 . . . 52 B3
Poole BH13. . . . . 104 C3
Claire Ct **6** BH23 . . . . . . 80 A2
Clare Lodge Cl BH23. . . . 108 C3
Claremont Ave BH9 . . . . . . 52 B1
Claremont Rd BH9. . . . . . . 52 B1
Clarence Park Rd BH7 . . 74 A1
Clarence Pl BH23 . . . . 75 C3
Clarence Rd **3** BH14. . . . 92 A3
Clarendon Cl BH18 . . . . . 46 A4

Clarendon Ct **3** BH2. . . . 95 A2
Clarendon Pk SO41 . . . . . 110 C3
Clarendon Rd
Bournemouth BH4 . . . . . . 95 A3
Broadstone BH18. . . . . . 45 C4
Christchurch BH23 . . . . . 76 A2
Clark's Cl BH24 . . . . 13 B3
Clayford Ave BH10. . . . . . . 26 B3
Clayford Cl BH17 . . . . 47 A2
Claylake Dr BH31 . . . . 5 A1
Cleasby Grange **2** BH5 . 97 C2
Cleeve Ho BH25 . . . . 81 C2
Cleeves Cl BH12 . . . . 49 A2
Clematis Cl BH23 . . . . 78 C3
Clement Mews BH4. . . . . . 94 B3
Cleveland Cl BH25. . . . . . . 81 A2
Cleveland Ct **4** BH25 . . . 92 A2
Cleveland Gdns BH1 . . . . 96 C4
Cleveland Rd BH1 . . . . 97 A4
Cliff Cres BH25 . . . . 81 C2
Cliff Dr
Christchurch BH23. . . . . . 78 C1
Poole BH13. . . . . 104 B2
Cliffe Rd BH25. . . . . 81 B2
Clifford Rd BH9. . . . . 72 A4
Cliff Rd SO41. . . . . 86 B2
Cliff Wlk **17** BH4 . . . . 94 C2
Clifton Ct
1 Bournemouth BH7 . . . 97 C3
Hamworthy BH15 . . . . . . 89 A4
3 New Milton BH25 . . . . 82 A3
Clifton Gdns BH22 . . . . . . 34 C4
Clifton Rd
Bournemouth BH6 . . . . . . 99 A2
Poole BH14. . . . . 93 B2
Clingan Rd BH6 . . . . 75 A2
Clinton Cl BH23 . . . . 60 B1
Clinton Rd SO41 . . . . 111 A4
Clive Ct **22** BH4 . . . . 94 C3
Cliveden Cl BH22 . . . . 26 C3
Clive Rd
Bournemouth BH9 . . . . . . 51 C1
Christchurch BH23 . . . . . 59 B1
Cloisters The
3 Christchurch BH23 . . . 76 B1
Lymington SO41 . . . . . . 111 A2
Ringwood BH24 . . . . 14 A2
Close The
Barton on S BH25. . . . . . 82 B2
Broadstone BH18. . . . . . 45 B3
Ringwood BH24 . . . . 13 A3
St Leonards, Avon Castle
BH24. . . . . 20 B4
St Leonards, St Ives
BH24. . . . . 19 B4
Sway SO41. . . . . 107 A3
Clough's Rd BH24 . . . . . . 13 C3
Clover Cl BH23 . . . . 78 B3
Clover Ct BH25 . . . . 63 A2
Clover Dr BH17 . . . . 45 C1
Clovers The BH12. . . . . . . 70 A4
Clowes Ave BH6 . . . . 100 B2
Clyde Rd BH17. . . . . 46 B2
Coach House Mews
BH22. . . . . 27 C3
Coach House Pl BH11. . . 96 A4
Coastguard Cotts
Barton on S BH25. . . . . . 81 B3
Lymington SO41 . . . . . . 111 C1
Coastguard Way
BH23. . . . . 101 C4
Cobbs La BH15 . . . . 67 B2
Cobb's Rd BH21 . . . . 23 B2
Cobham Rd
Bournemouth BH9 . . . . . . 52 A2
Ferndown BH21. . . . . 26 A4
Cobham Way BH21 . . . . . . 31 B1
Cockerell Cl BH21 . . . . . . 31 C1
Codogan Ct **3** BH1. . . . . 96 B2
Cogdean Cl BH21 . . . . 37 B4
Cogdean Elms BH21 . . . . 37 B4
Cogdean Way BH21 . . . . . 37 B4
Cogdean Wlk BH21 . . . . . 37 B4
Colborne Ave BH21 . . . . . 23 C2
Colborne Cl
Lymington SO41 . . . . . . 111 A4
Poole BH15. . . . . 90 C3
Colbourne Cl BH23 . . . . . 108 C2
COLEHILL 24 B4
Colehill Cres BH9. . . . . 52 B2

Colehill Fst Sch BH21. . . 24 A3
Colehill La Colehill BH21 . 23 C4
Wimborne Minster BH21 . . 24 A4
Coleman Rd BH11 . . . . . . 50 C3
Colemere Gdns BH23 . . . 79 C3
Colemore Rd BH7 . . . . 74 C2
Coleridge Gn BH23 . . . . . 77 C3
Coles Ave BH15. . . . . 89 B2
Coles Gdns BH15 . . . . 89 B2
Colin Cl BH21. . . . . 37 A1
College Rd
Bournemouth BH5 . . . . . . 98 A3
Ringwood BH24 . . . . 13 B3
Collingbourne Ave BH6 . 75 A2
Collingwood Rd BH21 . . . 31 A2
Collins La BH24. . . . . 13 B3
Collwood Cl BH15 . . . . . . 66 C3
Colman Ct BH1. . . . . 96 C2
Colonnade Rd **3** BH5. . . 98 A4
Colonnade Road W **2**
BH5. . . . . 98 A4
Colt Cl BH21. . . . . 20 C2
Columbian Way BH10 . . . 50 C2
Columbia Rd BH10. . . . . . 50 C3
Columbia Trees La
BH10. . . . . 50 C1
Columbine Cl BH23 . . . . . 78 B4
Colville Cl **4** BH5. . . . . . . 98 A4
Colville Rd **5** BH5. . . . . . 98 A4
Comber Rd **1** BH9 . . . . . 52 A2
Comet Way BH23 . . . . 78 A1
Comley Rd BH9. . . . . 51 C2
Commercial Rd
Bournemouth BH2 . . . . . 112 A2
Poole BH14. . . . . 93 A2
Compton Acres Gdns★
BH13. . . . . 104 B3
Compton Ave BH14 . . . . . 93 A1
Compton Beeches
BH24. . . . . 11 B1
Compton Cl BH31. . . . . . . 2 C2
Compton Cres BH22 . . . . 17 C1
Compton Ct
4 Bournemouth BH6 . . . 99 C3
Poole BH14. . . . . 93 A3
Compton Dr BH14 . . . . . . 92 C2
Compton Gdns BH14. . . . 92 C2
Compton Lo **26** BH4 . . . 94 C3
Compton Rd BH25 . . . . . . 82 A4
Condor Cl BH21 . . . . 9 C1
Coneygar La BH22. . . . . . . 34 B3
Conference Pl **5**
SO41. . . . . 111 B1
Conifer Ave BH14. . . . . . . 92 B2
Conifer Cl
Christchurch BH23. . . . . . 55 A2
Ferndown BH22 . . . . 35 C1
St Leonards BH24 . . . . . . 18 B4
Conifer Cres SO41 . . . . . 110 A2
Conifers **4** BH13 . . . . . . 94 B3
Coniston Ave BH11 . . . . . 41 C2
Coniston Cl BH31 . . . . 2 B1
Coniston Rd BH24 . . . . . . 13 C2
Connaught Cl BH25. . . . . 81 B4
Connaught Cres BH12 . . 69 B2
Connaught Rd BH5 . . . . . 98 B4
Connell Rd BH15 . . . . 66 C1
Consort Cl BH12. . . . . 68 C1
Consort Ho BH22 . . . . 27 A2
Constable Cl BH22. . . . . . 34 C4
Constitution Hill Gdns
BH14. . . . . 68 A1
Constitution Hill Rd
BH14. . . . . 68 A1
Convent Meadow Mobile
Home Site BH23 . . . . . 100 C4
Conway Cl BH25. . . . . 62 B1
Conway **10** BH25 . . . . . . 62 B1
Conways Dr BH14. . . . . . . 92 A4
Cook Cl BH24. . . . . 14 A4
Cooke Gdns BH12 . . . . . . 69 C2
Cooke Rd BH12. . . . . 69 C2
Cook Row BH21. . . . . 30 B4
Coolhurst BH14. . . . . 103 C3
Coombe Ave BH10 . . . . . . 51 B3
Coombe Gdns BH10 . . . . 51 B2
Cooper Dean Dr BH8 . . . 73 C4

Cooper Dean Rdbt The BH7, BH8 ..... 74 A4
Coopers La BH11 ..... 2 C4
Copeland Dr BH14 ..... 92 B2
Copper Beech Cl BH14 ..... 94 A4
Copper Beeches BH2 ..... 112 B3
Copper Beech Gdns BH10 ..... 51 A2
Coppercourt Leaze **5** BH21 ..... 30 C4
Coppice Ave BH22 ..... 26 B3
Coppice Cl
 New Milton BH25 ..... 63 A2
 St Leonards BH24 ..... 19 A4
Coppice The BH23 ..... 78 B1
Coppice View BH10 ..... 51 B3
Copse Ave BH25 ..... 82 B4
Copse Cl BH14 ..... 91 C3
Copse Rd
 New Milton BH25 ..... 82 B4
 Verwood BH31 ..... 2 C2
Copse The BH24 ..... 28 C4
Copse Way BH23 ..... 79 B3
Copsewood Ave BH8 ..... 73 B4
Copythorne Cl BH8 ..... 53 A1
Coral Ct **2** BH13 ..... 94 A4
Corbar Rd BH23 ..... 75 B3
Corbiere Ave BH12 ..... 49 A1
Corbin Ave BH22 ..... 28 A2
Corbin Ct SO41 ..... 110 A1
Corbin Rd SO41 ..... 110 A1
Corfe Halt Cl BH21 ..... 29 B1
Corfe Hills Sch BH18 ..... 37 C2
Corfe Lodge Rd BH18 ..... 45 A3
Corfe Mews BH15 ..... 91 A4
CORFE MULLEN 36 C2
Corfe View Rd
 Corfe Mullen BH21 ..... 36 C1
 Poole BH14 ..... 92 C3
Corfe Way BH18 ..... 45 B3
Corfu BH13 ..... 104 B2
Corhampton Rd BH6 ..... 74 C1
Cornelia Cres BH12 ..... 70 A2
Cornerways Ct **3** BH25 ..... 82 B4
Cornflower Dr BH23 ..... 78 C3
Cornford Way BH23 ..... 79 A3
Cornish Gdns BH10 ..... 51 A1
Cornmarket Ct **7** BH21 ..... 2 B2
Cornwallis Rd SO41 ..... 86 B2
Coronation Ave
 Bournemouth BH9 ..... 51 C2
 Upton BH16 ..... 64 B3
Coronation Cl BH31 ..... 2 C3
Coronation Rd BH31 ..... 2 C3
Corporation Rd BH1 ..... 96 C4
Corpus Christi RC Prim Sch BH5 ..... 98 A4
Corscombe Cl BH17 ..... 47 B2
Cortmerron **20** BH4 ..... 94 C2
Cortry Cl BH12 ..... 70 A3
Cotes Ave BH14 ..... 68 A1
Cotes Ct BH14 ..... 68 A1
Cotlands Rd BH8 ..... 96 B3
Cotswold Cl BH31 ..... 2 C1
Cotswold Ct **6** BH23 ..... 77 C3
Cottage Gdns BH12 ..... 68 C1
Cottagers La SO41 ..... 84 A3
Cotton Cl BH18 ..... 37 C1
Countess Cl BH21 ..... 39 B4
Countess Gdns BH7 ..... 73 C3
County Gates La **10** BH4 ..... 94 B4
Court Cl
 3 Christchurch BH23 ..... 77 B2
 Lymington SO41 ..... 110 C1
Courtenay Dr BH21 ..... 22 C2
Courtenay Pl SO41 ..... 111 A2
Courtenay Rd BH14 ..... 92 B4
Courthill Fst Sch BH14 ..... 93 A4
Courthill Rd BH14 ..... 92 C4
Courtlands **3** SO41 ..... 111 A3
Courtleigh Manor **6** BH5 ..... 97 A3
Courtney Pl BH21 ..... 36 C1
Court Rd BH9 ..... 72 B4
Court The SO41 ..... 110 C1
Courtyard The BH23 ..... 77 A1

Courtyard The BH12 ..... 48 C1
Courtyard The BH21 ..... 32 A1
Covena Rd BH6 ..... 75 B1
Coventry Cl BH11 ..... 44 C4
Coventry Cres BH17 ..... 46 A1
Cove Rd BH10 ..... 50 C2
Cowdrey Gdns BH8 ..... 53 C1
Cowdrys Field **2** BH21 ..... 22 B2
Cowell Dr BH7 ..... 74 B3
COWGROVE 29 A4
Cowgrove Rd BH21 ..... 21 C1
Cowley Rd
 Lymington SO41 ..... 110 B3
 Poole BH17 ..... 67 A4
Cowleys Rd BH23 ..... 56 C1
Cowper Ave BH25 ..... 82 A3
Cowper Rd BH9 ..... 51 C2
Cowpitts La BH24 ..... 7 B2
Cowslip Rd BH18 ..... 45 C2
Cox Ave BH9 ..... 52 B3
Cox Cl BH9 ..... 52 B3
Coxstone La **2** BH24 ..... 13 B2
Coy Pond Rd BH12 ..... 70 B1
CRAB ORCHARD 4 C2
Crab Orchard Way BH21 ..... 4 C2
Crabton Close Rd BH5 ..... 97 C3
Crabtree Cl BH23 ..... 56 C1
Craigmoor Ave BH8 ..... 73 C4
Craigmoor Cl BH8 ..... 73 C4
Craigmoor Way BH8 ..... 53 B1
Craigside Rd BH24 ..... 18 B4
Craigwood Dr BH22 ..... 35 B4
Cranborne Cts
Cranborne Ct
17 Bournemouth, Westbourne BH4 ..... 94 C3
 Bournemouth, Winton BH9 ..... 72 B3
Cranborne Pl BH25 ..... 61 B2
Cranborne Rd
 Bournemouth BH2 ..... 112 A1
 Wimborne Minster BH21 ..... 22 C3
Cranbourne Ct BH17 ..... 48 A2
Cranbrook Mews BH12 ..... 68 B2
Cranbrook Rd BH12 ..... 68 B2
Crane Cl BH31 ..... 2 B2
Crane Dr BH31 ..... 2 B2
Cranemoor Ave BH23 ..... 59 B1
Cranemoor Cl BH23 ..... 59 B1
Cranemoor Gdns BH33 ..... 59 C1
Cranes Mews BH15 ..... 91 A3
Crane Way BH21 ..... 9 C2
Cranfield Ave BH21 ..... 23 A1
Cranleigh Ct BH6 ..... 99 B4
Cranleigh Gdns BH6 ..... 99 B4
Cranleigh Rd BH6 ..... 99 A4
Cranmer Rd BH9 ..... 71 C4
Cransley Ct
 4 Bournemouth BH4 ..... 94 C2
 Bournemouth BH4 ..... 94 C2
Crantock Gr BH8 ..... 53 C1
Cranwell Cl
 Bournemouth BH11 ..... 49 B4
 Bransgore BH23 ..... 109 A3
Crawshaw Rd BH14 ..... 92 B2
Creasey Rd BH11 ..... 42 A1
Creech Rd BH12 ..... 68 C1
Creedy Dr BH23 ..... 100 B4
CREEKMOOR 65 C4
Creekmoor La BH17 ..... 66 A4
Crescent Ct
 Barton on S BH25 ..... 81 C2
 14 Bournemouth BH2 ..... 95 A2
Crescent Dr BH25 ..... 81 C2
Crescent Rd
 Bournemouth BH2 ..... 112 A2
 Poole BH14 ..... 93 B4
 Verwood BH31 ..... 3 A2
 Wimborne Minster BH21 ..... 30 C4
Crescent The
 Barton on S BH25 ..... 81 A3
 3 Bournemouth BH1 ..... 97 B3
 West Moors BH22 ..... 28 B4
Crescent Wlk BH22 ..... 35 B2
Cresta Gdns BH22 ..... 35 B2
Crest Rd BH12 ..... 68 C2
Cribb Ct BH17 ..... 67 B3
Crichel Mount Rd BH14 ..... 103 C3

Crichel Rd BH9 ..... 72 A3
Cricket Chambers BH1... 96 A3
Cricket Cl BH23 ..... 101 C4
Crimea Rd BH9 ..... 71 C3
Cringle Ave BH6 ..... 100 A3
Crispin Cl BH23 ..... 79 C3
Criterion Arc **18** BH1.. 112 B2
Crittall Cl SO41 ..... 107 C3
Crockford Cl BH25 ..... 62 B3
Croft Cl BH21 ..... 37 A3
Crofton Cl BH23 ..... 75 B4
Croft Rd
 Bournemouth BH9 ..... 51 C2
 Christchurch BH23 ..... 77 C2
 Poole BH12 ..... 68 B2
 Ringwood BH24 ..... 7 A1
Cromer Gdns BH12 ..... 69 C1
Cromer Rd
 Bournemouth BH8 ..... 73 A2
 Poole BH12 ..... 69 C1
Cromwell Pl **2** BH5 ..... 98 B4
Cromwell Rd
 Bournemouth BH5 ..... 98 B4
 Poole BH12 ..... 69 A1
4 Wimborne Minster BH21 ..... 31 A4
Crosby Rd BH4 ..... 94 C1
Crossmead Ave BH25 ..... 82 A4
Cross Way BH23 ..... 75 A4
Crossways SO41 ..... 86 B3
Crossways BH21 ..... 85 B3
Crossways The BH16 ..... 64 C3
Crow Arch La BH24 ..... 13 C2
Crow Arch Lane Ind Est BH24 ..... 13 C1
Crowe Hill Ct **2** BH15... 91 B4
Crow La BH24 ..... 14 A1
Crown Cl SO41 ..... 68 C1
Crown Ct **4** BH21 ..... 22 B1
Crown Mead BH21 ..... 30 C4
Crusader Cl **3** BH4 ..... 94 B4
Crusader Rd BH11 ..... 49 A4
Cruse Cl SO41 ..... 107 B3
Cruxton Farm Cytd BH21 ..... 31 A2
Cucklington Gdns BH9.. 52 B3
Cuckoo Hill Way BH23 ..... 109 B3
Cuckoo Rd BH12 ..... 68 A4
Cudnell Ave BH11 ..... 42 A2
Cul-De-Sac BH25 ..... 80 C3
Culford Cl BH8 ..... 53 C1
Culford Ct **1** BH8 ..... 96 A4
Cull Cl BH12 ..... 70 C4
Culliford Cres BH17 ..... 47 B2
Cull La BH25 ..... 62 B3
Cullwood La BH25 ..... 62 B3
Culverhayes Cl **5** BH21 ..... 22 B2
Culverhayes Pl BH21 ..... 22 B2
Culverhayes Rd BH21 ..... 22 B2
Culver Rd BH25 ..... 61 C1
Cumnor Rd BH1 ..... 96 A2
Cunningham Cl
 Bournemouth BH11 ..... 50 A3
 Christchurch BH23 ..... 78 A1
 Ringwood BH24 ..... 14 A4
Cunningham Cres BH11... 50 B3
Cunningham Ct BH12 ..... 61 C2
Cunningham Pl BH11 ..... 50 A3
Curlew Cl BH22 ..... 26 B3
Curlew Rd
 Bournemouth BH8 ..... 53 A1
 Christchurch BH23 ..... 78 A1
Curlews The BH31 ..... 3 A1
Curlieu Rd BH15 ..... 67 B2
Curtis Rd BH12 ..... 68 C1
Curzon Ct **16** BH4 ..... 94 C3
Curzon Pl SO41 ..... 110 C1
Curzon Rd
 Bournemouth BH1 ..... 73 A1
 Poole BH14 ..... 92 A3
Curzon Way BH23 ..... 79 A3
Cuthbura Rd BH21 ..... 30 C4
Cuthbury Cl BH21 ..... 30 A4
Cuthbury Gdns BH21 ..... 22 A1
Cutler Cl
 New Milton BH25 ..... 62 C1
 Poole BH12 ..... 70 C3
Cutlers Pl BH21 ..... 24 A1

Cynthia Cl BH12 ..... 68 B3
Cynthia Ho BH12 ..... 68 B3
Cynthia Rd BH12 ..... 68 B3
Cypress Gr SO41 ..... 85 B2
Cyril Rd BH8 ..... 72 C1

D

Dacombe Cl BH16 ..... 64 C3
Dacombe Dr BH16 ..... 64 C3
Dacres Wlk **3** SO41 ..... 87 A3
Dahlia Cl BH15 ..... 67 B2
Dairy Cl
 Christchurch BH23 ..... 77 A2
 Corfe Mullen BH21 ..... 44 B4
Daisy Cl BH15 ..... 67 A2
Dakota Cl BH23 ..... 78 B2
Dale Cl BH15 ..... 67 C2
Dale Rd BH15 ..... 67 C2
Dales Cl BH21 ..... 24 C2
Dales Dr BH21 ..... 24 B1
Dale Valley Rd BH15 ..... 67 C2
Dalewood Ave BH11 ..... 41 B1
Dalkeith Arc BH1 ..... 112 B2
Dalkeith Rd
 Corfe Mullen BH21 ..... 45 A4
 Poole BH13 ..... 94 A1
Dalling Rd BH12 ..... 70 A1
Dalmeny Rd BH6 ..... 100 A2
Damerham Rd BH8 ..... 73 B4
Danecourt Cl BH14 ..... 91 C4
Danecourt Rd BH14 ..... 91 C4
Danecrest Rd SO41 ..... 63 C1
Dane Ct BH14 ..... 92 A4
Dane Dr BH22 ..... 35 B3
Danehurst Cl SO41 ..... 86 A4
Dane Rd SO41 ..... 86 A4
Danesbury Ave BH6... 99 C3
Danesbury Mdws BH25 ..... 62 C3
Danes Cl BH25 ..... 82 A1
Danestead Ho **3** BH25 ..... 82 A1
Danestream Cl SO41 ..... 87 A2
Danestream Ct SO41 ..... 87 B2
Daneswood Rd BH25 ..... 62 C1
Daniel Gdns **2** BH15 ..... 90 C1
Daniell's Cl SO41 ..... 111 A2
Daniell's Wlk SO41 ..... 111 A2
Dansie Cl BH14 ..... 92 B4
Darby's Cl BH15 ..... 67 C2
Darby's Cnr BH17 ..... 46 C2
Darby's La BH15 ..... 67 A4
Darby's La N BH17 ..... 67 A4
Dark La BH21 ..... 60 A3
Darley Rd BH22 ..... 34 C3
Darracott Rd BH5 ..... 98 B4
Darrian Ct BH16 ..... 64 B3
Darwin Ave BH23 ..... 75 B4
Darwin Ct **4** BH11 ..... 94 A4
Davenport Cl BH16 ..... 64 C3
David's La BH24 ..... 12 B1
David Way BH15 ..... 89 A2
Davis Ct BH12 ..... 69 B1
Davis Field BH25 ..... 61 C1
Davis Rd BH12 ..... 69 B1
Dawkins Bsns Ctr BH15 .. 89 A3
Dawkins Rd BH15 ..... 89 A3
Dawkins Way BH25 ..... 82 A4
Dawn Cl BH10 ..... 50 C2
Daws Ave BH11 ..... 50 B2
Daylesford Cl BH14 ..... 92 A2
Day's Ct SO41 ..... 87 A3
Day's Ct BH21 ..... 31 A4
Daytona Rd BH14 ..... 103 C3
Deacon Gdns BH11 ..... 42 A1
Deacon Rd BH11 ..... 42 A1
Dean Cl BH15 ..... 89 B3
Dean Court (Bournemouth FC) BH7... 73 C1
DEAN PARK 96 A3
Dean Park Cres BH1 ..... 112 B2
Dean Park Rd BH1 ..... 112 B3
Deans Court La BH21 ..... 30 C4
Deanscroft Rd BH10 ..... 51 B4
Deans Ct SO41 ..... 87 A3
Deans Gr BH21 ..... 23 A3
Deansleigh Rd BH7 ..... 74 B4
Dean's Rd **6** BH5 ..... 98 B4
Deans The BH11 ..... 112 B3
Dean Swift Cres BH14.. 103 C4
Dear Hay La BH15 ..... 90 C2

Decies Rd BH14 ..... 68 B1
De Courtenai Cl BH11... 41 B1
Deepdene La BH11 ..... 41 B1
Deerleap Way BH25 ..... 62 B3
Deer Park Cl BH25 ..... 61 C3
Dee Way BH15 ..... 90 B1
De Haviland Cl BH21 ..... 31 C2
De Havilland Ho BH23 ..... 78 A1
De Havilland Way BH23 ..... 78 A1
Delamere Gdns BH10 ..... 51 B3
De La Warr Rd SO41 ..... 86 C2
Delft Mews BH23 ..... 77 A1
Delhi Cl BH14 ..... 93 A3
Delhi Rd BH9 ..... 51 C2
Delilah Rd BH15 ..... 89 A2
De Lisle Rd BH3 ..... 71 C3
Delkeith Ct BH22 ..... 35 A4
Dell Cl BH18 ..... 45 B4
Dell The BH23 ..... 80 C3
Delph Rd BH21 ..... 39 A4
Delph Woods Woodland Trail* BH18, BH21...... 38 C3
Delta Cl BH23 ..... 78 A2
De Mauley Ct BH13 ..... 104 B4
De Mauley Rd BH13 ..... 104 B4
De Montfort Rd BH21 ..... 31 A1
De Mowbray Way SO41 ..... 110 C1
Denby Rd BH15 ..... 91 B4
Dene Cl BH24 ..... 7 A1
Denecote Lodge BH13 ..... 105 B4
Dene The BH13 ..... 94 A2
Deneve Ave BH17 ..... 46 C1
Dene Wlk BH22 ..... 35 B1
Denewood Copse BH22 ..... 16 B3
Denewood Rd
 Bournemouth BH4 ..... 94 B3
 West Moors BH22 ..... 16 B4
Denham Cl BH17 ..... 47 B3
Denham Dr BH23 ..... 79 C4
Denholm Cl BH24 ..... 7 B1
Denison Rd BH17 ..... 46 C1
Denmark La BH15 ..... 91 A3
Denmark Rd
 Bournemouth BH9 ..... 51 C1
 Poole BH15 ..... 91 A3
Denmark Terr BH1 ..... 73 B1
Denmead BH25 ..... 63 A2
Denmead Rd BH6 ..... 75 A2
Dennis Rd BH21 ..... 37 A1
Dennistoun Ave BH23 ..... 77 C2
Derby Rd BH1 ..... 96 C3
De Redvers Rd BH14 ..... 92 C2
Dereham Way BH12 ..... 69 C2
Derrybrian Gdns BH25 ..... 82 A4
Derwent Cl
 Bournemouth BH9 ..... 52 A1
 Ferndown BH22 ..... 28 A2
Derwent Rd BH25 ..... 62 B3
Derwentwater Rd BH21 ..... 30 C2
Deverel Cl BH23 ..... 76 A3
Devon Rd
 Christchurch BH23 ..... 75 B3
 Poole BH15 ..... 67 B1
Deweys La BH24 ..... 13 A3
Dewlands Pk BH31 ..... 2 A2
Dewlands Rd BH31 ..... 2 A2
Dewlands Way BH31 ..... 2 B2
Dewlish Cl BH17 ..... 48 A2
Dial Cl BH23 ..... 109 C4
Diana Cl BH22 ..... 27 A2
Diana Ct **7** BH23 ..... 80 A2
Diana Way BH21 ..... 37 B3
Dibden Cl BH8 ..... 53 A2
Dickens Rd BH6 ..... 75 A2
Didcot Rd BH17 ..... 67 A3
Dilly La BH25 ..... 82 A1
Dingle Rd BH5 ..... 98 B3
Dingley Rd BH15 ..... 67 A2
Dinham Ct BH25 ..... 63 A2
Dinham Rd BH25 ..... 63 A2
Diprose Rd BH12 ..... 69 C2
Discovery Court Bsns Ctr BH12 ..... 49 B2
Disraeli Rd BH23 ..... 77 A1
Doe Copse Way BH25 ..... 61 B3
Dogdean BH21 ..... 22 C4
Dogwood Rd BH18 ..... 45 B2
Dolbery Rd N BH12 ..... 49 A2

Dolbery Rd S BH12 . . . . . 48 C1
Dolphin Ave BH10 . . . . . . 43 B1
Dolphin Cl BH3 . . . . 94 B2
Dolphin Ctr 3 BH15 . . . . 90 C2
Dolphin Pl BH25 . . . . 82 A1
Dolphin Quays 10 BH15 . 90 C1
Dominion Ctr BH11 . . . . . 49 B3
Dominion Rd BH11 . . . . . 49 B3
Donnelly Rd BH6 . . . . 99 C4
Donnington Dr BH23 . . . . 78 B2
Donoughmore Rd 1
  BH1 . . . . 97 B3
Dorchester Gdns BH15 . . 67 B1
Dorchester Mans BH1 . . 97 A2
Dorchester Rd
  Poole BH15 . . . . 67 B2
  Upton BH16 . . . . 64 A3
Dormers The BH25 . . . . . 81 C4
Dornie Rd BH13 . . . . . . 104 B3
Dorset Ave BH22 . . . . 35 A3
Dorset Grange BH23 . . . 75 C2
Dorset Ho BH13 . . . . 94 B2
Dorset Lake Ave BH14. 103 B4
Dorset Lake Manor
  BH14. . . . . 92 A2
Dorset Rd
  Bournemouth BH4 . . . . . 70 C1
  Christchurch BH23 . . . . . 77 C3
Dorset Way BH17 . . . . . . 67 B3
Douglas Ave BH23 . . . . . 76 A1
Douglas Cl BH16. . . . . . . 64 C3
Douglas Gdns BH12. . . . 69 B1
Douglas Mews
  Bournemouth BH6 . . . . . 98 C4
  Upton BH16 . . . . 64 C4
Douglas Rd
  Bournemouth BH6 . . . . . 99 B3
  Poole BH12. . . . . 69 B1
Doulton Gdns BH14. . . . . 92 B2
Doussie Cl BH16. . . . . . . 64 B4
Dover Cl BH13 . . . . 94 A3
Dover Rd BH13 . . . . 94 A3
Doveshill Cres BH10 . . . 51 A3
Doveshill Gdns BH10 . . . 51 A3
Doveshill Mobile Home Pk
  BH10. . . . . 51 A3
Dowlands Cl BH10 . . . . . 51 A4
Dowlands Rd BH10 . . . . . 51 A4
Downey Cl BH11 . . . . 49 C2
Downlands Pl BH17. . . . . 67 C4
DOWNTON 83 C1
Downton Cl BH8. . . . . . . 53 A2
Downton Cvn Pk SO41. . 86 A4
Downton La SO41. . . . . . 83 C1
Doyne Rd BH14 . . . . 93 B4
Dragoon Way BH23 . . . . 75 C2
Drake Cl
  Christchurch BH23 . . . . . 77 C1
  New Milton BH25 . . . . . . 61 C2
  Ringwood BH24 . . . . 7 B1
Drake Ct 4 BH15 . . . . . . 90 C1
Drake Rd BH15 . . . . 90 C1
Drakes Rd BH22 . . . . 35 C3
Draper Rd
  Bournemouth BH11 . . . . 50 A4
  Christchurch BH23 . . . . . 77 B2
Draycott Rd BH10. . . . . . 51 A2
Dreswick Ct BH23. . . . . . 55 A3
Drew Cl BH12 . . . . 70 C3
Drew Grange BH15 . . . . . 89 B4
Drewitt Ind Est BH11 . . . 49 B3
Drive The
  Poole, Lilliput BH13 . . . 104 A3
  Poole, Upper Parkstone
    BH12. . . . . 69 A1
Droxford Rd BH6 . . . . . . 74 B1
Druids Cl BH22 . . . . 35 A2
Druitt Rd BH23 . . . . 77 C3
Drummond Rd BH1 . . . . . 97 A3
Drury Rd BH4 . . . . 94 B2
Dryden Cl BH24. . . . . 10 C1
Dryden Pl 4 SO41. . . . . . 87 A3
Duart Ct BH25 . . . . 62 C1
Ducking Stool La BH23 . 76 B1
Duck Island La 5 BH24 . 13 B2
Duck La BH11 . . . . 49 C4
Dudley Ave SO41 . . . . . . 63 C1
Dudley Gdns BH10 . . . . . 43 A1
Dudley Pl 3 BH25 . . . . . . 82 B3
Dudley Rd BH10 . . . . 43 A1

Dudmoor Farm Rd
  BH23. . . . . 55 C3
Dudmoor La BH23 . . . . . 55 C2
DUDSBURY 34 C1
Dudsbury Ave BH22. . . . 35 A4
Dudsbury Cres BH22. . . 35 B4
Dudsbury Gdns BH22 . . 43 B4
Dudsbury Rd BH22 . . . . 35 A1
Dudsway Ct BH22. . . . . . 35 A4
Dugdell Cl BH22 . . . . 27 C2
Dukes Cl BH6. . . . . 75 A1
Dukes Cl BH31. . . . . 2 C3
Dukes Dr BH11 . . . . 41 B1
Dukesfield BH23 . . . . . . 55 A1
Dulsie Rd BH3 . . . . 70 C3
Dumpton Sch BH21. . . . 23 A4
Dunbar Cres BH23 . . . . 59 C1
Dunbar Rd BH3 . . . . 71 B2
Duncan Rd BH25 . . . . . . 63 A2
Duncliff Rd BH6 . . . . . . 100 A3
Dundas Rd BH17. . . . . . . 67 B4
Dune Crest BH13 . . . . . 106 B3
Dunedin Cl BH22 . . . . . . 34 B3
Dunedin Dr BH22 . . . . . . 34 B3
Dunedin Gdns BH22 . . . 34 B3
Dunedin Gr BH23 . . . . . . 78 C2
Dunford Cl
  Barton on S BH25. . . . . . 81 B3
  Old Milton BH25. . . . . . . 81 B4
Dunford Rd BH12. . . . . . 69 A1
Dunkeld Rd BH3 . . . . . . 71 B2
Dunlin Cl BH23 . . . . 102 B4
Dunnock Cl BH22. . . . . . 26 B4
Dunstans La BH15 . . . . . 68 A2
Dunyeats Rd BH18 . . . . . 46 B4
Dunyeats Rdbt BH18. . . 39 A1
Duplock Ho BH25 . . . . . . 62 A1
Durdells Ave BH11 . . . . . 42 A1
Durdells Gdns BH11 . . . 42 A1
Durland Ct BH25. . . . . . . 82 A3
Durley Chine Ct 12
  BH2. . . . . 95 A2
Durley Chine Rd BH2 . . 95 A2
Durley Chine Rd S BH2. 95 A2
Durley Gdns BH2 . . . . . . 95 A2
Durley Rd BH2. . . . . . . 112 A1
Durley Rdbt BH2. . . . . . 112 A1
Durlston Court Sch
  BH25. . . . . 82 A2
Durlston Cres BH23. . . . 55 A3
Durlston Rd BH14. . . . . . 92 C2
Durnstown SO41. . . . . . 107 C3
Durrant Rd
  Bournemouth BH2 . . . . 112 A3
  Poole BH14. . . . . 92 C3
Durrant Way SO41. . . . 107 B3
Durrington Pl BH7. . . . . 74 B1
Durrington Rd BH7 . . . . 74 B2
Durweston Cl BH9 . . . . . 52 B2
Dymewood Rd BH21 . . . 8 C3

E

Eagle Rd BH13. . . . . 94 A4
Eagle Rise BH8. . . . . 73 A4
Eaglhurst 5 BH13 . . . . . 94 A4
Earle Rd BH4 . . . . 94 C1
Earley Ct SO41. . . . . . . 111 B3
Earlham Dr BH14 . . . . . . 92 C4
Earlsdon Way BH23 . . . 79 C3
Earlswood 10 BH4 . . . . . 94 C2
Earlswood Pk BH25. . . . 62 C2
East Ave
  Barton on S BH25. . . . . . 80 C2
  Bournemouth BH3 . . . . . 71 A2
East Avenue Rdbt BH3 . 71 B2
East Borough BH21 . . . . 22 B1
EAST BROOK 22 C1
Eastbrook Row BH21 . . 30 C4
Eastbury Ct BH23. . . . . 101 C3
East Cl BH25. . . . . 81 A3
East Cliff BH2 . . . . 112 B3
East Cliff Way BH7. . . . . 78 C2
Eastcott Cl BH7. . . . . . . 74 B3
East Dorset Trade Pk
  BH21. . . . . 25 C2
East Dr BH24 . . . . 28 B3
EAST END 29 B1
Eastern Rd SO41. . . . . . 110 C3
Eastern Way SO41. . . . . 87 C2

Easter Rd BH9 . . . . 52 A1
Eastfield Ct BH24 . . . . . . 14 A3
Eastfield La
  Ringwood, Hightown
    BH24. . . . . 14 A3
  Ringwood, Poulner
    BH24. . . . . 14 A4
East Hill SO41 . . . . 111 A3
EAST HOWE 50 C3
East Howe La BH10 . . . . 50 C4
East La SO41 . . . . 85 C3
Eastlake Ave BH12 . . . . 68 C2
Eastlands BH25. . . . . 82 B3
East Overcliff Dr BH1 . . 96 C2
East Quay 9 BH15. . . . . . 90 C1
East Quay Rd BH15 . . . . 90 C1
East St Poole BH15 . . . . 90 C1
  Wimborne Minster BH21 . 30 C4
East View Rd BH24 . . . . . 13 C3
East Way
  Bournemouth BH8 . . . . . 72 C4
  Corfe Mullen BH21. . . . . 37 A1
Eastwood Ave BH22. . . . 27 B2
Eastworth Rd BH31 . . . . 2 B3
Eaton Rd BH13 . . . . 94 A2
EBBLAKE 5 C3
Ebblake Cl BH31. . . . . . . 5 C3
Ebblake Ent Pk BH31 . . 3 C1
Ebblake Ind Est BH31 . . 5 C3
Ebenezer La BH24 . . . . . 13 A3
Ebor Cl BH22 . . . . 35 B2
Ebor Rd BH12 . . . . 69 A2
Ebury Ct 7 BH4. . . . . 94 C3
Eccles Rd BH15. . . . . 90 A2
Eden Ct
  9 Bournemouth BH1 . . . 96 B2
  11 Bournemouth,
    Westbourne BH4 . . . . . 94 C2
Eden Gr BH21 . . . . 31 A3
Edenhurst 12 BH4 . . . . . 94 C3
Edgarton Rd BH17 . . . . . 47 A3
Edgehill Rd BH9 . . . . 51 C1
Edgemoor Rd BH22 . . . . 17 C1
Edifred Rd BH9 . . . . 52 A3
Edmondsham Ho BH2 . 112 A2
Edmondsham Rd BH31. . 2 B4
Edmunds Cl 3 BH25. . . . 82 A3
Edward May Ct SO41. . . 54 A4
Edward Rd
  Bournemouth BH11 . . . . 50 B3
  Christchurch BH23 . . . . . 77 C3
  Poole BH14. . . . . 68 C1
Edwards Cl SO41 . . . . . . 110 A2
Edwards Ct BH23 . . . . . . 80 A3
Edwina Cl BH24 . . . . 7 A1
Edwina Dr BH17 . . . . 46 B2
Efford Ct SO41. . . . . 110 A1
Efford Way SO41. . . . . . . 110 A1
Egdon Cl BH22 . . . . 34 B3
Egdon Ct BH16 . . . . 64 B3
Egdon Dr BH21 . . . . 39 B4
Egerton Ct BH8. . . . . 73 A1
Egerton Gdns BH8. . . . . 73 A1
Egerton Rd BH8 . . . . 73 A1
Egmont Cl BH24 . . . . 20 B2
Egmont Dr BH24 . . . . . . 20 B2
Egmont Gdns BH24 . . . . 20 B2
Egmont Rd BH16 . . . . . . 88 B4
Elderberry La BH23 . . . . 77 C1
Eldon Ave BH25. . . . . 81 B3
Eldon Cl BH25. . . . . 81 B3
Eldon Ct 6 BH14 . . . . . . 92 A4
Eldon Pl BH4 . . . . 94 B3
Eldon Rd BH9 . . . . 51 B1
Eleanor Cl BH25. . . . . . . 81 C4
Eleanor Dr BH11. . . . . . . 41 A1
Eleanor Gdns BH23 . . . . 75 B3
Elfin Dr BH22 . . . . 26 C3
Elgar Cl SO41 . . . . 111 B3
Elgar Rd BH10 . . . . 51 A4
Elgin Rd
  Bournemouth BH4 . . . . . 71 A2
  Poole BH14. . . . . 92 C2
Elijah Cl BH15 . . . . 89 B2
Eliot Ho 8 BH25. . . . . . . 82 A4
Elise Ct BH17 . . . . 74 B3
Elizabeth Ave BH23 . . . . 75 C3
Elizabeth Cres SO41 . . . 84 B1
Elizabeth Ct
  1 Bournemouth BH1 . . . 96 B2

Elizabeth Ct continued
  Ferndown BH22 . . . . 27 A2
  8 New Milton BH25. . . . 82 B4
Elizabeth Gdns BH23. . . 79 A2
Elizabeth Rd
  Poole BH15. . . . . 91 A3
  Upton BH16 . . . . 64 C3
  Wimborne Minster BH21. . 22 C1
Elkhams Cl SO41 . . . . . . 85 B3
Ellery Gr SO41. . . . . 111 A4
Ellesfield Dr BH40 . . . . . 35 A2
Ellingham Rd BH25 . . . . 81 A3
Elliott Rd BH11 . . . . 49 C3
Elm Ave
  Christchurch BH23 . . . . . 75 B4
  New Milton BH25 . . . . . . 82 A4
Elm Cotts BH24 . . . . 13 B3
Elm Ct 5 BH25 . . . . 82 A4
Elmers Way BH23. . . . . . 109 A3
Elmes Rd BH9 . . . . 51 C2
Elmgate Dr BH7 . . . . 74 A2
Elm Gdns BH4. . . . . 70 C1
Elmhurst Rd
  Bournemouth BH11 . . . . 42 A1
  West Moors BH22 . . . . . 17 A2
Elmhurst Way BH22. . . . 17 A1
Elmore Dr BH24 . . . . 10 C2
Elmrise Prim Sch BH1. . 50 A4
Elms Ave BH14 . . . . 92 A1
Elms Cl BH14 . . . . 92 A1
Elmsdown Ct BH24 . . . . 13 A3
Elmstead Rd BH13 . . . . 104 C4
Elms Way BH6. . . . . 99 B3
Elm Tree Wlk BH22 . . . . 43 B4
Elmwood Way BH23 . . . 80 A2
Elphinstone Rd BH23 . . 80 B4
Eltham Cl BH7. . . . . 74 B3
Elvin Cl SO41. . . . . 63 C1
Elwyn Rd BH1, BH8. . . . 96 C4
Elysium Ct BH22. . . . . . . 35 B3
Embankment Way
  BH24. . . . . 13 C2
Emberley Cl BH22 . . . . . 28 A2
Emerald Cl BH24 . . . . . . 10 C2
Emerson Cl 12 BH15 . . . 90 C2
Emerson Rd BH15 . . . . . 91 A2
Emily Cl BH23 . . . . 76 A4
Emily Ct BH14 . . . . 69 B1
Emmanuel CE Mid Sch
  BH31. . . . . 2 B1
Emsworth Rd SO41 . . . . 111 A3
Encombe Cl BH12 . . . . . 69 C4
Endeavour Pk BH24 . . . . 13 C2
Endfield Cl BH23 . . . . . . 75 C4
Endfield Rd
  Bournemouth BH9 . . . . . 52 A1
  Christchurch BH23 . . . . . 75 B4
Enfield Ave BH15 . . . . . . 67 B2
Enfield Cres BH15 . . . . . 67 B2
Enfield Rd BH15 . . . . 67 B2
Englands Way BH11. . . . 49 A4
English Ct 15 BH2 . . . . . 95 A4
ENSBURY 43 C2
Ensbury Ave BH10 . . . . . 51 A1
Ensbury Cl BH10. . . . . . . 51 A1
Ensbury Ct BH10. . . . . . . 51 A1
ENSBURY PARK. 50 C2
Ensbury Park Rd BH9 . . 51 C1
Epiphany CE Prim Sch
  The BH9 . . . . 52 B3
Erica Dr BH21 . . . . 37 A2
Ericksen Rd BH11. . . . . . 50 C3
Erinbank Mans BH1. . . . 96 C2
Erpingham Rd BH12 . . . 70 A1
Esmonde Way BH17 . . . 67 C4
Esplanade BH13 . . . . . . 104 C3
Essex Ave BH23. . . . . . . 75 C4
Ethelbert Rd BH1 . . . . . . 31 A4
Eton Gdns BH4 . . . . 94 C4
Eton Mans 2 BH4 . . . . . 99 B2
Ettrick Rd BH13 . . . . 94 A2
Eucalyptus Ave BH24 . . 19 B2
Euston Gr BH24. . . . . 13 B2
Evans Cl
  Bournemouth BH11 . . . . 49 C1
  St Leonards BH24 . . . . . 10 C2
Evelyn Mews 1 BH9. . . . 51 C1
Evelyn Rd BH9. . . . . 51 A1
Evening Glade BH22 . . . 35 B4
Eventide Homes BH8 . . 53 B1

Everdene Cl BH22 . . . . . 34 C2
Everest Rd BH23 . . . . . . 77 B3
Everglades Cl BH22 . . . 27 A3
Evergreen Cl BH21. . . . . 8 C4
Evergreens BH24 . . . . . . 10 C1
Evering Ave BH12 . . . . . 49 A1
Evering Gdns BH12 . . . . 48 C1
Everlea Cl SO41 . . . . 85 B3
Everon Gdns BH25 . . . . 82 B3
Evershot Rd BH8 . . . . . . 53 B1
Eversleigh 10 BH2 . . . . . 95 A2
EVERTON 85 C3
Everton Rd SO41. . . . . . 84 B1
Evesham Cl BH7 . . . . . . 74 B3
Evesham Ct BH13. . . . . . 94 A1
Exbourne Manor BH1 . . 96 C2
Exbury Dr BH11. . . . . 41 C1
Excelsior Rd BH14 . . . . . 92 C3
Exeter Cres BH2 . . . . . . 112 B2
Exeter Ct 5 BH23 . . . . . . 80 B2
Exeter La BH2 . . . . 112 B2
Exeter Park Mans
  BH2. . . . . 112 B1
Exeter Park Rd BH2. . . . 112 B1
Exeter Rd BH2 . . . . 112 B2
Exton Rd BH6 . . . . 75 A2
Eynon Mews BH24 . . . . . 13 A2

F

Factory Rd BH16. . . . . . . 64 C2
Faircourt 8 BH25 . . . . . . 62 B1
Fairfield BH23 . . . . 76 B2
Fairfield Cl
  Christchurch BH23 . . . . . 76 B2
  Lymington SO41. . . . . . 111 A2
  Wimborne Minster BH21. . 23 C1
Fairfield Rd
  Barton on S BH25. . . . . . 81 B2
  Wimborne Minster BH21. . 31 A4
Fairhaven Ct 9 BH5 . . . . 97 B3
Fairies Dr BH22. . . . . 35 C3
Fairlawn BH22. . . . . 27 A1
Fair Lea BH2 . . . . 112 A1
Fairlea Rd SO41 . . . . . . 111 A4
Fairlie BH24 . . . . 7 A1
Fairlie Pk BH24. . . . . 6 C1
FAIRMILE. 75 C4
Fairmile Par BH23 . . . . . 75 C4
Fairmile Rd BH23 . . . . . . 75 C4
Fairthorn Ct BH2 . . . . . 112 B3
Fairview Cres BH18 . . . . 38 A1
Fairview Dr BH18 . . . . . . 38 A1
Fairview Pk BH14 . . . . . 92 C3
Fairview Rd BH18 . . . . . . 38 A1
Fairway Dr BH23. . . . . . . 75 C1
Fairway Rd BH14 . . . . . 103 C4
Fairways BH22 . . . . 27 C2
Fairway The BH25. . . . . . 82 B1
Fairwinds BH13. . . . . . . 106 A3
Falcon Dr BH23 . . . . . . 102 A4
Falconer Dr BH15. . . . . . 89 B4
Falkland Sq 2 BH15. . . . 90 C2
Fallows The BH25. . . . . . 62 B3
Fancy Rd BH12 . . . . 68 B4
Farcroft Rd BH12 . . . . . . 68 B1
Far Ends 4 BH14 . . . . . . 92 B4
Farm Cl BH24. . . . . 13 B4
Farm Ct BH21 . . . . 32 A4
Farmdene Cl BH23. . . . . 79 A3
Farmers Wlk
  Hordle SO41. . . . . 85 B2
  1 Wimborne Minster
    BH21. . . . . 22 B2
Farm La BH23 . . . . 102 A4
Farm La BH25 . . . . 82 A2
Farm La S BH25 . . . . 82 A2
Farm Rd BH22. . . . . 16 B2
Farnham Rd BH12 . . . . . 70 A3
Farnleys Mead SO41. . 111 A1
Farriers Cl BH21. . . . . . . 24 B2
Farrington 24 BH24 . . . . 94 C2
Farthings Ct The 13
  BH1. . . . . 96 A2
Farwell Cl BH23 . . . . 56 C2
Farwell Rd BH12. . . . . . . 48 C2

Faversham 🟑 BH2 . . . . **95** A2
Fawcett Rd BH25 . . . . **61** C1
Fawley Gn BH8 . . . . **53** A2
Fawn Gdns BH25 . . . . **61** C3
Fayrewood Ct BH31 . . . . **2** C3
Felton Cres BH23 . . . . **79** C3
Felton Cl BH14 . . . . **67** C1
Felton Rd BH14 . . . . **67** C1
Fenleigh Cl BH25 . . . . **82** B3
Fennel Gdns SO41 . . . . . . **111** A4
Fenton Rd BH6 . . . . **98** C4
Fenwick Ct BH8 . . . . **96** B4
Fern Bank
  🟝 Bournemouth
  BH2 . . . . **112** B2
  Three Legged Cross BH21 . . **8** C3
Fern Barrow BH12 . . . . **70** B3
Fern Cl BH23 . . . . **56** C1
Ferncroft Gdns BH10 . . . . **43** A1
Ferncroft Rd BH10 . . . . . . **43** A1
Ferndale Rd BH25 . . . . **62** B2
FERNDOWN **26** B1
Ferndown Fst Sch
  BH22 . . . . **26** C1
Ferndown Ind Est
  BH21 . . . . **25** C3
Ferndown Mid Sch
  BH22 . . . . **26** C1
Ferndown Upper Sch
  BH22 . . . . **26** B2
Fernglade BH25 . . . . **62** A1
Fernheath Cl BH11 . . . . . . **50** A3
Fernheath Rd BH11 . . . . . . **50** A3
Fernhill Cl BH17 . . . . **48** A2
Fernhill Flats 🟨 BH2 . . **112** B2
Fernhill Gate BH25 . . . . . . **62** A3
Fernhill La BH25 . . . . **62** A2
Fernhill Rd BH25 . . . . **62** A1
Fernlea BH23 . . . . **77** A1
Fernlea Ave BH22 . . . . **35** A4
Fernlea Cl
  Ferndown BH22 . . . . **35** A4
  St Leonards BH24 . . . . . . **18** C4
Fernlea Gdns BH22 . . . . . . **35** A4
Fernside Ave BH14 . . . . . . **91** C4
Fernside Bsns Pk BH22 . **26** A3
Fernside Ct BH15 . . . . **91** B4
Fernside Rd
  Bournemouth BH9 . . . . . . **71** B4
  Poole BH15 . . . . **91** B4
  West Moors BH22 . . . . . . **16** C2
Fernway Cl BH21 . . . . **32** B4
Fernwood Cl BH24 . . . . . . **11** C1
Ferris Ave BH8 . . . . **53** A1
Ferris Cl BH8 . . . . **53** A1
Ferris Pl BH8 . . . . **53** A1
Ferrypoint SO41 . . . . **111** C3
Ferry Rd
  Bournemouth BH6 . . . . . . **99** C2
  Poole, Lower Hamworthy
  BH15 . . . . **90** B1
Ferry Way BH13 . . . . **106** A3
Feversham Ave BH8 . . . . . **73** B4
Field Pl
  Barton on S BH25 . . . . . . **81** A3
  Verwood BH31 . . . . **2** B3
Fields The BH31 . . . . **2** C3
Fieldway BH24 . . . . **13** C4
Field Way
  Christchurch BH23 . . . . . . **79** A4
  Corfe Mullen BH21 . . . . . . **37** B4
Field Wlk SO41 . . . . **110** C4
Filton Rd SO41 . . . . **110** C3
Finchfield Ave BH11 . . . . . **41** C2
Fineshade 🟨 BH13 . . . . . **104** C3
Fir Ave BH25 . . . . **82** B4
Firbank Rd BH9 . . . . **72** B3
Fir Cl BH22 . . . . **16** C3
Firmain Rd BH12 . . . . **49** A1
Firmount Cl SO41 . . . . **85** C3
Firs Glen Rd
  Bournemouth BH9 . . . . . . **71** B4
  Verwood BH31 . . . . **5** A4
  West Moors BH22 . . . . . . **16** C2
Firshill BH23 . . . . **79** B3
Firside Rd BH21 . . . . **44** C4
Firs La BH14 . . . . **103** B4

Firs The BH1 . . . . **96** A3
First Marine Ave BH25 . . **81** C2
Firsway BH16 . . . . **64** C3
Fir Tree Cl BH24 . . . . **18** B2
Firtree Cres SO41 . . . . **63** C1
Fir Tree La BH23 . . . . **79** A4
Fir Vale Rd BH1 . . . . **112** B2
Fisherman's Ave BH5 . . . . **98** B3
Fisherman's Bank
  BH23 . . . . **101** B4
Fishermans Rd BH15 . . . . **90** C1
Fisherman's Wlk BH5 . . . . **98** B3
Fitzharris Ave BH9 . . . . . . **72** A2
Fitzmaurice Rd BH23 . . . . **75** B3
Fitzpain Cl BH22 . . . . **35** A2
Fitzpain Rd BH22 . . . . **35** A2
Fitzwilliam Cl BH11 . . . . . **41** B1
Fitzworth Ave BH16 . . . . . **88** C4
Flaghead BH13 . . . . **104** B2
Flaghead Chine Rd
  BH13 . . . . **104** B2
Flaghead Rd BH13 . . . . . . **104** B3
Flambard Ave BH23 . . . . . **76** A4
Flambard Rd BH14 . . . . . . **92** C2
Flazen Cl BH11 . . . . **49** A3
Fleetsbridge Bsns Ctr
  BH17 . . . . **66** B3
Fleet's Cnr BH17 . . . . **66** B3
Fleets Est BH15 . . . . **66** B2
Fleets La BH15 . . . . **66** C2
Fleetspoint Bsns Ctr
  BH15 . . . . **66** B1
Fleetwood Ct BH15 . . . . . . **66** C3
Fletcher Cl BH10 . . . . **51** A3
Fletcher Rd BH10 . . . . **51** A3
Floral Farm BH21 . . . . **32** A2
Florence Rd
  Bournemouth BH5 . . . . . . **97** C3
  Poole BH14 . . . . **93** A4
Floriston Gdns BH25 . . . . **63** A1
Flower Ct BH21 . . . . **31** A3
Flushards SO41 . . . . **111** B2
Folly Farm La BH24 . . . . . **12** A2
Fontmell Rd BH18 . . . . **46** C3
Footners La BH23 . . . . **56** C1
Ford Cl BH22 . . . . **27** C3
Ford La BH22 . . . . **28** A3
Foreland Cl BH23 . . . . **55** A3
Foreland Rd BH16 . . . . . . **88** C4
Forelle Ctr The BH31 . . . . . **5** C4
Forest Cl BH23 . . . . **79** A4
Forest Ct
  Lymington SO41 . . . . **110** A1
  New Milton BH25 . . . . . . **82** B4
Forest Edge Cl
  St Leonards BH24 . . . . . . **10** B1
  Sway SO41 . . . . **107** A4
Forest Edge Dr BH24 . . . . **10** B2
Forest Edge Rd BH24 . . . . **14** C1
Forest Hills BH24 . . . . **14** B2
Forest Ho 🟨 BH1 . . . . **96** A2
Forest La
  Ringwood BH24 . . . . **15** A2
  Verwood BH31 . . . . **2** B3
Forestlake Ave BH24 . . . . **14** B2
Forest Oak Dr BH25 . . . . . **62** A3
Forest Pines BH25 . . . . . . **62** A2
Forest Rd Poole BH13 . . . . **94** A2
  West Moors BH22 . . . . . . **17** A3
Forest Rise BH23 . . . . **59** A1
Forest Side Gdns BH24 . . . **7** A1
Forest View BH25 . . . . **61** A4
Forest View Cl BH9 . . . . . . **52** A1
Forest View Dr BH21 . . . . **26** A1
Forest View Rd BH9 . . . . . **52** A2
Forest Way
  Christchurch BH23 . . . . . . **79** A4
  Everton SO41 . . . . **85** B3
  Ferndown BH21 . . . . **26** A1
Forsyth Gdns BH10 . . . . . **50** C1
Fort Cumberland Cl
  BH15 . . . . **89** A2
Fortescue Rd
  Bournemouth BH3 . . . . . . **72** A1
  Poole BH12 . . . . **69** A2
Forton Cl BH10 . . . . **51** B4
Forward Dr SO41 . . . . **110** B1
FOULFORD **15** B3
Fountain Ct BH13 . . . . **94** B2

Fountain Rdbt BH23 . . . . **76** B1
Fountain Way BH23 . . . . . **76** B1
Four Wells Rd BH21 . . . . . **24** A3
Foxcote Gdns BH25 . . . . . **61** C2
Foxcroft Dr BH21 . . . . **24** B1
Foxdale Ct 🟨 BH2 . . . . . **112** A2
Foxes Cl BH31 . . . . **2** C1
Fox Field SO41 . . . . **85** B3
Foxglove Cl BH23 . . . . **78** C3
Foxglove Pl BH25 . . . . **63** A2
Foxgloves BH16 . . . . **64** B3
Foxhills BH31 . . . . **3** B2
FOXHOLES **68** A2
Foxholes 🟨 BH6 . . . . **99** C3
Foxholes Rd
  Bournemouth BH6 . . . . . . **99** C3
  Poole BH15 . . . . **67** C2
Fox La BH21 . . . . **24** C1
Foxwood Ave BH23 . . . . . **101** C4
Frampton Cl BH25 . . . . . . **62** C3
Frampton Pl BH24 . . . . **13** B3
Frampton Rd BH9 . . . . **72** A3
Francesca Ct 🟨 BH23 . . . **77** B2
Francesca Grange 🟨
  BH23 . . . . **77** B2
Francesca Lo 🟦 BH23 . . **77** B1
Frances Ct 🟨 BH23 . . . . . **80** B2
Frances Rd BH1 . . . . **96** C3
Francis Ave BH11 . . . . **49** A3
Francis Avenue Ind Est
  BH11 . . . . **49** A3
Francis Rd BH12 . . . . **49** A3
Frankland Cres BH14 . . . . **93** B3
Franklin Rd
  Bournemouth BH9 . . . . . . **52** A2
  New Milton BH25 . . . . . . **62** C2
Franklyn Cl BH16 . . . . **64** B3
Frankston Rd BH6 . . . . . . **98** C3
Franks Way BH17 . . . . **47** B4
Frank Wareham Cottage
  Homes The BH9 . . . . **52** A3
Fraser Ct BH25 . . . . **61** C2
Fraser Rd BH12 . . . . **69** C4
Freda Rd BH23 . . . . **75** C1
Frederica Rd BH9 . . . . **71** B4
Freemans Cl BH21 . . . . . . **24** B2
Freemans La BH21 . . . . . . **24** B2
Fremington Ct 🟨 BH25 . . **62** B1
French Rd BH17 . . . . **46** B1
French's Farm Rd BH16 . . **64** A3
Frensham Cl BH10 . . . . . . **51** B3
Freshwater Dr BH15 . . . . . **89** A3
Freshwater Rd BH23 . . . . . **78** C1
FRIARS CLIFF **79** A2
Friars Gate BH23 . . . . **78** B1
Friars Rd BH23 . . . . **78** B1
Friars Wlk BH25 . . . . **82** A2
Friday's Ct BH24 . . . . **13** A3
Frinton Ct 🟨 BH14 . . . . . **92** A4
Fritham Gdns BH8 . . . . . . **53** A2
Frobisher Ave BH12 . . . . . **49** C1
Frobisher Cl
  Christchurch BH23 . . . . . . **77** C1
  Ringwood BH24 . . . . **7** A1
Fromond Cl SO41 . . . . . . **111** A4
Frost Rd BH11 . . . . **49** C3
Froud Way BH21 . . . . **44** C4
Fryer Cl BH11 . . . . **42** B1
Fryers Copse BH21 . . . . . . **24** C2
Fryers Rd BH21 . . . . **8** A4
Frys La SO41 . . . . **85** B3
Fulcrum Ctr The BH12 . . . **48** C2
Fullerton Rd SO41 . . . . . . **110** B3
Fulmar Rd BH23 . . . . **102** A4
Fulwood Ave BH11 . . . . . . **41** B1
Furlong Mews BH24 . . . . . **13** A3
Furlong The BH24 . . . . **13** A3
Furnell Rd BH15 . . . . **91** A1
Furzebrook Cl BH17 . . . . . **47** B3
Furze Croft BH25 . . . . **82** A4
Furzehill BH21 . . . . **22** C4
Furze Hill Dr BH14 . . . . . . **92** C1
Furzelands Rd BH21 . . . . . **8** C4
Furzey Rd BH16 . . . . **64** B2
Furzy Whistlers Cl
  BH23 . . . . **109** A3

G

Gablehurst BH16 . . . . **64** C3

Gadbridge Ct 🟩 BH4 . . . **94** C2
Gainsborough Ave
  BH25 . . . . **62** B3
Gainsborough Ct
  🟨 Bournemouth BH5 . . . **98** B4
  Lymington SO41 . . . . **110** C1
Gainsborough Rd
  Bournemouth BH7 . . . . . . **73** C2
  St Leonards BH24 . . . . . . **11** A1
Gallop Way BH12 . . . . **70** C3
Galloway Rd BH15 . . . . . . **89** A4
Gallows Dr BH22 . . . . **35** B1
Galton Ave BH23 . . . . **75** C1
Garden Cl BH25 . . . . **82** A3
Garden Court Cotts
  BH22 . . . . **16** B3
Garden Cl BH1 . . . . **73** A1
Garden Ho 🟨 BH1 . . . . . . **96** B2
Garden-La BH24 . . . . **18** C3
Gardens Cres BH14 . . . . . **103** B4
Gardens Ct 🟩 BH15 . . . . **91** B3
Gardens Rd BH14 . . . . . . **103** B4
Garden Wlk BH22 . . . . **27** B3
Gardner Ct BH23 . . . . **75** B3
Gardner Rd
  Christchurch BH23 . . . . . . **75** B3
  Ringwood BH24 . . . . **13** C2
Garfield Ave BH1 . . . . **97** A4
Garland Rd BH15 . . . . **91** A4
Garrow Dr SO41 . . . . **111** A4
Garsdale Cl BH11 . . . . **42** A2
Garth Cl BH24 . . . . **18** B4
Garth Rd BH9 . . . . **72** A4
Gateway The BH13 . . . . . . **93** C4
Gaydon Rise BH11 . . . . . . **49** B4
Geneva Ave BH6 . . . . **99** A4
George Mews The
  BH24 . . . . **13** A3
George Rd SO41 . . . . **86** C3
George Rdbt The BH15 . . . **90** C1
Georges Mews BH21 . . . . **37** A3
Georgian Cl BH23 . . . . **13** B4
Georgian Way BH10 . . . . . **51** C4
Georgina Cl BH12 . . . . **70** C4
Georgina Talbot Ho
  BH12 . . . . **70** B4
Gerald Rd BH3 . . . . **72** A1
Germaine Cl BH23 . . . . . . **79** C3
Gervis Cres BH14 . . . . **92** A4
Gervis Rd BH1 . . . . **112** B2
Gervis Rd BH1 . . . . **96** B2
Gibson Rd BH17 . . . . **67** B3
Giddylake BH21 . . . . **23** A2
Gilbert Cl SO41 . . . . **110** C1
Gilbert Rd BH8 . . . . **73** A1
Gillam Rd BH10 . . . . **43** A1
Gillett Rd BH12 . . . . **70** C3
Gillingham Cl BH9 . . . . . . **52** C3
Gillingham Rd SO41 . . . . . **87** A2
Gillion Ct 🟨 BH23 . . . . . . **77** B1
Gilpin Hill SO41 . . . . **107** B3
Gilpins Folly SO41 . . . . . . **107** A4
Gladdis Rd BH11 . . . . **49** C3
Gladelands Cl BH18 . . . . . **45** B4
Gladelands Pk BH22 . . . . . **27** C3
Gladelands Way BH18 . . . **45** B4
Glade The
  Christchurch BH23 . . . . . . **75** B4
  St Leonards BH24 . . . . . . **10** C1
Gladstone Cl BH23 . . . . . . **77** A1
Gladstone Rd
  Bournemouth BH7 . . . . . . **97** C4
  Poole BH12 . . . . **68** C1
Gladstone Rd E BH7 . . . . . **97** C4
Gladstone Rd W BH1 . . . . **97** B4
Glamis Ave BH10 . . . . **43** B1
Gleadowe Ave BH23 . . . . . **76** A1
Glebefields 🟨 SO41 . . . . **87** A3
Glenair Ave BH14 . . . . **92** A3
Glenair Cres BH14 . . . . . . **92** A3
Glenair Rd BH14 . . . . **92** A3
Glenavon BH25 . . . . **82** C4
Glenavon Rd BH23 . . . . . . **79** C4
Glen Cl BH25 . . . . **81** A3
Glencoe Rd
  Bournemouth BH7 . . . . . . **73** C2
  Poole BH12 . . . . **69** A1
Glendale Ave BH22 . . . . . . **27** B2
Glendale Cl
  Christchurch BH23 . . . . . . **55** A2

Glendale Cl continued
  Wimborne Minster BH21 . . **22** C1
Glendale Ct BH23 . . . . **55** A2
Glendale Rd BH6 . . . . **100** A3
Glendon Ave BH10 . . . . . . **42** C2
Glendrive BH25 . . . . **80** C3
Gleneagles
  Christchurch BH23 . . . . . . **75** C1
  Poole BH13 . . . . **94** B2
Gleneagles Ave BH4 . . . . . **93** A2
Gleneagles Cl BH22 . . . . . **27** C2
Glenferness Ave BH4 . . . . **71** A1
Glen Fern Rd BH1 . . . . **96** A2
Glengariff Rd BH14 . . . . . . **92** C2
Glengarry BH25 . . . . **82** C4
Glengarry Way BH23 . . . . **78** C1
Glenives Cl BH24 . . . . **19** B4
Glenmeadows Dr BH10 . . **42** B1
Glenmoor Cl BH10 . . . . . . **51** A1
Glenmoor Rd
  Bournemouth BH9 . . . . . . **71** B4
  Ferndown BH22 . . . . **35** A3
Glenmoor Sch BH10 . . . . . **51** A1
Glenmount Dr BH14 . . . . . **92** B4
Glen Rd
  Bournemouth BH5 . . . . . . **97** C3
  Poole BH14 . . . . **92** B4
Glenroyd Gdns BH6 . . . . . **99** B3
Glenside BH23, BH25 . . . . **80** B2
Glen Spey BH25 . . . . **83** A4
Glen The Poole BH14 . . . . . **69** A2
  Poole, Canford Cliffs
  BH13 . . . . **104** B4
Glenville Cl BH23 . . . . **60** B1
Glenville Gdns BH10 . . . . **50** C2
Glenville Rd
  Bournemouth BH10 . . . . . **50** C1
  Walkford BH23 . . . . **60** B1
Glenwood Cl BH22 . . . . . . **16** C2
Glenwood La BH22 . . . . . . **16** C2
Glenwood Rd
  Verwood BH31 . . . . **2** C1
  West Moors BH22 . . . . . . **16** C2
Glenwood Way BH22 . . . . **16** C2
Glissons BH22 . . . . **34** A2
Globe La BH15 . . . . **90** C2
Gloucester Rd
  Bournemouth BH7 . . . . . . **97** C4
  Poole BH12 . . . . **69** B1
Glynville Cl BH21 . . . . **24** A3
Glynville Ct BH21 . . . . **24** A3
Glynville Rd BH21 . . . . **24** A3
Goathorn Cl BH16 . . . . **89** A4
Godmanston Cl BH17 . . . . **48** A1
Godshill Cl BH8 . . . . **53** A2
GODWINSCROFT **58** C4
Golden Cres SO41 . . . . **85** B3
Golden Gates BH13 . . . . . **106** A3
Goldenleas Ct BH11 . . . . . **49** A3
Goldenleas Dr BH11 . . . . . **49** A3
Golden Sands BH13 . . . . . **106** A3
Goldfinch Cl BH25 . . . . **61** C1
Goldfinch Rd BH17 . . . . . . **65** B4
Gold Mead Cl 🟨
  SO41 . . . . **111** A1
Golf Links Rd
  Broadstone BH18 . . . . **38** C1
  Ferndown BH22 . . . . **35** B4
Goliath Rd BH15 . . . . **89** A2
Good Rd BH12 . . . . **68** C3
Gooseberry La BH24 . . . . . **13** A3
Gordon Ct 🟨 BH4 . . . . . . **94** C4
Gordon Mount BH23 . . . . . **80** B3
Gordon Rd
  Bournemouth BH1 . . . . . . **97** A3
  Christchurch BH23 . . . . . . **80** A3
  Lymington SO41 . . . . **110** B2
  Poole BH12 . . . . **70** A1
  Wimborne Minster BH21 . . **31** B4
Gordon Rd S BH12 . . . . . . **70** A1
Gordon Way BH23 . . . . . . **77** A4
Gore Grange BH25 . . . . . . **61** C1
Gore Rd BH25 . . . . **61** A3
Gore Rd Ind Est BH25 . . **61** C1
Gorey Rd BH12 . . . . **49** A1
Gorleston Rd BH12 . . . . . . **69** C1
Gorley Rd BH24 . . . . **7** A1
Gorse Cl
  New Milton BH25 . . . . **63** A2
  St Leonards BH24 . . . . . . **18** B4

Gorsecliff Ct **7** BH5 . . . . . . 97 A3
Gorsecliff Rd BH10 . . . . . . 51 A1
Gorsefield Rd BH25 . . . . . . 62 B2
Gorse Hill Cl BH15 . . . . . . 67 C1
Gorse Hill Cres BH15 . . . . 67 B1
Gorse Hill Rd BH15 . . . . . . 67 C1
Gorse Knoll Dr BH31 . . . . . 2 B3
Gorse La BH16 . . . . 65 A3
Gorseland Ct BH22 . . . . . . 35 B3
Gorse Rd BH21 . . . . 36 C1
Gort Rd
  Bournemouth BH11 . . . . . 50 B3
  Poole BH17 . . . . 46 A1
Gosling Cl BH17 . . . . 67 C3
Gosport St SO41 . . . . . . 111 B3
Gough Cres BH17 . . . . 46 B2
Grace Darling Ho BH15 . . 91 A1
Grafton Cl
  Bournemouth BH3 . . . . . . 72 A2
  Christchurch BH23 . . . . . . 77 A1
Grafton Rd BH3 . . . . 72 A1
Grammar School La
  BH21 . . . . 30 B4
Granary Mews BH24 . . . . 13 A3
Granary The BH24 . . . . . . 13 A3
Granby Rd BH9 . . . . 52 A3
Grand Ave BH6 . . . . 98 C3
Grand Par **13** BH15 . . . . . . 90 B1
Grange Cl SO41 . . . . 85 C2
Grange Ct **5** BH1 . . . . 96 B2
Grange Gdns BH12 . . . . . . 69 B4
Grange Rd
  Bournemouth BH6 . . . . . . 99 A2
  Broadstone BH18 . . . . . . 46 A4
  Christchurch BH23 . . . . . . 78 B2
  St Leonards BH24 . . . . . . 18 C1
Grange Road Bsns Ctr
  BH23 . . . . 78 A2
Grange The SO41 . . . . . . 85 C2
Grangewood Hall BH21 . . 23 A1
Grantham Rd BH1 . . . . . . 97 B4
Grantley Rd **3** BH5 . . . . . . 97 C3
Grant's Ave BH1 . . . . 73 A1
Grants Cl BH1 . . . . 73 B1
Granville Pl BH1 . . . . 112 B2
Granville Rd
  Bournemouth BH5 . . . . . . 98 A4
  Poole BH12 . . . . 68 B1
Grasmere Cl BH23 . . . . . . 55 A2
Grasmere Gdns BH25 . . . . 62 B3
Grasmere Rd
  Bournemouth BH5 . . . . . . 98 A3
  Poole BH13 . . . . 106 A3
Gravel Hill BH17, BH18,
  BH21 . . . . 39 A1
Gravel La BH24 . . . . 13 A4
Gray Cl BH17 . . . . 67 C4
Graycot Cl BH10 . . . . 42 C1
Gray's Yd **5** BH15 . . . . . . 90 C1
Greaves Cl BH10 . . . . 50 C3
Grebe Cl
  Broadstone BH17 . . . . . . 65 B4
  Christchurch BH23 . . . . . . 78 A1
  Milford on S SO41 . . . . . . 87 B2
Greenacre BH25 . . . . 82 A2
Greenacre Cl BH16 . . . . . 64 C2
Greenacres **52** BH4 . . . . . 94 C3
Greenacres BH23 . . . . . . 77 C2
Greenacres Cl BH10 . . . . 43 B2
Green Acres Cl BH24 . . . . 12 B1
Greenbanks Cl SO41 . . . . 87 A3
Green Bottom BH21 . . . . 24 A3
Green Cl BH15 . . . . 91 A1
Greenclose La BH21 . . . . 31 A4
Greenfield Gdns BH25 . . 82 B2
Greenfield Rd BH15 . . . . . 67 B3
Greenfields **1** BH12 . . . . . 69 C3
Greenfinch Cl BH17 . . . . 45 C1
Greenfinch Wlk BH24 . . . 14 A2
Green Gdns BH15 . . . . . . 91 A1
Greenhayes BH18 . . . . . . 46 C2
Greenhays Rise BH22 . . . 12 C1
Greenhill Cl BH21 . . . . . . 23 A2
Greenhill La BH21 . . . . . . 23 A2
Greenhill Rd BH21 . . . . . 23 A2
Green La
  Barton on S BH25 . . . . . . 82 B2
  Bournemouth BH10 . . . . . 51 A3
  Ferndown BH22 . . . . 34 A1

Green La continued
  Ringwood BH24 . . . . 13 B3
Green Loaning BH23 . . . 101 C4
Greenmead Ave SO41 . . . 85 B3
Green Pk BH1 . . . . 97 A2
Green Rd
  Bournemouth BH9 . . . . . . 72 A3
  Poole BH15 . . . . 91 A1
Greensleeves Ave BH18 . 38 B2
Greensome Dr BH22 . . . . 27 C2
Green The BH23 . . . . 57 A1
Greenway Cl SO41 . . . . 110 B2
Greenway Cres BH16 . . . 64 C3
Greenways
  Christchurch BH23 . . . . . . 79 C3
  Milford on S SO41 . . . . . . 86 C3
Greenways Ave BH8 . . . . 52 C2
Greenways Ct BH22 . . . . 35 B3
Greenwood Ave
  Ferndown BH22 . . . . 27 B2
  Poole BH14 . . . . 103 C4
Greenwood Copse
  BH24 . . . . 19 B4
Greenwood Rd BH9 . . . . 71 B4
Greenwoods **6** BH25 . . . 82 B3
Greenwood Way BH24 . . 19 B4
Grenfell Rd BH9 . . . . 51 C3
Grenville Cl BH24 . . . . 7 B1
Grenville Ct
  11 Bournemouth BH4 . . 95 A4
  15 Poole BH15 . . . . 90 C2
Grenville Rd BH21 . . . . . . 31 A4
Gresham Rd BH9 . . . . 72 B4
Greycot Cl BH21 . . . . 8 C4
Greystoke Ave BH11 . . . . 41 C1
Griffin Ct BH21 . . . . 31 A3
Griffiths Gdns BH10 . . . . 42 B1
Grosvenor Cl BH24 . . . . . . 10 B1
Grosvenor Ct
  8 Bournemouth BH1 . . 96 B2
  2 Bournemouth,
    Springbourne BH1 . . . . 97 A3
  Christchurch BH23 . . . . . . 80 B3
Grosvenor Gdns BH1 . . . . 97 B3
Grosvenor Ho **6** BH4 . . 94 C3
Grosvenor Lo **8** BH4 . . 94 C3
Grosvenor Mews
  SO41 . . . . 110 C4
Grosvenor Pines **13**
  BH4 . . . . 94 C3
Grosvenor Rd BH4 . . . . . 94 C3
Grove Gdns BH25 . . . . . . 82 A1
Groveley Bsns Ctr
  BH23 . . . . 77 B1
Groveley Rd
  Bournemouth BH4 . . . . . . 94 B2
  Christchurch BH23 . . . . . . 77 B1
Grovely Ave BH5 . . . . 97 C2
Grove Mans **10** BH1 . . . 96 B2
Grove Pastures SO41 . . 111 A2
Grove Pl SO41 . . . . 111 A2
Grove Rd
  Barton on S BH25 . . . . . . 82 A1
  Bournemouth BH1 . . . . . . 96 B2
  Lymington SO41 . . . . . . 111 B2
  Poole BH12 . . . . 68 B2
  Wimborne Minster BH21 . . 31 A4
Grove Road E BH23 . . . . . 76 A3
Grove Road W BH23 . . . . 75 C3
Grove The
  Bournemouth BH9 . . . . . . 51 C3
  Christchurch BH23 . . . . . . 75 B4
  Ferndown BH22 . . . . 34 C4
  Wimborne WH31 . . . . 3 A1
Grower Gdns BH11 . . . . . 50 A4
Guernsey Rd BH12 . . . . . . 49 A1
Guest Ave BH12 . . . . 70 A2
Guest Cl BH12 . . . . 70 A2
Guest Rd BH16 . . . . 64 B3
Guildford Ct **2** BH4 . . . 94 C4
Guildhall Ct BH15 . . . . . . 90 B2
Guildhall Mus* BH15 . . . 90 B2
Guildhill Rd BH6 . . . . 99 B3
Gulliver Cl BH14 . . . . . . 103 C4
Gulliver Ct **1** BH21 . . . . 22 C1
Gunville Cres BH9 . . . . . . 52 B2
Gurjun Cl BH16 . . . . 64 A4
Gurney Rd BH21 . . . . 37 B2
Gussage Rd BH12 . . . . . . 69 C4
Guy's Cl BH24 . . . . 13 C2

Gwenlyn Rd BH16 . . . . . . 64 C2
Gwynne Rd BH12 . . . . . . 69 B1
Gypsy La BH24 . . . . 13 C4

H

Haarlem Mews BH23 . . . . 77 A2
Hadden Rd BH8 . . . . 73 A3
HADDON HILL 73 B4
Haddons Dr BH21 . . . . 8 B3
Hadley Way BH18 . . . . . . 45 B3
Hadow Rd BH10 . . . . 50 C3
Hadrian Cl BH22 . . . . 35 A2
Hadrian Way BH21 . . . . . 37 B4
Haglane Copse SO41 . . 110 B1
Hahnemann Rd BH2 . . . 112 A1
Haig Ave BH13 . . . . 93 B1
Hainault Dr BH31 . . . . 3 A2
Haking Rd BH23 . . . . 77 A2
Halcyon Ct BH15 . . . . 66 C2
Hale Ave BH25 . . . . 82 B4
Hale Gdns BH25 . . . . 82 B4
Halewood Way BH23 . . . 75 C3
Halifax Way BH23 . . . . . . 78 B2
Hall Rd BH11 . . . . 49 C3
Halstock Cres BH17 . . . . 47 A2
Halter Path BH15 . . . . . . 89 B3
Halter Rise BH21 . . . . . . 24 C2
Halton Cl BH23 . . . . 109 A2
Hambledon Gdns BH6 . . 74 C1
Hambledon Rd
  Bournemouth BH7 . . . . . . 74 C1
  Bournemouth, West
    Southbourne BH6 . . . . . 74 C1
Hamble Rd BH15 . . . . 68 A2
Hamblin Way BH8 . . . . . . 53 B1
Hamilton Bsns Pk BH25. 61 B3
Hamilton Cl
  Bournemouth BH1 . . . . . . 97 A4
  Christchurch BH23 . . . . . 101 C3
  Hamworthy BH15 . . . . . . 89 B2
Hamilton Cres BH15 . . . . 89 B2
Hamilton Ct
  1 Bournemouth BH8 . . 96 B4
  Milford on S SO41 . . . . . . 86 C2
  1 Wimborne Minster
    BH21 . . . . 22 B1
Hamilton Mews
  Bransgore BH23 . . . . . . 109 A2
  Lymington SO41 . . . . . . 111 B3
Hamilton Pl SO41 . . . . . 110 C2
Hamilton Rd
  Bournemouth BH1 . . . . . . 97 A3
  Corfe Mullen BH21 . . . . . 37 B1
  Hamworthy BH15 . . . . . . 89 B2
Hamilton Way BH25 . . . . 61 B1
Ham La
  Hampreston BH21 . . . . . . 33 B3
  Wimborne Minster BH21 . . 24 C1
Hampden La BH6 . . . . . . 98 B4
HAMPRESTON 33 B2
Hampreston CE Fst Sch
  BH21 . . . . 33 B3
Hampshire Cl BH23 . . . . 55 C1
Hampshire Ct **3** BH2 . 112 B2
Hampshire Ho **2** BH2 . 112 B2
Hampton Cl **5** BH22 . . . 95 A4
Hampton Dr BH24 . . . . 6 C1
HAMWORTHY 88 C3
Hamworthy Fst Sch
  BH15 . . . . 89 C1
Hamworthy LODGE
  BH15 . . . . 89 C2
Hamworthy Mid Sch
  BH15 . . . . 89 C1
Hamworthy Sta BH16 . . 89 A4
Handley Cl BH24 . . . . 13 A3
Handley Lodge **2**
  BH12 . . . . 69 C3
HANGERSLEY 7 C2
Hanham Ct BH12 . . . . . . 70 B4
Hanham Rd
  Corfe Mullen BH21 . . . . . 37 A1
  Wimborne Minster BH21 . . 22 C1
Hankinson Rd BH9 . . . . . 72 A3
Hanlon Cl BH11 . . . . 50 B4
Hannington Pl BH7 . . . . . 98 A4
Hannington Rd BH7 . . . . 98 A4
Hanover Gn BH17 . . . . . . 67 C3
Hanover Ho BH15 . . . . . . 91 A3

HAPPY BOTTOM 29 C1
Harbeck Rd BH8 . . . . 52 C2
Harbour Cl BH13 . . . . . . 104 A2
Harbour Cres BH23 . . . . 101 B4
Harbour Ct
  Barton on S BH25 . . . . . . 81 B2
  Christchurch BH23 . . . . . . 77 B1
  Poole BH13 . . . . 104 B2
Harbour Hill Cres BH15 . 67 B1
Harbour Hill Rd BH15 . . . 67 B1
Harbour Hospl The
  BH15 . . . . 91 A3
Harbour Lights BH15 . . . 91 B4
Harbour Prospect
  BH14 . . . . 103 C4
Harbour Rd BH6 . . . . . . 100 A2
Harbour View Cl BH14 . . 68 A1
Harbour View Ct
  BH23 . . . . 100 B4
Harbour View Rd BH14 . 68 A1
Harbour Watch BH14 . . 103 C3
Harcombe Cl BH17 . . . . . 47 B3
Harcourt Mews **6** BH5 . 98 A4
Harcourt Rd BH5 . . . . . . 98 A4
Hardy Cl
  New Milton BH25 . . . . . . 61 C2
  West Moors BH22 . . . . . . 17 A1
Hardy Cres BH21 . . . . . . 31 A4
Hardy Rd Poole BH14 . . . 93 A4
  West Moors BH22 . . . . . . 17 A1
Hare La BH25, SO41 . . . . 63 B1
Hares Gn BH7 . . . . 74 A3
Harewood Ave BH7 . . . . . 74 A1
Harewood Cres BH7 . . . . 73 C3
Harewood Gdns BH7 . . . 73 C2
Harewood Pl BH7 . . . . . . 74 A1
Harford Rd BH12 . . . . 68 C4
Harkwood Dr BH15 . . . . . 89 B4
Harland Rd BH6 . . . . 100 A2
Harleston Villas **5**
  BH21 . . . . 31 A4
Harness Cl BH21 . . . . 24 B2
Harraby Gn BH18 . . . . . . 46 A3
Harrier Dr BH21 . . . . 31 A2
Harriers Cl BH23 . . . . 79 A3
Harrington Ct BH23 . . . . 79 C2
Harrison Ave BH1 . . . . . . 73 A1
Harrison Cl BH23 . . . . . . 56 C2
Harrison Way BH22 . . . . 16 C3
Harris Way BH25 . . . . 62 B4
Harrow Cl BH23 . . . . 109 A1
Harry Barrow Cl **1**
  BH24 . . . . 13 B2
Hart Cl BH25 . . . . 61 C3
Harting Rd BH6 . . . . 75 A2
Hartnell Ct BH21 . . . . 37 A1
Hartsbourne Dr BH7 . . . . 74 B3
Harts Way SO41 . . . . 85 B3
Harvey Rd
  Bournemouth BH5 . . . . . . 98 A4
  Oakley BH21 . . . . 39 B4
Harwell Rd BH17 . . . . 67 A3
Harwood Ct BH25 . . . . . . 61 C2
Haskells Rd BH12 . . . . . . 68 B3
Haslemere Ave BH23 . . . 80 A3
Haslemere Pl BH23 . . . . . 80 A3
Hasler Rd BH17 . . . . 47 A2
Haslop Rd BH21 . . . . 24 A3
Hastings Rd
  Bournemouth BH8 . . . . . . 53 C1
  Poole BH17 . . . . 46 B2
Hatch Pond Rd BH17 . . . 66 C4
Hatfield Ct BH25 . . . . 61 B2
Hatfield Gdns BH7 . . . . . 74 B3
Hathaway Rd BH6 . . . . . . 99 A3
Hatherden Ave BH14 . . . 67 C1
Havelock Rd BH12 . . . . . 70 A1
Havelock Way BH23 . . . . 59 A1
Haven Cotts BH23 . . . . . 102 A3
Haven Ct
  4 Bournemouth BH5 . . 98 C2
  Poole BH13 . . . . 106 A3
Haven Gdns BH25 . . . . . . 82 B4
Havenhurst BH13 . . . . . . 104 B2
Haven Rd
  Corfe Mullen BH21 . . . . . 36 C2
  Poole BH13 . . . . 104 B3
Haverstock Rd BH9 . . . . 52 B1
Haviland Mews BH7 . . . . 97 C4

Gor – Hea 121

Haviland Rd
  Bournemouth BH7 . . . . . . 97 C4
  Ferndown BH21 . . . . 26 A3
Haviland Rd E BH7 . . . . . 97 C4
Haviland Rd W BH1 . . . . 97 C4
Hawden Rd BH11 . . . . 50 A1
Hawkchurch Gdns
  BH17 . . . . 47 B2
Hawk Cl BH21 . . . . 24 A3
Hawker Cl BH21 . . . . 31 C1
Hawkins Cl BH24 . . . . 7 A1
Hawkins Rd BH12 . . . . . . 49 C1
Hawkwood Rd BH1,
  BH5 . . . . 97 C3
Haworth Cl BH23 . . . . . . 76 A4
Hawthorn Cl BH25 . . . . . 62 C2
Hawthorn Dr
  Broadstone BH17 . . . . . . 45 C1
  Sway SO41 . . . . 107 B3
Hawthorn Rd
  Bournemouth BH9 . . . . . . 71 C4
  Burton BH23 . . . . 57 B3
Hawthorns The BH25 . . . 77 C1
Haydens Ct SO41 . . . . . 111 B3
Haydon Rd BH13 . . . . 94 B1
Hayes Ave BH7 . . . . 73 B1
Hayes Cl BH21 . . . . 32 A4
Hayes La BH21 . . . . 24 B1
Hayeswood Fst Sch
  BH21 . . . . 24 B2
Hayeswood Rd BH21 . . . 24 A2
HAYMOOR BOTTOM . . . 47 C1
Haymoor Mid Sch
  BH17 . . . . 47 B1
Haymoor Rd BH15 . . . . . 68 A3
Haynes Ave BH15 . . . . . . 91 A4
Haysoms Cl BH25 . . . . . . 82 B3
Hayward Cres BH31 . . . . . 2 C3
Haywards Farm Cl BH31 . .2 B1
Haywards La BH21 . . . . . 36 C3
Hayward Way BH31 . . . . . 2 C3
Hazel Cl BH23 . . . . 78 C4
Hazel Ct
  Bournemouth BH9 . . . . . . 52 C3
  1 New Milton BH25 . . . 82 B3
Hazel Dr BH22 . . . . 27 A4
Hazell Ave BH10 . . . . 50 B2
Hazelton Cl BH7 . . . . 74 A3
Hazelwood Ave BH25 . . . 61 C3
Hazelwood Dr BH31 . . . . . 5 B4
Hazlebury Rd BH17 . . . . 66 A3
Hazlemere Dr BH24 . . . . 18 C3
Headingley **9** BH13 . . . 94 B3
Headlands Bsns Pk
  BH24 . . . . .6 B2
Headless Cross BH10 . . . 43 A1
Heads Farm Cl BH10 . . . 43 B1
Head's La BH10 . . . . 43 B1
Headswell Ave BH10 . . . 51 B4
Headswell Cres BH10 . . . 51 B4
Headswell Gdns BH10 . . 51 A4
Heanor Cl BH10 . . . . 50 C2
Hearts of Oak Mews
  SO41 . . . . 110 C3
Heath Ave BH15 . . . . 67 A2
Heath Cl BH21 . . . . 24 B3
Heathcote Ct **2** BH7 . . 99 C3
Heathcote Rd BH5, BH7 . 97 C3
Heatherbank Rd BH4 . . . 94 C3
Heatherbrae La BH16 . . . 64 B2
Heather Cl
  Bournemouth BH8 . . . . . . 53 A3
  Corfe Mullen BH21 . . . . . 37 B2
  Hordle SO41 . . . . 84 A2
  St Leonards BH24 . . . . . . 18 C3
  Walkford BH23 . . . . 60 A1
Heatherdell BH16 . . . . . . 64 B2
Heatherdown Rd BH22 . . 17 B1
Heatherdown Way
  BH22 . . . . 17 B1
Heather Dr BH22 . . . . . . 27 A3
Heatherlands Fst Sch
  BH12 . . . . 69 B1
Heatherlands Rise
  BH12 . . . . 69 A1
Heatherlea Rd BH6 . . . . 99 A3
Heather Lo **1** BH25 . . . 62 A1

Heather Rd BH10 . . . . 51 A3
Heather View Rd BH12 . . 69 C3
Heather Way BH22 . . . . . . 27 A3
Heath Farm Cl BH22 . . . . 34 C3
Heath Farm Rd BH22 . . . . 34 C3
Heath Farm Way BH22 . . 34 C3
Heathfield Ave BH12 . . . . 70 A4
Heathfield Rd BH22 . . . . . 17 B1
Heathfield Way BH22 . . . . 17 A1
Heathlands Ave BH22 . . . . 35 A2
Heathlands Cl
  Burton BH23 . . . . 56 C2
  Verwood BH31 . . . . 3 A2
Heathlands Prim Sch
  BH11 . . . . 50 A3
Heath Rd Hordle SO41 . . . 63 C1
  St Leonards BH24 . . . . . . 18 B4
  Walkford BH23 . . . . 80 B4
Heathwood Ave BH25 . . . 81 B3
Heathwood Rd BH9 . . . . . 71 B4
Heathy Cl BH25 . . . . 81 C3
Heaton Rd BH10 . . . . 50 B2
Heavytree Rd BH14 . . . . . 92 B4
Heckford La BH15 . . . . 91 A3
Heckford Rd
  Corfe Mullen BH21 . . . . . 36 C1
  Poole BH15 . . . . 91 A4
Hedgerley BH25 . . . . 82 B2
Heights App BH16 . . . . . . 64 C3
Heights Rd BH16 . . . . 64 C4
Helic Ho **2** BH21 . . . . 22 C1
Helyar Rd BH8 . . . . 53 C1
Henbest Cl BH21 . . . . 24 C1
Henbury Cl
  Corfe Mullen BH21 . . . . . 37 A2
  Poole BH17 . . . . 48 A2
Henbury Rise BH21 . . . . . 37 A2
Henbury View Fst Sch
  BH21 . . . . 36 C2
Henbury View Rd BH21 . . 37 A2
Henchard Cl BH22 . . . . . . 34 C2
Hendford Gdns BH10 . . . . 51 A2
Hendford Rd BH10 . . . . . . 51 A2
Hengistbury Head Nature
  Reserve* BH6 . . . . 101 B3
Hengistbury Head Nature
  Trail* BH6 . . . . 100 C2
Hengistbury Rd
  Barton on S BH25 . . . . . . 81 B3
  Bournemouth BH6 . . . . . 100 A2
Hengist Cvn Pk BH6 . . . . 100 B3
Hengist Rd BH1 . . . . 97 A3
Henley Ct SO41 . . . . 87 B1
Henley Gdns BH7 . . . . 74 A2
Henning's Park Rd
  BH15 . . . . 67 B1
Henville Rd **6** BH8 . . . . . 96 C4
Herbert Ave BH12 . . . . . . 69 A3
Herbert Ct BH12 . . . . 69 A3
Herbert Hospl BH4 . . . . . . 94 B2
Herberton Rd BH6 . . . . . . 98 C4
Herbert Rd
  New Milton BH25 . . . . . . 62 B1
  Poole BH4 . . . . 94 B2
Hercules Rd BH15 . . . . . . 89 A3
Heritage Ct BH13 . . . . . . 104 C3
Hermitage Cl BH21 . . . . . . 8 C4
Hermitage Rd BH14 . . . . . 68 A1
Hermitage The BH14 . . . . 68 A1
Herm Rd BH12 . . . . 49 A1
Heron Cl SO41 . . . . 107 B3
Heron Court Rd BH3,
  BH9 . . . . 72 A2
Heron Dr BH21 . . . . 24 A4
Herstone Cl BH17 . . . . . . 47 C1
Hertford Ct **6** BH23 . . . . 80 B2
Hesketh Cl BH24 . . . . 11 B1
Hestan Cl BH23 . . . . 55 A3
Heston Way BH22 . . . . . . 16 B3
Hewitt Rd BH15 . . . . 89 B4
Heysham Rd BH18 . . . . . . 46 A3
Heytesbury Rd BH6 . . . . . 99 A4
Hibbard Cl BH10 . . . . 51 A1
Hibberd Way BH10 . . . . . . 51 A1
Hibbs Cl BH16 . . . . 64 C3
Hickes Cl BH11 . . . . 49 C4
Hickory Cl BH16 . . . . 64 A4

Highbridge Rd BH14 . . . . 92 C3
High Brow BH22 . . . . 27 A1
Highbury Cl BH25 . . . . . . 82 B4
HIGHCLIFFE 79 B3
Highcliffe Castle*
  BH23 . . . . 79 B2
Highcliffe Cnr BH23 . . . . 80 B3
Highcliffe Rd BH23 . . . . . 78 C2
Highcliffe St Mark's Prim
  Sch BH23 . . . . 79 C4
Highcliffe Sch BH23 . . . . 79 A4
Higher Blandford Rd BH18,
  BH21 . . . . 37 C2
Higher Merley La BH21 . . 37 B4
Highfield SO41 . . . . 110 C2
Highfield Ave
  Lymington SO41 . . . . . . 110 B2
  Ringwood BH24 . . . . 13 B4
Highfield Cl
  Corfe Mullen BH21 . . . . . 37 B1
  Sway SO41 . . . . 107 B3
Highfield Dr BH24 . . . . . . 13 B4
Highfield Gdns SO41 . . . . 107 B3
Highfield Ho **3** BH14 . . . 92 B4
Highfield Rd
  Bournemouth BH9 . . . . . 51 B2
  Corfe Mullen BH21 . . . . . 37 B1
  Lymington SO41 . . . . . . 110 B2
  Ringwood BH24 . . . . 13 B4
  West Moors BH22 . . . . . 16 C4
High Howe Cl BH11 . . . . . 49 B4
High Howe Gdns BH11 . . 49 B4
High Howe La BH11 . . . . . 49 B4
Highland Ave BH23 . . . . . 80 B4
Highland Rd Poole BH14 . 68 B1
  Wimborne Minster BH21 . 23 A2
Highlands Cres BH10 . . . . 50 C4
Highlands Rd BH25 . . . . . 82 A2
Highland View Cl BH21 . . 23 A1
High Marryats BH25 . . . . 82 A1
High Mead La BH22 . . . . . 34 A1
High Mead BH22 . . . . 34 A2
Highmoor Cl
  Corfe Mullen BH21 . . . . . 37 A1
  Poole BH14 . . . . 92 B3
Highmoor Rd
  Bournemouth BH11 . . . . . 50 A1
  Corfe Mullen BH21 . . . . . 37 A1
  Poole BH14 . . . . 92 B3
High Oaks Gdns BH11 . . . 49 B4
High Park Rd BH18 . . . . . 45 B4
High Pines BH23 . . . . 79 A2
High Ridge Cres BH25 . . . 82 C4
HIGHROWN 14 A3
High St N BH15 . . . . 91 A3
High St
  Christchurch BH23 . . . . . 76 B1
  Lymington SO41 . . . . . . 111 A3
  Milford on S SO41 . . . . . 87 A2
  Poole BH15 . . . . 90 C2
  Ringwood BH24 . . . . 13 A3
  St Leonards BH24 . . . . . 11 A2
  Wimborne Minster BH21 . 38 B4
Hightown Gdns BH24 . . . 14 A2
Hightown Hill BH24 . . . . . 15 A3
Hightown Ind Est BH24 . . 13 C2
Hightown Rd
  Ringwood, Hightown
  BH24 . . . . 14 A2
  Ringwood, Moortown
  BH24 . . . . 13 B2
High Trees BH13 . . . . 105 A4
Hightrees Ave BH8 . . . . . 73 C4
High Trees Wlk BH22 . . . 27 A3
Highview Cl BH23 . . . . . . 55 B2
Highview Gdns BH12 . . . . 68 C3
High Way BH18 . . . . 45 C3
HIGH WOOD 7 B3
Highwood La BH24 . . . . . . 7 C3
Highwood Rd BH14 . . . . . 93 B4
Hilary Rd BH17 . . . . 46 C1
Hilda Rd BH12 . . . . 69 B3
Hiley Rd BH15 . . . . 66 C2
Hillary Rd BH23 . . . . 77 B3
HILLBOURNE 46 B2
Hillbourne Com Fst & Mid
  Schs BH17 . . . . 46 B2
Hillbourne Rd BH17 . . . . . 46 A2
Hillbrow Rd BH6 . . . . 74 B1
HILLBUTTS 21 C2

Hill Cl BH23 . . . . 108 C2
Hillcrest Ave BH22 . . . . . 26 C4
Hillcrest Cl BH9 . . . . 52 A2
Hillcrest Hospl BH10 . . . . 51 A1
Hillcrest Rd
  Bournemouth BH9 . . . . . 52 A2
  Corfe Mullen BH21 . . . . . 36 C1
  Poole BH12 . . . . 68 A1
Hillcroft Cl SO41 . . . . . . 111 A3
Hill La Bransgore BH23 . . 108 C2
  Burton BH23 . . . . 57 C1
Hillman Rd BH14 . . . . 69 A1
Hillmeadow BH31 . . . . 5 A4
Hillside Dr BH23 . . . . 55 A2
Hillside Fst Sch BH31 . . . 2 C3
Hillside Gdns BH21 . . . . . 44 C4
Hillside Mews BH21 . . . . 44 C4
Hillside Rd
  Corfe Mullen BH21 . . . . . 36 C1
  Lymington SO41 . . . . . . 110 B2
  Poole BH12 . . . . 49 C1
  Verwood BH31 . . . . 2 C3
Hill St BH15 . . . . 90 C2
Hill Terr BH21 . . . . 32 A2
Hilltop Cl BH22 . . . . 26 B3
Hilltop Rd
  Corfe Mullen BH21 . . . . . 36 C1
  Ferndown BH22 . . . . 26 B3
HILL VIEW 45 A4
Hill View Prim Sch
  BH10 . . . . 51 B3
Hillview Rd BH10 . . . . 51 A3
Hill View Rd BH22 . . . . . . 26 C3
Hill Way BH24 . . . . 11 A1
Hiltom Rd BH24 . . . . 13 C3
Hilton Cl BH15 . . . . 68 A2
Hilton Rd BH25 . . . . 62 B2
Hinchliffe Cl BH15 . . . . . 89 C2
Hinchliffe Rd BH15 . . . . . 89 C2
HINTON 60 A2
Hinton Admiral Mews
  BH23 . . . . 59 B1
Hinton Admiral Sta
  BH23 . . . . 59 B1
Hinton Rd BH1 . . . . 112 B2
Hinton Wood BH1 . . . . . . 96 A1
Hinton Wood Ave BH23 . . 79 B4
Hintonwood La BH23 . . . . 59 B1
Hive Gdns BH13 . . . . 104 A2
Hobart Rd BH25 . . . . 61 C1
Hobbs Pk BH24 . . . . 19 A4
Hobbs Rd BH12 . . . . 68 C4
Hoburne Ct BH23 . . . . . . 78 C4
Hoburne Cvn Pk BH23 . . 78 C3
Hoburne Gdns BH23 . . . . 78 C3
Hoburne La BH23 . . . . . . 78 C3
Hodges Cl BH17 . . . . 67 B3
Hogarth Way BH8 . . . . . . 54 A1
Hogue Ave BH10 . . . . 43 A1
Holburne Naish BH25 . . . 81 A3
Holbury Cl BH8 . . . . 53 B2
Holcombe Rd BH16 . . . . . 64 B2
HOLDENHURST 54 B2
Holdenhurst Ave BH7 . . . 74 C2
Holdenhurst Rd
  Bournemouth BH8 . . . . . 96 C4
  Bournemouth, Holdenhurst
  BH8 . . . . 54 B2
Holdings The BH24 . . . . . 13 C1
Holes Bay North Rdbt
  BH17 . . . . 66 A2
Holes Bay Pk BH15 . . . . . 90 B4
Holes Bay Rd BH15 . . . . . 90 B4
Holes Bay Rdbt BH15 . . . 66 B1
Holes Cl SO41 . . . . 63 C2
Hollands Wood Dr
  BH25 . . . . 62 B3
Holland Way BH18 . . . . . . 37 C1
Hollenden **9** BH13 . . . . . 94 A4
Hollies Cl SO41 . . . . 107 B2
Holloway Ave BH11 . . . . . 41 C1
Holly Cl
  St Leonards BH24 . . . . . 18 B4
  Upton BH16 . . . . 64 A3
  West Moors BH22 . . . . . 16 B2
Holly Ct
  Lymington SO41 . . . . . . 110 A1
  Poole BH15 . . . . 91 A4
  West Moors BH22 . . . . . 16 B2
Holly Gdns Burton BH23 . 77 A4

Holly Gdns continued
  Milford on S SO41 . . . . . 86 C3
Holly Gr BH31 . . . . 2 C2
Holly Green Rise BH11 . . 49 B4
Holly Hedge La BH17 . . . 66 C4
Holly La
  New Milton BH25 . . . . . . 62 C2
  Walkford BH23 . . . . 60 C1
Holly Lo **13** BH13 . . . . . . 94 A4
Hollywood Cl SO41 . . . . 110 C4
Hollywood La SO41 . . . . 110 C4
Holm Cl BH24 . . . . 7 A1
Holme Rd BH23 . . . . 80 B3
Holmfield Ave BH7 . . . . . 74 C2
Holmhurst Ave BH23 . . . . 79 C4
Holm Oak Cl BH31 . . . . . . 2 B4
Holmsley Cl SO41 . . . . . 110 A1
Holmwood Garth BH24 . . 14 B2
Holnest Rd BH17 . . . . 47 A1
Holt Ho BH8 . . . . 97 A4
Holt Pl BH22 . . . . 27 C3
Holt Rd Poole BH12 . . . . . 69 C2
  Three Legged Cross BH21 . 8 B4
Holworth Cl BH11 . . . . . . 49 B3
Holyrood Cl BH17 . . . . . . 66 A4
Holywell Cl BH17 . . . . . . 47 A3
Homecliffe Ho BH23 . . . . 80 B3
Homecorfe Ho BH18 . . . . 38 B1
Homedale Ho BH2 . . . . . . 71 C1
Homedene Ho BH15 . . . . 91 A3
Home Farm BH25 . . . . . . 83 B2
Home Farm Rd BH31 . . . . 2 B3
Home Farm Way BH31 . . 2 B2
Homefield Ho **7** BH25 . . 82 A4
Homefield Ind Prep Sch
  BH6 . . . . 99 C4
Homegrange Ho SO41 . . 87 A2
Homelake Ho BH14 . . . . . 92 B3
Homelands Est BH20 . . . . 75 A2
Homelands Ho BH22 . . . . 27 A1
Homeleigh Ho **5** BH8 . . . 96 A4
Homelife Ho BH23 . . . . . . 96 B3
Homemill Ho **5** BH25 . . . 62 A1
Homeoaks Ho BH2 . . . . . . 71 C1
Home Rd BH11 . . . . 42 B2
Homeside Rd BH9 . . . . . . 52 A1
Homestour Ho **1** BH23 . . 76 C1
Homeview Ho BH15 . . . . . 91 A3
Homewood Cl BH25 . . . . . 62 C1
Homewood Ho SO41 . . . 110 B1
Honeybourne Cres
  BH6 . . . . 100 A3
Honeysuckle Gdns
  SO41 . . . . 85 A3
Honeysuckle La BH17 . . . 45 C1
Honeysuckle Way BH23 . 78 B3
Honeywood Rd BH14 . . . 103 C3
Hood Cl BH10 . . . . 50 B1
Hood Cres BH10 . . . . 50 B1
Hooke Cl BH17 . . . . 48 A2
Hop Cl BH16 . . . . 64 A3
Hopkins Cl BH8 . . . . 54 A1
Horace Rd **7** BH5 . . . . . . 97 B3
HORDLE 63 C1
Hordle CE Prim Sch
  SO41 . . . . 84 A2
Hordle La SO41 . . . . 84 A1
Hornbeam Sq BH15 . . . . 91 A2
Hornbeam Way BH21 . . . 23 B1
Horning Rd BH12 . . . . . . 69 C1
Horsa Cl BH6 . . . . 99 B3
Horsa Ct BH6 . . . . 99 B3
Horsa Rd BH6 . . . . 99 B3
Horseshoe Cl BH21 . . . . 24 B2
Horseshoe Common
  BH1 . . . . 112 B3
Horseshoe Common Rdbt
  BH1 . . . . 112 B2
Horseshoe Ct BH1 . . . . . 112 B3
Horseshoe The BH13 . . 106 B4
Horsham Ave BH10 . . . . . 42 C2
Horton Cl BH9 . . . . 52 C2
Horton Ho BH22 . . . . 27 C3
Horton Rd
  Ringwood BH24 . . . . 12 A2
  St Leonards BH24 . . . . . 10 C2
Horton Way BH31 . . . . 2 A1
Hosker Rd BH5 . . . . 98 B4
Houlton Rd BH15 . . . . 91 B4
HOUND HILL 21 B3

Hounds Way BH21 . . . . . 24 B1
Hounslow Cl BH15 . . . . . 89 C1
Howard Cl BH23 . . . . 77 C1
Howard Rd
  Bournemouth BH8 . . . . . 72 C3
  Verwood BH31 . . . . 2 C2
Howards Mead SO41 . . . 110 A1
Howe Cl
  Christchurch BH23 . . . . 101 C4
  New Milton BH25 . . . . . . 61 C2
Howe La BH31 . . . . 2 C1
Howell Ho BH21 . . . . 23 C3
Howeth Cl BH10 . . . . 51 A3
Howeth Rd BH10 . . . . 51 A3
Howlett Cl SO41 . . . . . . 110 B3
Howton Cl BH10 . . . . 42 C1
Howton Rd BH10 . . . . 42 C1
Hoxley Rd BH10 . . . . 51 A4
Hoyal Rd BH15 . . . . 89 A3
Hudson Cl Poole BH12 . . 48 C2
  Ringwood BH24 . . . . 14 A4
Hughes Bsns Ctr BH23 . 78 A2
Hull Cres BH11 . . . . 49 A4
Hull Rd BH11 . . . . 49 B4
Hull Way BH11 . . . . 49 B4
Humber Rd BH22 . . . . . . 28 A2
Hungerfield Cl BH23 . . . 108 C3
Hungerford Rd BH8 . . . . 53 A2
Hunger Hill BH15 . . . . . . 90 C2
Hunter Cl
  Christchurch BH23 . . . . . 78 A2
  Wimborne Minster BH21 . 24 C2
Hunters Cl BH31 . . . . 3 C1
Huntfield Rd BH9 . . . . . . 52 B1
Huntingdon Dr BH21 . . . . 31 B1
Huntingdon Gdns BH23 . 56 A1
Huntly Rd BH3 . . . . 71 A3
Hunt Rd
  Christchurch BH23 . . . . . 77 C3
  St Leonards BH24 . . . . . 20 A3
Hurn Way BH23 . . . . 75 A4
Hursley Cl BH7 . . . . 74 C3
Hurstbourne Ave BH23 . . 79 B4
Hurst Cl
  Barton on S BH25 . . . . . . 81 A3
  Walkford BH23 . . . . 60 C1
Hurst Ct
  4 Christchurch BH23 . . 80 A2
  5 Milford on S SO41 . . 86 C2
Hurstdene Rd BH8 . . . . . . 52 C1
Hurst Hill BH14 . . . . 103 C4
Hurst Rd
  Milford on S SO41 . . . . . 87 B1
  Ringwood BH24 . . . . 6 B1
Hussar Cl BH23 . . . . 75 C2
Hyacinth Cl BH17 . . . . . . 45 C1
Hyde Cl SO41 . . . . 107 B3
Hyde Rd BH10 . . . . 42 C1
Hyde The BH25 . . . . 61 B3
Hynesbury Rd BH23 . . . . 78 C1
Hythe Rd BH15 . . . . 68 A3

I

Ibbertson Cl BH8 . . . . . . 53 C1
Ibbertson Rd BH8 . . . . . . 53 C1
Ibbertson Way BH8 . . . . . 53 C1
Ibbett Rd BH10 . . . . 50 C3
Ibsley Cl BH8 . . . . 72 C1
Iddesleigh Rd BH3 . . . . . 72 A1
IFORD 75 A2
Iford Bridge Home Pk
  BH6 . . . . 75 A2
Iford Gdns BH7 . . . . 74 C2
Iford La BH6 . . . . 75 B1
Ilford Cl BH6 . . . . 99 C4
Imber Dr BH23 . . . . 79 C3
Imbrecourt BH13 . . . . . . 104 B3
Imperial Cl **4** BH13 . . . 104 C3
Ingarth **7** BH6 . . . . 99 B2

Inglegreen Cl BH25 . . . . . 81 C4
Inglesham Way BH15 . . . 89 B4
Inglewood Ave BH8. . . . . 73 C4
Inglewood Dr BH25. . . . . 82 B4
Ingram Wlk **1** BH21. . . . . 31 A4
Ingworth Rd BH12 . . . . . . 70 A1
Insley Cres BH18. . . . . . . 37 B1
Inveravon BH23. . . . . 101 C3
Inverclyde Rd BH14. . . . . 92 B4
Inverclyde Rd BH14. . . . . 92 C4
Inverleigh Rd BH6 . . . . . . 74 C1
Inverness Rd BH13. . . . . 104 B3
Ivamy Pl BH11 . . . . 49 C2
Ivor Rd
  Corfe Mullen BH21. . . . . 45 A4
  Poole BH15. . . . . 90 A1
Ivy Cl BH24. . . . . 18 B4
Ivy La BH24 . . . . 6 C4
Ivy Rd BH21. . . . . 39 A4
Iwerne Cl BH9 . . . . 52 B3

J

Jacey Ho **6** BH1. . . . . 96 A2
Jacklin Ct BH18 . . . . 38 B1
Jackson Gdns BH12. . . . . 68 C2
Jackson Rd BH12 . . . . 68 C2
Jacmar Ct **4** BH25 . . . . . . 82 B4
Jacobean Cl BH23 . . . . . . 80 B4
Jacobs Rd BH15 . . . . 89 B2
Jacqueline Rd BH12 . . . . . 68 C3
Jameson Rd BH9 . . . . 51 C1
James Rd BH12. . . . . 70 A1
Janred Ct BH25. . . . . 81 B2
Jasmine Ct SO41 . . . . . . 110 B3
Jaundrells Cl BH25 . . . . . 62 C1
Jay's Ct BH23. . . . . 80 B3
Jefferson Ave BH1. . . . . . 73 A1
Jellicoe Cl BH14 . . . . 67 C1
Jellicoe Dr BH23 . . . . 77 C1
Jenner Cl BH31. . . . . 2 B3
Jennings Rd BH14 . . . . . . 92 C2
Jephcote Rd BH11. . . . . . 49 C4
Jersey Cl BH12 . . . . 49 A1
Jersey Rd BH12. . . . . 49 A1
Jesmond Ave BH23 . . . . . 79 C3
Jessica Ave BH1. . . . . . . 2 A3
Jessopp Cl BH10. . . . . . . 51 C4
Jessopp Ho **6** BH21 . . . . 22 C1
Jessopp Rd BH21. . . . . . . 24 B2
Jewell Rd BH8. . . . . 54 A1
Jimmy Brown Ave BH21. . 9 A1
Johnson Rd BH21. . . . . . . 26 A4
Johnstone Rd BH23. . . . . 77 B1
Johnston Rd BH15 . . . . . . 67 A3
Jolliffe Ave BH15 . . . . 91 A4
Jolliffe Rd BH15. . . . . 91 A4
Jonathan Cl SO41. . . . . . 111 A4
Jopps Cnr BH23 . . . . 56 C3
Jordans La SO41. . . . . . . 107 C3
Joshua Cl BH15. . . . . 89 B2
Jowitt Dr BH25 . . . . 61 C1
Joyce Dickson Cl BH24 . 13 C2
Joys Rd BH21. . . . . 8 C4
Jubilee Cl
  Corfe Mullen BH21. . . . . 37 B3
  Ringwood BH24 . . . . 14 A4
Jubilee Cres BH12 . . . . . . 69 A1
Jubilee Ct SO41 . . . . 107 B2
Jubilee Gdns BH10 . . . . . 51 A2
Jubilee Rd
  Corfe Mullen BH21. . . . . 37 B3
  Poole BH12. . . . . 69 A1
Julia Cl BH23 . . . . 79 C3
Julian's Rd BH21. . . . . . . 30 A4
Julyan Ave BH12. . . . . . . 70 A4
Jumpers Ave BH23. . . . . . 75 B3
JUMPERS COMMON . . . 75 B4

Jumpers Rd BH23 . . . . . . 75 C3
Junction Rd
  Bournemouth BH9 . . . . . 71 C4
  Hamworthy BH16. . . . . . 89 A4
Juniper Cl
  Ferndown BH22 . . . . 26 C4
  Lymington SO41. . . . . . 110 A1
  Three Legged Cross BH21. . 8 C4
Juniper Flats BH23 . . . . . 75 B3
Jupiter Way BH7 . . . . 37 B4
Justin Gdns BH10. . . . . . . 51 B4

K

Kamptee Copse BH25. . . 62 B4
Kangaw Pl BH15. . . . . . . 89 A2
Katherine Chance Cl
  BH23. . . . . 56 C2
Katterns Cl BH23 . . . . . . 55 B1
Kay Cl BH23 . . . . 77 B1
K&B Est BH17 . . . . 66 B4
Keats Ave SO41. . . . . . . 87 A3
Keats Ho **1** BH25. . . . . . . 82 A3
Keeble Cl BH10. . . . . 43 A2
Keeble Cres BH10. . . . . . 43 A2
Keeble Rd BH10 . . . . 43 A2
Keepers La BH21 . . . . 33 C4
Keighley Ave BH18. . . . . 45 C1
Keith Rd BH3. . . . . 71 A3
Kellaway Rd BH17 . . . . . . 67 C4
Kelly Cl BH17. . . . . 67 C4
Kelsall Gdns BH25 . . . . . 62 A1
Kemp Rd BH9 . . . . 71 C4
Kemp Welch Ct BH12 . . . 70 B4
Kenilworth Cl BH25 . . . . 62 B1
Kenilworth Ct
  2 Christchurch BH23 . . 76 A2
  1 Poole BH13. . . . . 104 C4
Kennard Ct BH25 . . . . . . 61 C2
Kennard Rd BH25. . . . . . . 61 C2
Kennart Rd BH17 . . . . 66 B3
Kenneth Ct **9** BH23. . . . . 80 B2
Kennington Rd BH17. . . . 67 A4
Ken Rd BH6 . . . . 99 B3
Kensington Ct **14** BH13. . 94 B3
Kensington Dr **1** BH2 . . . 95 A4
Kensington Pk SO41 . . . . 86 C2
Kent Ho **28** BH4. . . . . 94 C3
Kent Rd BH12. . . . . 69 B2
Kenyon Cl BH15 . . . . 92 B3
Kenyon Rd BH15. . . . . . . 67 B3
Keppel Cl BH24. . . . . 13 C3
Kerley Rd BH12. . . . . 112 A1
Kernells Ct **2** BH4. . . . . . 94 B4
Kerry Cl SO41 . . . . 110 B2
Kestrel Cl
  Ferndown BH22 . . . . 26 B3
  Upton BH16 . . . . 64 B4
Kestrel Ct BH24. . . . . 13 B4
Kestrel Dr BH23 . . . . 78 A1
Keswick Ct BH25 . . . . . . 62 B3
Keswick Rd
  Bournemouth BH5 . . . . . 97 C3
  New Milton BH25. . . . . . 62 B3
Keswick Way BH31. . . . . . 2 B1
Keverstone Ct BH1 . . . . . 97 A2
Keyes Cl
  Christchurch BH23. . . . . 77 C1
  Poole BH12. . . . . 49 C1
Keysworth Ave BH25. . . . 81 C3
Keysworth Rd BH16. . . . . 88 C4
Khyber Rd BH12 . . . . 69 A1
Killock **6** BH13. . . . . 104 C3
Kilmarnock Rd BH9 . . . . . 52 A2
Kilmington Way BH23. . . 79 C3
Kiln Cl BH21. . . . . 44 C4
Kiln Way BH31. . . . . 5 C3
Kimberley Cl BH23 . . . . . 75 C3
Kimberley Rd
  Bournemouth BH6 . . . . . 98 C4
  Poole BH14. . . . . 92 B3
Kimber Rd BH11. . . . . 49 C3
Kimmeridge Ave BH12 . . 68 C4
King Cl BH24 . . . . 19 A4
Kingcup Cl BH18. . . . . . . 45 B2
King Edward Ave BH9. . . 52 A1
King Edward Ct BH9 . . . . 51 C2
Kingfisher Cl
  Bournemouth BH6 . . . . . 75 B1
  West Moors BH22 . . . . . 17 A2

Kingfisher Ct BH8 . . . . . . 73 A1
Kingfisher Park Homes 3
  BH10. . . . . 51 C4
Kingfisher Pk BH21. . . . . 8 C2
Kingfishers **4** BH23 . . . 100 A4
Kingfishers The BH31 . . . 3 A1
Kingfisher Way
  Christchurch BH23 . . . . 102 A4
  Ringwood BH24 . . . . 6 C1
King George Ave BH9 . . . 51 C2
King George Mobile
  Home Pk BH25 . . . . 81 C4
King John Ave BH11 . . . . 41 A1
King John Cl BH11. . . . . . 41 A2
Kingland Cres **4** BH15. . 90 C2
Kingland Rd BH15 . . . . . . 91 A2
King Richard Dr BH11. . . 41 A1
Kings Arms La BH24 . . . . 13 A3
Kings Arms Row BH24 . . 13 A3
Kings Ave BH14. . . . . 93 A2
King's Ave BH23 . . . . 75 C1
Kingsbere Ave BH10 . . . . 50 B2
Kingsbere Gdns BH23. . . 80 A3
Kingsbere Rd BH15 . . . . . 67 B1
Kingsbridge Rd BH14 . . . 92 C3
Kingsbury's La BH24. . . . 13 A3
Kings Cl
  Lymington SO41 . . . . . . 110 C3
  Poole BH15. . . . . 67 A1
  West Moors BH22 . . . . . 16 C1
Kings Cres SO41. . . . . . . 110 C3
King's Cres BH14 . . . . . . 93 B2
Kingsfield
  Lymington SO41. . . . . . 111 C1
  Ringwood BH24 . . . . 13 B3
Kingsgate **10** BH13. . . . . 94 B3
Kings Grange **11** BH4 . . . 95 A2
Kings High Sch BH10 . . . 50 C3
Kingsland Ct BH13 . . . . . 104 C3
Kingsleigh Prim Sch
  BH10. . . . . 50 C3
Kingsley Ave BH6. . . . . . 100 A3
Kingsley Cl BH6 . . . . 100 A3
Kingsmead Ct **5** BH21. . . 22 B1
Kingsmill Rd BH17 . . . . . 67 B3
Kings Park Com Hospl
  BH7. . . . . 97 C3
King's Park Dr BH7,
  BH1. . . . . 73 B1
King's Park Prim Sch
  BH1. . . . . 97 B4
King's Park Rd BH7 . . . . . 73 B1
Kings Rd
  Lymington SO41 . . . . . . 110 C3
  New Milton BH25. . . . . . 62 C1
  Ver Rd BH3 . . . . 72 A2
King's Saltern Rd
  SO41. . . . . 111 C1
King St BH21 . . . . 30 B4
Kingston Pk SO41 . . . . . 110 C1
Kingston Rd BH15 . . . . . . 91 A4
Kingsway BH22. . . . . 26 B4
Kingsway Cl BH23 . . . . . . 75 C4
Kingswell Cl BH10 . . . . . 51 A2
Kingswell Gdns BH10 . . . 50 B2
Kingswell Gr BH10. . . . . . 50 B2
Kingswell Rd BH10 . . . . . 50 C2
Kingswood **15** BH4. . . . . . 94 C2
Kinross Rd BH10 . . . . 71 B2
Kinsbourne Ave BH10. . . 51 A2
Kiosks The **9** BH15. . . . . 90 C1
Kipling Rd BH14 . . . . 68 B1
Kirby Cl BH15 . . . . 67 C2
Kirby Way BH6 . . . . 99 A3
Kirkham Ave BH23 . . . . . 56 C2
Kirkway BH18 . . . . 46 B4
Kitchener Cres BH17. . . . 46 B2
Kitchers Cl SO41. . . . . . . 107 B3
Kitscroft Rd BH10. . . . . . 42 C1
Kittiwake Cl BH6 . . . . 75 A1
Kitwalls La SO41. . . . . . . 87 A3
Kivernell Pl **1** SO41 . . . . 86 C2

Kivernell Rd SO41 . . . . . . 87 A2
Kiwi Cl BH15 . . . . 91 B3
Knapp Cl BH23 . . . . 76 A3
Knapp Mill Ave BH23. . . . 76 A3
Knightcrest Pk SO41. . . . 85 C3
KNIGHTON 41 A4
Knighton Cvn Pk SO41 . . 85 C3
Knighton Heath Cl
  BH11. . . . . 49 B4
Knighton Heath Ind Est
  BH11. . . . . 49 B2
Knighton Heath Rd
  BH11. . . . . 49 B4
Knighton La BH21 . . . . . . 41 A3
Knighton Pk BH25 . . . . . . 81 B3
Knightsbridge Ct BH2. . 112 A1
Knights Rd BH11. . . . . . . 41 A1
Knightstone Gr BH22 . . . 16 B2
Knightwood Cl BH23. . . . 79 A3
Knobcrook Rd **3** BH21 . . 22 B2
Knole Ct **5** BH1. . . . . 97 A3
Knole Gdns BH1. . . . . 97 A3
Knole Rd BH1 . . . . 97 A3
Knoll Gdns* BH21. . . . . . 33 C4
Knoll Gdns BH24. . . . . . . 19 A4
Knoll La BH21 . . . . 36 B3
Knoll Manor BH2 . . . . 71 C1
Knowland Dr SO41. . . . . . 87 A3
Knowles Cl BH23 . . . . . . 77 B2
Knowlton Gdns BH9 . . . . 52 B2
Knowlton Rd BH17. . . . . . 47 C2
Knyveton Ho BH1. . . . . . 96 B3
Knyveton Rd BH1. . . . . . 96 C3
Kyrchil La BH21. . . . . 23 C2
Kyrchil Way BH21. . . . . . 23 C3

L

Labrador Dr BH15 . . . . . . 91 A1
Laburnum Cl
  Ferndown BH22 . . . . 26 B2
  Verwood BH31 . . . . 3 C1
Laburnum Dr SO41 . . . . . 85 B2
Laburnum Ho **8** BH10 . . 51 C4
Lacey Cres BH15 . . . . 68 A2
Lacy Cl BH21 . . . . 22 C2
Lacy Dr BH21 . . . . 22 C2
Ladysmith Cl BH23. . . . . 77 B2
Lagado Cl BH14 . . . . 103 C4
Lagland Ct **14** BH15. . . . . 90 C2
Lagland St BH15 . . . . 90 C2
Lagoon Cl BH14 . . . . 103 B4
Lagoon Rd BH14. . . . . . . 103 B4
Laidlaw Cl BH12 . . . . 70 B4
LAKE 89 A1
Lake Ave BH15. . . . . 89 A1
Lake Cres BH15. . . . . 89 B3
Lake Dr
  Hamworthy BH15. . . . . . 89 A1
  Poole BH15. . . . . 89 A2
Lake Farm Cl BH22 . . . . . 44 A2
Lake Grove Rd BH25 . . . . 62 A2
Lake Rd
  Bournemouth BH11 . . . . 42 C2
  Hamworthy BH15. . . . . . 89 B2
  Verwood BH31 . . . . 3 B1
Lakeside BH24. . . . . 14 A2
Lakeside Pines BH25. . . . 62 A2
Lakeside Rd BH13 . . . . . . 94 A1
Lakeview Dr BH24 . . . . . . 14 A2
Lake View Manor BH25. . 62 A1
Lakewood Rd BH23 . . . . . 79 C4
Lambs Cl BH17 . . . . 46 C1
LAMBS' GREEN 29 C2
Lambsgreen La BH21 . . . 29 C2
Lampton Gdns **5** BH9 . . . 51 C1
Lanark Cl BH14 . . . . 92 A3
Lancaster Cl
  Christchurch BH23. . . . . 78 C2
  Corfe Mullen BH18. . . . . 37 C1
Lancaster Dr
  Corfe Mullen BH18. . . . . 37 C1
  Verwood BH31 . . . . 3 B2
Lancaster Rd BH21 . . . . . 26 A4
Lancer Cl BH23 . . . . 75 C2
Lander Cl BH15 . . . . 91 A1
Landford Gdns BH8. . . . . 53 A1
Landford Way BH8. . . . . . 53 A1
Landseer Rd **1** BH4 . . . . 94 C3

Lane Lowther Gdns The
  BH8. . . . . 96 C4
Lanes The BH25. . . . . 62 A3
Langdon Ct BH14 . . . . . . 93 A4
Langdon Rd BH14 . . . . . . 93 A4
Langham Ct BH23 . . . . . . 75 C4
Langley Chase BH24 . . . . 11 B1
Langley Rd
  Christchurch BH23 . . . . . 79 B4
  Poole BH14. . . . . 93 C4
Langside Ave BH12 . . . . . 70 A4
Langside Sch BH12 . . . . . 70 A4
Langton Cl BH25. . . . . . . 82 B2
Langton Rd BH7 . . . . 97 C4
Lansdell Ct **4** BH15. . . . . 91 B3
Lansdowne Cres BH1. . . 96 B2
Lansdowne Gdns BH1. . . 96 A3
Lansdowne Rd BH1. . . . . 96 A4
Lansdowne Rdbt The
  BH1. . . . . 96 A2
Lapwing Rd BH21. . . . . . 24 A3
Lara Cl BH8 . . . . 53 A2
Larch Cl
  Broadstone BH17. . . . . . 45 B1
  Hordle SO41. . . . . 63 C1
  St Leonards BH24 . . . . . 19 B4
Larch Way BH22 . . . . 26 C3
Lark Rd BH23. . . . . 78 A1
Larks Cl BH22. . . . . 26 B3
Larksfield Ave BH9 . . . . . 52 C2
Larkshill Cl BH25 . . . . . . 62 B2
Larks Rise BH22 . . . . 26 B3
Lascelles Ct **1** BH7. . . . . 74 B1
Lascelles Rd BH7 . . . . . . 74 B1
Latch Farm Ave BH23 . . . 76 A3
Latimer Rd BH9 . . . . 71 C4
Latimers Cl BH23 . . . . . . 79 C4
Laundry La SO41. . . . . . . 87 B2
Laurel Cl
  Christchurch BH23 . . . . . 79 A4
  Corfe Mullen BH21. . . . . 37 A2
  Hordle SO41. . . . . 63 B2
  St Leonards BH24 . . . . . 18 C3
Laurel Dr BH18 . . . . 46 C4
Laurel Gdns BH18. . . . . . 46 C4
Laurel La BH24 . . . . 18 C3
Laurels The
  Broadstone BH18. . . . . . 46 B4
  Ferndown BH22 . . . . 26 C3
Lavender Cl BH31. . . . . . . 3 C1
Lavender Rd
  Bournemouth BH8 . . . . . 53 A3
  Hordle SO41. . . . . 63 B1
Lavender Villas BH21. . . 80 A3
Lavender Way BH18 . . . . 45 A3
Lavender Wlk BH8. . . . . . 53 A3
Laverstock **3** BH5. . . . . . 97 C2
Lavinia Rd BH12 . . . . 68 C3
Lawford Rd BH9 . . . . 52 A3
Lawn Cl SO41. . . . . 87 B2
Lawn Ct **13** BH22 . . . . . . 95 A4
Lawn Rd
  Lymington SO41 . . . . . . 110 A2
  Milford on S SO41 . . . . . 87 B2
Lawns Cl BH21 . . . . 24 C2
Lawns Rd BH21 . . . . 24 B2
Lawns The BH23 . . . . 80 B3
Lawn View BH25 . . . . 61 A4
Lawrence Ct BH8 . . . . . . 72 C1
Lawrence Dr BH13. . . . . . 93 B1
Lawrence Rd BH24. . . . . . 7 B2
Lawson Rd BH12. . . . . . . 68 B2
Layard Dr BH21 . . . . 31 A1
Laymoor La BH21. . . . . . 25 A1
Layton Cl BH21 . . . . 69 A1
Layton Rd BH12 . . . . 69 A1
Leamington Rd BH9 . . . . 72 A2
Leaphill Rd BH7 . . . . 74 B1
Learoyd Rd BH17 . . . . . . 67 B3
Lea The BH31. . . . . 3 A1
Lea Way BH11. . . . . 41 B2
Lechlade Gdns BH7. . . . . 74 B3
Ledbury Rd BH23 . . . . . . 101 C4
Ledgard Ct BH14. . . . . . . 92 B4
Lee Ct BH22 . . . . 35 A4
Leedam Rd BH10 . . . . . . 51 A4
Lees Cl BH23 . . . . 55 A3

Leeson Dr BH22 . . . . 26 B4
Leeson Rd BH7 . . . . 73 B2
Legg La BH21 . . . . 31 A4
Legion Cl BH15 . . . . 89 B2
Legion Rd BH15 . . . . 89 B2
Leicester Rd BH13 . . . . . 93 C3
LEIGH 31 C4
Leigham Vale Rd BH6 . . . 99 A3
Leigh Cl BH21 . . . . 31 B4
Leigh Comm BH21 . . . . . 23 B1
Leigh Gdns BH21 . . . . . . 31 A4
Leigh La BH21 . . . . 23 C1
LEIGH PARK 31 B4
Leigh Pk SO41 . . . . 110 B2
Leigh Rd
  New Milton BH25 . . . . . . 62 A1
  Wimborne Minster BH21 . 31 B4
Leighton Lo 3 BH21 . . . . 95 A4
Lentham Cl BH17 . . . . . . 47 A1
Lentune Way SO41 . . . . 110 C1
Le Patourel Cl BH23 . . . . 77 A2
Leslie Rd
  Bournemouth BH9 . . . . . 71 C3
  Poole BH14 . . . . 92 A3
Leven Ave BH4 . . . . 71 A1
Leven Cl BH4 . . . . 95 A4
Levet's La BH15 . . . . 90 B1
Lewens Cl BH21 . . . . 30 C4
Lewens La BH21 . . . . 30 C4
Lewesdon Dr BH18 . . . . . 45 C4
Leybourne Ave BH10 . . . 51 A4
Leybourne Cl BH10 . . . . . 42 C1
Leydene Ave BH8 . . . . . . 73 C4
Leydene Cl BH8 . . . . 73 C4
Leyland Rd BH12 . . . . . . 49 B2
Leyside BH23 . . . . 77 C1
Leyton Conyers 11
  BH13 . . . . 104 C3
Liberty Cl BH21 . . . . 9 C2
Liberty Ct BH23 . . . . 75 C2
Library Mews BH12 . . . . 69 A1
Library Rd
  Bournemouth BH9 . . . . . 51 C1
  Ferndown BH22 . . . . 27 A1
  Poole BH12 . . . . 69 B1
Liederbach Dr BH31 . . . . 5 C4
Lights Cl BH23 . . . . 76 B2
Lilac Cl BH24 . . . . 13 C4
LILLIPUT 103 C4
Lilliput CE Fst Sch
  BH14 . . . . 103 C4
Lilliput Cl BH14 . . . . 92 B3
Lilliput Rd BH14 . . . . . . 104 A4
Lime Cl BH15 . . . . 67 C2
Lime Gr SO41 . . . . 85 B2
Lime Tree Ho 11
  SO41 . . . . 111 A3
Limited Rd BH9 . . . . 72 A4
Linbrook Ct BH24 . . . . . . 6 B1
Lin Brook Dr BH24 . . . . . 7 A2
Lincoln Ave
  Bournemouth BH1 . . . . . 97 A4
  Christchurch BH23 . . . . 55 C1
Lincoln Rd BH12 . . . . . . 69 A3
Lindbergh Rd BH21 . . . . 26 A4
Linden Cl BH22 . . . . 35 A1
Linden Ct BH24 . . . . 13 A4
Linden Gdns BH24 . . . . . 13 A4
Linden Rd
  Bournemouth BH9 . . . . . 52 A1
  Ferndown BH22 . . . . 35 A1
  Poole BH12 . . . . 68 C2
Lindens The BH23 . . . . . 57 A2
Linden Way SO41 . . . . . 110 B3
Lindsay Ct 19 BH13 . . . . 94 A4
Lindsay Manor 11
  BH13 . . . . 94 A4
Lindsay Pk 15 BH13 . . . . 94 A4
Lindsay Rd BH13 . . . . . . 93 C4
Lindum Ct 3 BH13 . . . . . 94 A4
Lineside BH23 . . . . 76 C3
Linford Cl BH25 . . . . 62 B2
Linford Rd BH24 . . . . 7 B1
Lingdale Rd BH6 . . . . . . 75 A1
Lingfield Grange 11
  BH13 . . . . 94 B3
Ling Rd BH12 . . . . 48 B1

Lingwood Ave BH23 . . . . 77 C1
Linhorns La BH25 . . . . . . 62 A3
Link Rd BH24 . . . . 14 A4
Link Rise BH21 . . . . 37 B2
Links Dr BH23 . . . . 75 A4
Linkside Ave BH7 . . . . . . 73 C3
Links Rd BH14 . . . . 93 A2
Links View Ave BH14 . . . 93 B2
Linmead Dr BH11 . . . . . . 42 A2
Linnet Cl BH24 . . . . 14 A2
Linnet Ct BH25 . . . . 61 C2
Linnet Rd BH17 . . . . 65 C4
Linthorpe Rd BH15 . . . . . 91 B4
Linton Lawns BH22 . . . . 35 B3
Linwood Rd BH9 . . . . . . 72 B2
Linwood Sch BH9 . . . . . 72 A2
Lionheart Cl BH11 . . . . . 41 A1
Lions La BH24 . . . . 10 B1
Lions Wood BH24 . . . . . 18 C4
Lisle Cl SO41 . . . . 110 C2
Lissenden 11 BH13 . . . . 94 B3
Litchford Rd BH25 . . . . . 62 C1
Little Barrs Dr BH25 . . . . 62 B2
Little Burn SO41 . . . . . . 107 B3
LITTLE CANFORD 33 A4
Littlecroft Ave BH9 . . . . 52 B2
Little Croft Rd BH12 . . . . 68 B2
Little Ct Poole BH14 . . . 103 C3
  Poole, Canford Cliffs
  BH13 . . . . 104 C4
Little Dene Copse
  SO41 . . . . 110 A1
Little Dewlands BH31 . . . 2 A2
LITTLEDOWN 74 A2
Littledown Ave BH7 . . . . 73 C2
Littledown Dr BH7 . . . . . 73 C2
Little Forest Mans 12
  BH1 . . . . 96 A2
Little Forest Rd BH4 . . . 71 B1
Little Fosters BH13 . . . . 104 B2
Little Lonnen
  Colehill BH21 . . . . 23 C4
  Wimborne Minster BH21 . 24 A4
Littlemead Cl BH17 . . . . 66 A3
Littlemoor Ave BH11 . . . 49 A4
LITTLE PAMPHILL 21 C1
Livingstone Rd
  Bournemouth BH5 . . . . . 98 B4
  Christchurch BH23 . . . . 77 A2
  Poole BH12 . . . . 68 C2
  Wimborne Minster BH21 . 31 B4
Llewellin Cl BH16 . . . . . . 64 C3
Llewelyn Cl BH16 . . . . . . 64 C3
Loaders Cl BH9 . . . . 72 A3
Loch Rd BH14 . . . . 69 B1
Lockerley Cl SO41 . . . . . 111 A1
Locksley Dr BH22 . . . . . . 34 C3
Lockyers Dr BH22 . . . . . 27 C2
Lockyer's Mid Sch
  BH21 . . . . 37 A4
Lockyers Rd BH21 . . . . . 37 B4
Loders Cl BH17 . . . . 47 A3
Lodge Cl BH14 . . . . 93 B4
Lodge Ct BH14 . . . . 93 B4
Lodge Rd
  Christchurch BH23 . . . . 75 B3
  Lymington SO41 . . . . . 110 A2
Lodge The BH12 . . . . . . 112 A3
Loewy Cres BH12 . . . . . 49 A2
Lombard Ave BH6 . . . . . 99 A4
Lombardy Cl BH31 . . . . . 3 B1
London Tavern Cvn Pk
  The BH24 . . . . 14 A4
Lone Pine Dr BH22 . . . . . 35 B3
Lone Pine Pk BH22 . . . . 35 C3
Lone Pine Way BH22 . . . 35 C2
Longacre Dr BH22 . . . . . 34 C4
Longbarrow Cl BH8 . . . . 74 A4
Longespee Rd BH21 . . . . 39 B4
Longfield Dr
  Bournemouth BH11 . . . . 42 A2
  Ferndown BH22 . . . . 34 B4
Longfield Rd SO41 . . . . . 84 B2
LONGFLEET 91 A4
Longfleet CE Comb Sch
  BH15 . . . . 91 A4
Longfleet Rd BH15 . . . . . 91 B4
LONGHAM 34 A1
Longham Bsns Ctr
  BH22 . . . . 34 B2

Long La BH21 . . . . 23 B4
Longleat Gdns BH25 . . . . 61 B2
Long Meadow Ind Est
  BH21 . . . . 8 C3
Longmeadow La BH17 . . 65 B4
Long Rd BH10 . . . . 42 C1
Longspee Sch BH17 . . . . 67 A3
Lonnen Rd BH21 . . . . . . 24 A4
Lonnen Wood Cl BH21 . . 24 A4
Lonsdale Rd BH3 . . . . . . 71 C2
Loraine Ave BH23 . . . . . 80 C3
Lord Cl BH17 . . . . 67 C3
Lorne Park Rd BH1 . . . . . 96 A2
Love La SO41 . . . . 87 A3
Lower Ashley Rd BH25 . . 83 A4
Lower Blandford Rd
  BH18 . . . . 46 B3
LOWER BUCKLAND . . . 111 A4
Lower Buckland Rd
  SO41 . . . . 110 C4
Lower Common La BH21 . .9 B3
Lower Gardens* BH2 . . 112 B2
Lower Golf Links Rd
  BH18 . . . . 38 B1
LOWER HAMWORTHY . . 90 A1
Lower Meadend Rd
  SO41 . . . . 107 A1
LOWER PARKSTONE . . . 92 B3
Lowesmore Ct BH14 . . . . 92 C4
Lowther Gdns 3 BH8 . . . 96 C4
Lowther Rd BH8 . . . . 72 B1
Lucas Rd Poole BH15 . . . 90 B1
  Poole, Upper Parkstone
  BH12 . . . . 68 C2
Lucerne Ave BH6 . . . . . . 99 A4
Lucerne Rd SO41 . . . . . . 87 A2
Luckham Cl BH9 . . . . 52 B1
Luckham Gdns BH9 . . . . 52 C1
Luckham Pl BH9 . . . . 52 B1
Luckham Rd BH9 . . . . . . 52 B1
Luckham Rd E BH9 . . . . . 52 B1
Lulworth Ave BH15 . . . . . 89 B1
Lulworth Cl BH15 . . . . . . 89 B1
Lulworth Cres BH15 . . . . 89 B1
Lulworth Ct BH15 . . . . . . 89 B2
Lumby Dr BH24 . . . . 13 C4
Lumby Drive Mobile
  Home Pk 2 BH24 . . . . . 13 C4
Luscombe Rd BH14 . . . . 92 C2
Luther Rd BH9 . . . . 71 C4
Lych Gate Ct BH14 . . . . . 14 A2
Lydford Gdns BH11 . . . . 50 A2
Lydford Rd BH11 . . . . . . 50 A2
Lydgate SO41 . . . . 86 A3
Lydlinch Cl BH22 . . . . . . 35 A1
Lydwell Cl BH11 . . . . 41 C1
Lyell Rd BH12 . . . . 68 C2
Lyme Cres BH23 . . . . . . 79 C3
Lymefields SO41 . . . . . . 87 B4
LYMINGTON 110 B4
Lymington CE Inf Sch
  SO41 . . . . 110 C3
Lymington Hospl
  SO41 . . . . 110 C3
Lymington Jun Sch
  SO41 . . . . 110 C3
Lymington Pier Sta
  SO41 . . . . 111 C2
Lymington Rd
  Christchurch BH23 . . . . 79 C2
  Milford on S SO41 . . . . 87 B4
  New Milton BH25 . . . . . 82 C3
Lymington Rehabilitation
  Unit SO41 . . . . 111 A3
Lymington Town Sta
  SO41 . . . . 111 B3
Lymington Vineyard*
  SO41 . . . . 110 A1
Lymore La SO41 . . . . . . 87 C4
Lymore Valley SO41 . . . . 87 B4
Lyndale Cl SO41 . . . . . . 87 B3
Lyndhurst Rd
  Christchurch BH23 . . . . 57 C4
  Christchurch BH23 . . . . 59 A1
Lyndon Ct BH23 . . . . 75 C4
Lynes La BH24 . . . . 13 A3
Lynn Rd BH17 . . . . 47 C1
Lynric Cl BH25 . . . . 82 A1
Lynton Cres BH23 . . . . . 55 B2
Lynwood Cl BH22 . . . . . . 27 A3

Lynwood Ct SO41 . . . . . 110 C2
Lynwood Dr BH21 . . . . . . 39 B4
Lyon Ave BH25 . . . . 62 B1
Lyon Rd BH12 . . . . 49 B2
Lysander Cl BH23 . . . . . . 78 C2
Lystra Rd BH9 . . . . 52 A2
Lytchett Dr BH18 . . . . . . 45 C2
Lytchett Way BH16 . . . . . 64 B2
Lyteltane Rd SO41 . . . . . 110 C1
Lytham Rd BH18 . . . . . . 46 A3
Lytton Rd BH1, BH8 . . . . 96 C4

M

Mabey Ave BH10 . . . . . . 51 A2
MacAndrew Rd BH13 . . 104 C3
MacAulay Rd BH18 . . . . 46 A4
McKinley Rd BH4 . . . . . . 94 C2
MacLaren Rd BH9 . . . . . 51 C3
Maclean Rd BH11 . . . . . . 49 C3
Madeira Rd
  Bournemouth BH1 . . . . . 96 A3
  Poole BH14 . . . . 69 A1
Madeline Cl BH12 . . . . . 68 B3
Madeline Cres BH12 . . . 68 B3
Madison Ave BH1 . . . . . . 73 A1
Madrisa Ct SO41 . . . . . 111 A3
Magdalen La BH23 . . . . . 76 A1
Magna Cl BH11 . . . . 41 C2
Magna Gdns BH11 . . . . . 41 C2
Magna Rd BH21 . . . . 40 C3
Magnolia Cl
  Bournemouth BH10 . . . 100 A4
  Verwood BH31 . . . . 5 C4
Magnolia Ho 6 BH10 . . . 51 C4
Magpie Cl BH8 . . . . 52 C2
Magpie Gr BH25 . . . . 61 C1
Mag's Barrow BH22 . . . . 35 B2
Maidment Cl BH11 . . . . . 49 B4
Maitland Ct SO41 . . . . . 110 C2
Maitlands The 2 BH2 . . . 95 A2
Majorca Mans 4 BH2 . . 112 A2
Malan Cl BH17 . . . . 67 B4
Malcomb Cl BH6 . . . . . . 100 A3
Mallard Bldgs 6 BH25 . . 62 A1
Mallard Cl
  Bournemouth BH8 . . . . . 72 C2
  Christchurch BH23 . . . . 78 A1
  Hordle SO41 . . . . 84 A2
Mallard Rd
  Bournemouth BH8 . . . . . 73 A4
  Wimborne Minster BH21 . 24 A3
Mallory Cl BH23 . . . . 77 C3
Mallow Cl
  Broadstone BH18 . . . . . 45 B3
  Christchurch BH23 . . . . 78 C3
Mallows The BH25 . . . . . 63 A2
Malmesbury Ct BH8 . . . . 72 C1
Malmesbury Park Pl 7
  BH8 . . . . 96 C4
Malmesbury Park Prim
  Sch BH8 . . . . 96 B4
Malmesbury Park Rd
  BH8 . . . . 72 B1
Malmesbury Rd BH24 . . . 18 C3
Malmsbury Cl 6
  BH23 . . . . 100 A4
Maloren Way BH22 . . . . . 17 B1
Malthouse 7 BH15 . . . . . 90 C2
Maltings The
  Bournemouth BH11 . . . . 41 C2
  3 Poole BH15 . . . . 91 B3
Malvern Cl BH9 . . . . 52 A2
Malvern Ct
  4 Bournemouth BH9 . . . 52 A1
  2 Christchurch BH23 . . . 77 C3
Malvern Rd BH9 . . . . 52 A1
Manchester Rd SO41 . . . 107 B2
Mandalay Cl BH31 . . . . . 2 B1
Mandale Cl BH11 . . . . . . 50 A3
Mandale Rd BH11 . . . . . 49 C3
Manderley SO41 . . . . . . 87 B1
Manington Hall 5 BH4 . . 94 C2
Manning Ave BH23 . . . . 78 C4
Mannings Heath Rd
  BH12 . . . . 48 B1
Mannings Heath Rdbt
  BH17 . . . . 48 B2

Mannings Heath Ret Pk
  BH12 . . . . 68 A4
Mannington Pl 12
  BH2 . . . . 112 A2
Mannington Way BH22 . . 16 B2
Manor Ave BH12 . . . . . . 48 C1
Manor Cl
  Ferndown BH22 . . . . 27 B1
  Milford on S SO41 . . . . 87 A4
Manor Ct
  Ringwood BH24 . . . . . . 13 A4
  Verwood BH31 . . . . 2 C2
Manor Farm Cl BH25 . . . 81 C4
Manor Farm Rd BH10 . . . 42 C3
Manor Farmyard BH8 . . . 54 B2
Manor Gdns
  Bournemouth BH24 . . . . 13 A4
  Verwood BH31 . . . . 2 C2
Manor Ho BH18 . . . . 46 A4
Manor La BH31 . . . . 2 C1
Manor Pk BH15 . . . . 66 B1
Manor Rd
  Bournemouth BH1 . . . . . 96 C2
  Christchurch BH23 . . . . 76 A1
  Milford on S SO41 . . . . 87 A4
  New Milton BH25 . . . . . 62 B1
  Ringwood BH24 . . . . . . 13 C3
  Verwood BH31 . . . . 2 C2
Manorside Comb Sch
  BH12 . . . . 49 A1
Manor Way BH31 . . . . . . 2 C3
Mansard Ct BH13 . . . . . 106 A3
Mansel Cl BH12 . . . . 70 C3
Mansfield Ave BH14 . . . . 92 C4
Mansfield Cl
  Ferndown BH22 . . . . 35 A2
  Poole BH14 . . . . 92 C4
Mansfield Rd
  Bournemouth BH9 . . . . . 51 B1
  Poole BH14 . . . . 92 C4
  Ringwood BH24 . . . . . . 13 A3
Manton Cl BH15 . . . . 89 B3
Manton Rd BH15 . . . . . . 89 B3
Maple Bsns Pk BH25 . . . 25 C3
Maple Cl
  Barton on Sea BH25 . . . 82 B1
  Christchurch BH23 . . . . 79 C2
Maple Ct SO41 . . . . 110 A1
Maple Dr BH22 . . . . 26 C4
Maple Lo BH16 . . . . 64 C3
Maple Rd
  Bournemouth BH9 . . . . . 71 C4
  Poole BH15 . . . . 91 A3
Mapperton Cl BH17 . . . . 47 C2
Marabout Cl BH23 . . . . . 77 A2
Marchwood Rd BH10 . . . 50 C3
Margards La BH31 . . . . . . 2 B1
Marian Cl BH21 . . . . 44 C4
Marianne Rd
  Poole BH12 . . . . 70 C4
  Wimborne Minster BH21 . 24 A3
Marian Rd BH21 . . . . . . 44 C4
Marie Cl BH12 . . . . 69 A3
Marina Ct
  2 Bournemouth BH5 . . . 97 B2
  Christchurch BH23 . . . . 80 A2
Marina Dr BH14 . . . . 92 B1
Marina The BH7 . . . . 97 B2
Marina Twrs 5 BH5 . . . . 97 B2
Marina View 11 BH23 . . 100 A4
Marine Ct BH25 . . . . 81 A2
Marine Dr BH25 . . . . 81 B2
Marine Drive W BH25 . . . 81 B2
Marine Point BH25 . . . . . 81 C2
Marine Prospect BH25 . . 81 C2
Marine Rd BH6 . . . . 99 A4
Mariners Ct
  Christchurch BH23 . . . . 78 A1
  Lymington SO41 . . . . . 111 B1
Market Cl BH15 . . . . 90 C2
Market Pl BH24 . . . . 13 A3
Market St BH15 . . . . 90 B2
Market Way BH21 . . . . . 31 A4
Markham Ave BH10 . . . . 43 A3
Markham Cl BH10 . . . . . 43 A2
Markham Rd BH9 . . . . . . 72 A3
Mark's La BH25 . . . . 62 A4
Marks Rd BH9 . . . . 51 C3
Marlborough Ct
  30 Bournemouth BH4 . . . 94 C3

Marlborough Ct continued
3 Wimborne Minster
BH21. . . . . **22** C1
Marlborough Mans 2
BH7. . . . . **74** B1
Marlborough Pines 25
BH4. . . . . **94** C3
Marlborough Pl
Lymington SO41. . . . . . . **110** C4
Wimborne Minster BH21. . **23** A1
Marlborough Rd
Bournemouth BH4. . . . . . **94** C3
Poole BH14. . . . . **92** C4
Marler Ho 8 BH4. . . . . . **94** B4
Marley Ave BH25. . . . . . **61** C2
Marley Cl BH25. . . . . . . **61** C2
Marline Rd BH12. . . . . . **69** A2
Marlott Rd BH15. . . . . . **66** C1
Marlow Dr BH23. . . . . . **55** B2
Marlpit Dr BH23. . . . . . **60** A1
Marmion Gn BH23. . . . . **77** C2
Marnhull Rd BH15. . . . . **91** A4
Marpet Cl BH11. . . . . . . **41** C2
Marquis Way BH11. . . . . **41** A1
Marram Cl SO41. . . . . . **111** A4
Marryat Ct
Christchurch BH23. . . . . . **80** B2
New Milton BH25. . . . . . **61** C2
Marryat Rd BH25. . . . . . **61** C2
Marshal Rd BH17. . . . . . **46** B1
Marshfield BH21. . . . . . **23** C3
Marsh La
Christchurch BH23. . . . . . **55** C1
Lymington SO41. . . . . . . **111** A4
Upton BH16. . . . . **64** A3
Marshlands Cl BH23. . . . **77** A1
Marshwood Ave BH17. . . **47** C3
Marston Cl BH23. . . . . . **62** B3
Marston Gr BH23. . . . . . **79** B4
Marston Rd
New Milton BH25. . . . . . **62** B3
Poole BH15. . . . . **90** B2
Martello Ho 5 BH13. . . **104** C4
Martello Pk BH13. . . . . **104** C3
Martello Rd BH13. . . . . . **93** C1
Martello Rd S BH13. . . . **104** C4
Martello Twrs BH13. . . . **104** C3
Martells The BH25. . . . . **82** B1
Martin Cl BH17. . . . . . . **46** B2
Martindale Ave BH21. . . **24** B1
Martingale Cl BH16. . . . **65** A3
Martins Cl BH22. . . . . . **27** B3
Martins Dr BH22. . . . . . **27** B3
Martins Hill La BH23. . . **76** C4
Martins La BH23. . . . . . **76** C4
Martins Way BH22. . . . . **27** B3
Marwell Cl BH7. . . . . . . **74** A2
Mary La BH22. . . . . **16** B2
Maryland Ct 3 SO41. . . **86** B2
Maryland Gdns SO41. . . **86** B2
Maryland Rd BH16. . . . . **88** C4
Mary Mitchell Cl BH24. . **13** A4
Masters Cl BH4. . . . . . . **95** A3
Masterson Cl BH23. . . . . **77** A2
Matlock Rd BH22. . . . . . **34** C3
Maturin Cl SO41. . . . . **110** C2
Maundeville Cres BH23. . **75** B3
Maundeville Rd BH23. . . **75** B3
Maureen Cl BH12. . . . . . **68** B4
Maurice Rd BH8. . . . . . . **73** A3
Mavis Rd BH9. . . . . **72** B4
Maxwell Rd
Bournemouth BH9. . . . . . **72** A2
Broadstone BH18. . . . . . **45** B3
Poole BH13. . . . . **104** C3
May Ave SO41. . . . . . . **110** C4
Mayfair BH4. . . . . **94** C2
Mayfair Cl BH13. . . . . . . **94** B2
Mayfair Gdns BH11. . . . . **50** A4
Mayfield Ave BH14. . . . . **93** B3
Mayfield Cl BH22. . . . . . **26** C2
Mayfield Dr BH22. . . . . . **26** C2
Mayfield Rd BH9. . . . . . **52** A1
Mayfield Way BH22. . . . . **26** C2
Mayflower Cl SO41. . . . **111** C1
Mayford Rd BH12. . . . . . **70** B2
May Gdns
Bournemouth BH11. . . . . **49** B4
Walkford BH23. . . . . **60** B1
Maylyn Rd BH16. . . . . . **44** A2

Mead Cl BH18. . . . . **46** A1
Meadowbank BH16. . . . . **64** C4
Meadow Cl
Bransgore BH23. . . . . . **108** C2
Ferndown BH22. . . . . . . **35** A1
Ringwood BH24. . . . . . . **13** C4
Meadow Court Cl BH9. . . **52** A2
Meadow Ct
2 Bournemouth BH9. . . **52** A2
Verwood BH31. . . . . **5** A4
3 Wimborne Minster
BH21. . . . . **31** A4
Meadow Farm La BH21. . **37** A4
Meadow Gr BH31. . . . . . **3** B1
Meadow La BH23. . . . . . **56** C1
Meadowland BH23. . . . . **77** C1
Meadowlands SO41. . . . **110** B3
Meadow Rd
Lymington SO41. . . . . . **110** B1
New Milton BH25. . . . . . **62** B2
Ringwood BH24. . . . . . . **13** C4
Meadow Rise BH18. . . . . **37** C1
Meadows Cl BH16. . . . . . **64** C3
Meadows Dr BH16. . . . . . **64** C3
Meadowsweet Rd BH17. . **65** B4
Meadow View Rd BH11. . **49** B4
Meadow Way
Barton on S BH25. . . . . . **82** A1
Ringwood BH24. . . . . . . **13** C4
Verwood BH31. . . . . **3** B1
Meadway The BH23. . . . . **59** A1
Medina Way BH23. . . . . . **78** C1
Medlar Cl BH23. . . . . . . **77** A4
Medway Rd BH22. . . . . . **28** A2
Meeting House La
BH24. . . . . **13** A3
Melbourne Rd
Bournemouth BH8. . . . . . **72** C1
Christchurch BH23. . . . . . **75** B4
Melbury Ave BH12. . . . . **69** B3
Melbury Cl
New Milton BH25. . . . . . **82** B4
Lymington SO41. . . . . . **110** C2
Melford Cl BH1. . . . . . . **96** A2
Mellstock Rd BH15. . . . . **67** A1
Melrose Ct BH25. . . . . . **62** C1
Melton Ct BH13. . . . . . . **93** C4
Melverley Gdns BH21. . . **23** A1
Melville Rd BH9. . . . . . . **71** B4
Mendip Cl
New Milton BH25. . . . . . **82** B4
Verwood BH31. . . . . **2** C1
Mendip Ct 4 BH31. . . . . **77** C3
Mendip Rd BH31. . . . . . **2** C2
Mentone Rd 2 BH14. . . **92** A3
Meon Rd BH7. . . . . **74** B2
Meredith Cl BH23. . . . . . **77** A2
Meriden Cl BH13. . . . . . **104** C3
Meridians The BH23. . . . **75** C1
Merino Way BH22. . . . . . **17** A1
Merlewood Cl BH21. . . . **112** B3
Merlewood Ct 9 BH25. . **62** B1
MERLEY. **31** A1
Merley Court Touring Pk
BH21. . . . . **30** C1
Merley Dr BH23. . . . . . . **80** A3
Merley Fst Sch BH21. . . . . **31** A1
Merley Gdns BH21. . . . . **31** B1
Merley Ho BH21. . . . . . . **31** A1
Merley House Holiday Pk
BH21. . . . . **30** B1
Merley House La BH21. . . **30** C1
Merley La BH21. . . . . . . **31** B1
Merley Park Rd
Ashington BH21. . . . . . . **38** B4
Corfe Mullen BH21. . . . . **37** C4
Merley BH21. . . . . **30** C1
Merley Ways BH21. . . . . **30** B1
Merlin Cl BH24. . . . . **14** A2
Merlin Way BH23. . . . . . **102** A4
Mermaid Ct 3 BH5. . . . . **97** B2
Merriefield Ave BH18. . . **38** B1
Merriefield Cl BH18. . . . . **38** B2
Merriefield Dr BH18. . . . . **38** B2
Merrifield BH21. . . . . . . **23** B4
Merrivale Ave BH6. . . . . . **99** B4
Merrow Ave BH12. . . . . . **70** B3
Merrow Chase 1
BH13. . . . . **104** C3

Merryfield Cl
Bransgore BH23. . . . . . **108** C2
Verwood BH31. . . . . **2** C2
Merryfield Ct BH10. . . . . **50** C4
Merryfield La BH10. . . . . **50** C4
Merryweather Est
BH24. . . . . **14** A4
Merton Ct
2 Christchurch BH23. . . **80** B2
2 Poole BH15. . . . . . . **91** B4
Merton Gr BH24. . . . . . . **13** A4
Merville Gdns BH9. . . . . **71** C3
Methuen Cl 2 BH8. . . . . **96** C4
Methuen Rd
Bournemouth BH8. . . . . . **96** B4
Poole BH17. . . . . **46** B2
Mews The
Bournemouth BH2. . . . . . **95** A3
Verwood BH31. . . . . **5** A4
Meyrick Cl BH23. . . . . . **109** C1
Meyrick Park Cres BH3. . **71** C2
Meyrick Park Mans
BH2. . . . . **112** B3
Meyrick Rd BH1. . . . . . . **96** A4
Michelgrove Rd BH5. . . . **97** B2
Michelmersh Gn BH8. . . . **53** A1
Mickleham Cl BH12. . . . . **70** B4
Middlebere Cres BH16. . . **88** C4
Middle Brook BH11. . . . . **42** A2
Middlehill Dr BH21. . . . . **24** B2
Middlehill Rd BH21. . . . . **24** A2
Middle La BH24. . . . . . . **13** B3
Middle Rd
Bournemouth BH10. . . . . **42** C1
Lymington SO41. . . . . . **110** C2
Poole BH15. . . . . **67** B2
Sway SO41. . . . . **107** B3
Middleton Mews BH25. . . **81** C4
Middleton Rd
Bournemouth BH9. . . . . . **51** B2
Ringwood BH24. . . . . . . **13** B4
Midland Rd BH9. . . . . . . **51** C1
Midway Path BH13. . . . **106** B3
Midwood Ave BH8. . . . . . **73** C4
Milborne Cres BH12. . . . **69** B4
Milbourne Rd BH22. . . . . **26** C2
Milburn Cl 3 BH4. . . . . . **94** C4
Milburn Rd BH4. . . . . . . **94** B4
Mildenhall 6 BH2. . . . . . **95** A2
Milestone Rd BH15. . . . . **67** A1
Milford Cl BH22. . . . . . . **17** A2
Milford Cres SO41. . . . . . **87** B2
Milford Dr BH11. . . . . . . **41** C1
Milford Ho SO41. . . . . . . **87** B3
MILFORD ON SEA. **87** B4
Milford on Sea CE Prim
Sch SO41. . . . . **87** B4
Milford Rd BH25. . . . . . . **82** C1
Milford Trad Est SO41. . . . **87** B3
Milky Down Back La
BH24. . . . . **14** C3
Milkbank Ho 5 BH21. . . . **22** C1
Miller Cl BH25. . . . . **62** C2
Miller Rd BH23. . . . . **77** A2
Millfield BH25. . . . . **61** B2
Millfield BH17. . . . . **66** A3
Millhams Cl BH10. . . . . . **42** B2
Millhams Dr BH10. . . . . . **42** B2
Millhams Rd BH10. . . . . . **42** B2
Millhams St BH23. . . . . . **76** B1
Millhams Street N 2
BH23. . . . . **76** B1
Mill Hill Cl BH14. . . . . . . **92** B3
Mill La
Christchurch BH23. . . . . . **80** B3
Lymington SO41. . . . . . **111** B3
Poole BH14. . . . . **92** B3
Wimborne Minster BH21. . **22** C1
Mill Mdw SO41. . . . . **87** A3
Mill Rd BH23. . . . . **76** A3
Mill Rd N BH8. . . . . **53** B2
Mill Rd S BH8. . . . . **53** A1
Mills The SO41. . . . . **69** B3
Millstream Cl
Poole BH17. . . . . **66** A4
Wimborne Minster BH21. . **30** C4
Millstream Trad Est
BH24. . . . . **13** B1
Millyford Cl BH25. . . . . . **81** A3

Milne Rd BH17. . . . . **46** B1
Milner Rd BH4. . . . . **94** C1
Milton Bsns Ctr BH25. . . . **61** B1
Milton Cl BH14. . . . . **93** A3
Milton Ct BH22. . . . . **27** A1
Milton Gr BH25. . . . . **82** B4
Milton Mead BH25. . . . . . **61** C1
Milton Rd
Bournemouth BH8. . . . . . **72** A1
Poole BH14. . . . . **93** A3
Wimborne Minster BH21. . **22** C2
Milton Villas BH8. . . . . . **96** A4
Milverton Cl BH23. . . . . . **79** B4
Mimosa Ave BH21. . . . . . **39** B4
Minstead Rd BH10. . . . . . **50** C3
Minster Pk BH21. . . . . **8** C1
Minster The BH21. . . . . . . **30** B4
Minster View BH21. . . . . **22** C1
Minster Way BH16. . . . . . **64** B3
Minterne Grange
BH14. . . . . **103** C3
Minterne Rd
3 Bournemouth BH9. . . **52** A1
Christchurch BH23. . . . . . **101** B4
Poole BH14. . . . . **103** C3
Minton Mews BH21. . . . . **71** C1
Mintys Yd 4 BH24. . . . . . **13** B2
Mission La BH18. . . . . . . **46** A2
Mission Rd BH18. . . . . . . **46** A2
Mitchell Cl BH25. . . . . . . **82** A1
Mitchell Rd
Ferndown BH21. . . . . . . **26** A3
Poole BH17. . . . . **67** C4
Mitre Ct 8 BH23. . . . . . . **76** A2
Moat Ct BH4. . . . . **70** C1
Moat La BH25. . . . . **81** C3
Moffat Rd BH23. . . . . **77** A2
Molefields SO41. . . . . . . **87** B3
Molyneux Rd BH25. . . . . **63** A1
Monaco Ct BH9. . . . . **72** B3
Monarch Ct 20 BH4. . . . **94** C3
Moneyfly Rd BH31. . . . . . **3** B1
Monks Cl BH22. . . . . **28** A4
Monks Ct 4 SO41. . . . . **111** B1
Monkshood BH23. . . . . . **78** B4
Monks Way BH11. . . . . . **41** A1
Monkswell Gn BH23. . . . . **77** A1
Monkton Cl BH22. . . . . . **27** A2
Monkton Cres BH12. . . . . **69** B4
Monkworthy Dr BH24. . . . **11** A1
Monmouth Cl BH31. . . . . **5** B4
Monmouth Ct
Lymington SO41. . . . . . **111** A2
Ringwood BH24. . . . . . . **13** A3
Monmouth Dr BH31. . . . . **5** B4
Monsal Ave BH22. . . . . . **34** C3
Montacute Sch BH17. . . . . **46** C2
Montacute Way BH21. . . . **39** B4
Montague Rd BH5. . . . . . **98** B3
Montagu Pk BH23. . . . . . **80** A2
Montagu Rd BH23. . . . . . **80** B3
Monteray Dr SO41. . . . . . **63** C2
Montgomery Ave BH11. . . **50** B3
Montrose Cl BH31. . . . . . **2** C1
Montrose Dr BH10. . . . . . **50** B2
Monument La SO41. . . . **111** C4
Moonrakers Way BH23. . . **79** B4
Moorcroft Ave BH23. . . . . **56** C1
MOORDOWN. **52** A1
Moordown St John's CE
Prim Sch BH9. . . . . **51** C1
Moore Ave BH11. . . . . . . **50** A4
Moore Cl BH25. . . . . **81** C4
Moorfield Gr BH9. . . . . . . **51** C1
Moorfields Rd BH13. . . . . **104** C4
Moorhaven BH22. . . . . . . **27** A2
Moorhills 2 BH21. . . . . . **31** A4
Moorings Cl BH15. . . . . . **89** C1
Moorings The 2
BH23. . . . . **100** A4
Moorland Ave BH25. . . . . **81** C3
Moorland Cres BH16. . . . . **64** B3
Moorland Ct BH22. . . . . . **16** B2
Moorland Gate BH24. . . . **13** B1
Moorland Par BH16. . . . . **64** B3
Moorland Rd BH1. . . . . . . **97** A3
Moorlands Rd
Verwood BH31. . . . . **2** C3
West Moors BH22. . . . . . **16** C3

Moorlands Rise BH22. . . . **17** A3
Moorland Way BH16. . . . . **64** B3
Moorlea 2 BH8. . . . . **96** B4
Moor Rd BH18. . . . . **38** B1
Moor Side BH24. . . . . . . **28** B4
Moorside Cl BH11. . . . . . **50** B3
Moorside Gdns BH11. . . . **50** B3
Moorside Rd
Bournemouth BH11. . . . . **50** B3
Corfe Mullen BH21. . . . . **37** A1
West Moors BH22. . . . . . **17** B1
Moors Valley Ctry Park
Visitor Ctr* BH24 . . . . . **10** B4
Moors Valley Railway*
BH24. . . . . **5** C1
MOORTOWN. **13** C1
Moortown Dr
Bournemouth BH11. . . . . **40** B4
Wimborne Minster BH21. . **32** B1
Moortown Farm BH21. . . . **40** B4
Moortown Ho BH24. . . . . **13** B1
Moorvale Rd BH9. . . . . . . **52** A1
Moor View Rd BH15. . . . . **67** B2
Morant Cl 4 BH25. . . . . . **62** B1
Morant Ct BH24. . . . . **6** C1
Moray Ct 11 BH21. . . . . . **22** B1
Morden Ave BH22. . . . . . **34** C4
Morden Rd BH9. . . . . **51** B1
Moreton Rd BH9. . . . . . . **52** B3
Moriconium Quay
BH15. . . . . **89** A1
Morington Ct 8 BH8. . . . **96** A4
Morley Cl
Bournemouth BH5. . . . . . **98** A4
Burton BH23. . . . . **56** C2
Morley Rd BH5. . . . . **98** A4
Morley Way BH22. . . . . . **35** C3
Mornish Rd BH13. . . . . . **93** C2
Morrison Ave BH12. . . . . **69** C2
Morris Rd BH17. . . . . **67** A4
Mortimer Cl BH23. . . . . . **78** A1
Mortimer Rd BH8. . . . . . . **72** B4
Mossley Ave
Poole BH12. . . . . **50** A1
Poole BH12. . . . . **70** A4
Motcombe Rd BH13. . . . . **94** A2
Mount Ave BH25. . . . . . . **82** A3
Mountbatten Cl BH23. . . **102** A4
Mountbatten Ct BH25. . . . **61** C2
Mountbatten Dr BH22. . . . **26** C1
Mountbatten Gdns BH8. . **53** C1
Mountbatten Rd BH13. . . **94** B1
Mount Cl BH25. . . . . **82** A3
Mount Grace Dr BH14. . . **104** A3
Mount Heatherbank 7
BH1. . . . . **112** B2
Mountjoy Cl BH21. . . . . . **31** C2
Mount Pleasant BH23. . . **102** A4
MOUNT PLEASANT. **13** B3
Mount Pleasant Dr
Bournemouth BH8. . . . . . **73** C4
Bransgore BH23. . . . . . **109** B3
Mount Pleasant Rd
BH15. . . . . **91** A3
Mount Rd
Bournemouth BH11. . . . . **50** B4
Poole BH14. . . . . **68** B1
Mount The BH24. . . . . . . **14** B4
MUDEFORD. **102** A4
Mudeford Com Inf Sch
BH23. . . . . **77** B1
Mudeford Green Cl
BH23. . . . . **101** C3
Mudeford Jun Sch
BH23. . . . . **77** C1
Mudeford La BH23. . . . . **77** C1
Mude Gdns BH23. . . . . . **102** A4
Mulberry Cl 4 BH23. . . . . **76** A2
Mulberry Gr SO41. . . . . . **85** B2
Mullins Cl BH12. . . . . . . **70** C4
Munster Rd BH14. . . . . . **93** A3
Murley Rd BH9. . . . . **72** A3
MUSCLIFFE. **52** C3
Muscliffe La BH9. . . . . . . **52** B4
Muscliffe Rd BH9. . . . . . . **51** C1

Muscliff Prim Sch BH9 . 52 C3
Mus of Electricity*
  BH23. . . . . 76 B2
Myrtle Cl SO41 . . . . 63 C2
Myrtle Rd BH8 . . . . 72 C1

N

Nada Rd BH23 . . . . 79 A4
Nairn Ct BH3 . . . . 71 B3
Nairn Rd
  Bournemouth BH3 . . . . . . 71 B2
  Poole BH13. . . . . 104 B3
Naish Rd BH25 . . . . 81 B2
Namu Rd BH9 . . . . 51 B1
Nansen Ave BH15 . . . . 67 A1
Napier Rd BH15 . . . . 88 C3

Narrow La
  Ringwood, North Poulner
  BH24. . . . . .7 B1
  Ringwood, Poulner BH24. . 14 B4
Naseby Rd BH9 . . . . 52 A1
Nathen Gdns BH15. . . . . . 89 A3
Navarac Ct BH14. . . . . 92 C3
Nea Cl BH23. . . . . 79 A3
Neacroft Cl BH25 . . . . 81 A3
Nea Rd BH23 . . . . 79 B3
Needles Ct [11] SO41 . . . . . 86 C2
Needles Point SO41. . . . . . 87 A1
Neighbourhood Ctr
  BH17. . . . . 47 B2
Nelson Cl BH9 . . . . 51 C2
Nelson Cl [13] BH15 . . . . . 90 C2
Nelson Dr BH23 . . . . 77 C1
Nelson Pl SO41 . . . . 111 B2
Nelson Rd BH4, BH12 . . . . 94 B4
Netherhall Gdns BH4 . . . . 94 C3
Netherwood Pl BH21. . . . . 22 A1
Netley Cl BH23 . . . . 68 A3
Nettleton Cl BH17 . . . . . . 67 B3
New Borough Rd BH21. . . 31 A3
Newbury Dr BH10. . . . . . . 51 A1
Newcombe Rd
  Bournemouth BH6 . . . . . . 99 B4
  West Moors BH22 . . . . . . 16 B3
New Cotts BH21 . . . . 33 B2
Newcroft Gdns BH23. . . . . 76 A3
New Ct BH24 . . . . 12 C3
Newenham Rd SO41 . . . . 111 A1
New Fields Bsns Pk
  BH17. . . . . 67 A4
Newfoundland Dr
  BH15. . . . . 91 A2
Newfoundland Drive Rdbt
  BH15. . . . . 91 A2
New Harbour Rd BH15 . . . 90 B1
New Harbour Road W
  BH15. . . . . 90 A1
New La SO41 . . . . 87 C1
Newlands Manor SO41. . . 85 B1
Newlands Rd
  Bournemouth BH7 . . . . . . 74 A1
  Christchurch BH23 . . . . . . 77 C2
  New Milton BH23 . . . . . . 82 B3
  Wimborne Minster BH21 . . 18 A3
Newlyn Way BH12 . . . . . . 69 B3
Newmans Cl
  West Moors BH21 . . . . 8 C1
  Wimborne Minster BH21 . . 31 A3
Newman's La BH22 . . . . . . 16 A4
New Merrifield BH21 . . . . 23 C3
NEW MILTON 61 B4
New Milton Inf Sch
  BH25. . . . . 82 A3
New Milton Jun Sch
  BH25. . . . . 82 A3
New Milton Sta BH25. . . . 62 A1
Newmorton Rd BH9 . . . . . 52 A3
New Orchard BH15 . . . . . . 90 B2
New Par BH10. . . . . 51 B3
New Park Rd BH6. . . . . 98 C3
New Quay Rd BH15 . . . . . . 90 B1
New Rd
  Bournemouth BH10 . . . . . 43 B3
  Ferndown BH22. . . . . 35 B3
  Poole BH12. . . . . 69 A2
New St Lymington SO41. . . 111 A3

New St continued
  [5] Poole BH15 . . . . 90 B1
  Ringwood BH24 . . . . 13 B2
Newstead Rd BH6 . . . . 99 A3
New Street Mews
  SO41. . . . . 111 A3
Newton Morrell BH14. . . . 93 A3
Newton Rd
  Barton on S BH25. . . . . . . 82 B2
  Poole BH13. . . . . 104 C4
NEWTOWN Corfe Mullen . 37 A3
  Poole 68 B3
Newtown Bsns Ctr
  BH12. . . . . 68 A3
Newtown La
  Corfe Mullen BH21. . . . . . 37 A4
  Verwood BH31 . . . . 3 A1
Newtown Rd
  Verwood BH31 . . . . 3 A1
  Verwood BH31 . . . . 3 A2
New Valley Rd SO41. . . . . 86 C3
Nichola Ct BH12 . . . . 68 B3
Nicholas Cl BH23 . . . . 60 B1
Nicholas Gdns BH10 . . . . . 50 C2
Nicholson Cl BH17 . . . . . . 67 B4
Nightingale Ct BH31 . . . . . 3 A1
Nightjar Cl BH17 . . . . 65 C4
Nimrod Way BH21 . . . . . . 25 C2
Noble Cl BH11 . . . . 49 C1
Noel Cl BH10 . . . . 50 B2
Noel The BH25 . . . . 62 C1
Noon Gdns BH31 . . . . 3 B2
Noon Hill Dr BH31 . . . . 3 B2
Noon Hill Rd BH31 . . . . 3 B2
Norcliffe Cl BH11 . . . . 50 B3
Norfolk Ave BH23 . . . . 55 C1
Norleywood BH23 . . . . 79 C3
Norman Ave BH12 . . . . . . 70 A2
Normandy Cl SO41. . . . . 107 A3
Normandy Dr BH23 . . . . . . 77 A2
Normandy Way BH15 . . . . 89 A2
Norman Gdns BH12 . . . . . 70 A2
Normanhurst Ave BH8 . . 73 B4
Normanton Ct BH23 . . . . . 75 C4
Norris Cl BH24. . . . . 18 C4
Norris Gdns BH25. . . . . . . 82 A3
Norrish Rd BH12. . . . . 68 C1
North Ave BH10. . . . . 43 A2
**NORTH
  BOCKHAMPTON** . . . 108 B1
NORTHBOURNE 51 B4
Northbourne Ave BH10 . 43 A1
Northbourne Gdns
  BH10. . . . . 43 B1
Northbourne Pl [3]
  BH10. . . . . 43 A1
Northbourne Rdbt
  BH10. . . . . 43 A1
Northbrook Rd BH18. . . . . 46 A2
North Cl SO41 . . . . 111 A3
Northcote Rd BH1 . . . . 96 C3
North Dr BH24. . . . . 28 B4
Northey Rd BH6 . . . . 75 B1
Northfield Rd
  Milford on S SO41 . . . . . . 87 C2
  Ringwood BH24 . . . . 6 C1
North Greenlands
  SO41. . . . . 110 B3
North Head SO41 . . . . . . 111 A1
Northleigh La BH21. . . . . . 23 B2
North Lodge Rd BH14 . . . 93 B4
Northmead Dr BH17 . . . . 65 C4
Northmere Dr BH12. . . . . 69 C3
Northmere Rd BH12 . . . . . 69 C3
Northover BH31 . . . . 2 B3
NORTH POULNER 7 B2
North Poulner Rd BH24 . . 6 C2
North Rd
  Bournemouth BH7 . . . . . . 97 B4
  Poole BH14. . . . . 92 A4
Northshore BH13 . . . . . . 106 B4
North St
  Lymington SO41 . . . . . . 110 B1
  Poole BH15. . . . . 90 C2
Northumberland Ct
  BH24. . . . . 13 A3
Nortoft Rd BH8. . . . . 72 B1
Norton Cl BH23. . . . . 77 A2
Norton Gdns BH9 . . . . 51 B1
Norton Rd BH9 . . . . 71 B4

Norton Way BH15. . . . . . . 90 A1
Norway Cl [3] BH9 . . . . . . 51 C1
Norwich Ave BH2 . . . . 95 A3
Norwich Ave W BH2 . . . . . 95 A3
Norwich Ct [5] BH2 . . . . . 112 A2
Norwich Mans BH2 . . . . . . 95 A3
Norwich Rd BH2. . . . . 112 A2
Norwood Pl BH5. . . . . 98 B4
Nouale La BH24 . . . . 14 B3
Noyce Gdns BH8 . . . . 54 B1
Nuffield Ind Est BH17 . . . 67 A4
Nuffield Rd BH17 . . . . 67 A3
Nugent Rd BH6 . . . . 100 A3
Nursery Rd
  Bournemouth BH9 . . . . . . 52 A2
  Ringwood BH24 . . . . 13 B2
Nursling Gn BH8. . . . . 53 A1
Nuthatch Cl
  Broadstone BH17. . . . . . . 65 C4
  Ferndown BH22. . . . . 26 B4
Nutley Cl BH11 . . . . 49 C4
Nutley Way BH11 . . . . 49 C4

O

Oak Ave BH23 . . . . 75 A3
Oak Cl
  Corfe Mullen BH21 . . . . . . 36 C1
  Ferndown BH22. . . . . 35 B1
Oak Ct SO41. . . . . 110 B1
OAKDALE. 67 A2
Oakdale Rd BH15 . . . . 67 B2
Oakdale South Road Mid
  Sch BH15 . . . . 66 C1
Oakdene Cl BH21 . . . . 23 A1
Oak Dr BH15 . . . . 91 A2
Oakenbrow SO41 . . . . . . 107 A3
Oakfield Rd BH15. . . . . . . 66 C2
Oakford Ct BH8. . . . . 53 A2
Oak Gdns
  Bournemouth BH11 . . . . . 50 B1
  Hordle SO41. . . . . 85 B2
Oakham Grange BH22 . . . 27 B1
Oakhurst BH23 . . . . 77 C2
Oakhurst Cl BH22 . . . . 17 A2
Oakhurst Com Fst Sch
  BH22. . . . . 17 A2
Oakhurst La BH22 . . . . 17 A2
Oakhurst Rd BH22 . . . . . . 17 A2
Oak La BH24. . . . . 14 C3
Oaklands SO41 . . . . 111 B1
Oaklands Cl BH31. . . . . 2 B2
Oakland Wlk BH23 . . . . . . 35 C1
Oakleigh Way BH23 . . . . . 79 C2
OAKLEY 31 B2
Oakley Gdns BH16 . . . . . . 64 A3
Oakley Hill BH21 . . . . 31 A2
Oakley La Merley BH21. . . 31 B2
  Wimborne Minster BH21 . . 32 A2
Oakley Rd BH21 . . . . 31 A2
Oakley Sh Ctr BH21. . . . . . 31 B1
Oakley Straight BH21 . . . . 31 B1
Oakmead Coll of Tech
  BH11. . . . . 49 C4
Oakmead Gdns BH11 . . . . 49 C4
Oakmead Rd BH17 . . . . . . 65 C3
Oak Mews BH12 . . . . 68 C1
Oak Rd
  Bournemouth BH8 . . . . . . 72 C1
  New Milton BH25 . . . . . . 62 C1
  Upton BH16 . . . . 64 C2
Oaks Dr BH24 . . . . 18 B3
Oaks Mead BH31 . . . . 3 A2
Oaks The BH31 . . . . 2 B3
Oaktree Ct SO41. . . . . 86 C2
Oaktree Par BH23 . . . . . . 109 A3
Oakwood BH3 . . . . 71 B3
Oakwood Ave BH25 . . . . . 62 C2
Oakwood Cl BH9 . . . . 52 B1
Oakwood Ct BH25 . . . . . . 62 B1
Oakwood Rd
  Bournemouth BH9 . . . . . . 52 B1
  Christchurch BH23 . . . . . . 79 B4
Oasis Mews BH16. . . . . . . 64 A3
Oasis The [12] BH13 . . . . . 94 A4
Oates Rd BH9 . . . . 51 B1
Oban Rd BH3 . . . . 71 B3
Oberland Ct SO41. . . . . . 110 C3
Oceanarium* BH2 . . . . . . 112 B1
Ocean Hts [4] BH5 . . . . . . 97 C2

Okeford Rd BH18 . . . . 46 C2
OK Mobile Home Pk
  BH23. . . . . 78 B3
Old Barn Cl
  Christchurch BH23 . . . . . . 55 A1
  Ringwood BH24 . . . . 14 A3
Old Barn Farm Rd BH21. . . 9 C2
Old Barn Rd BH23 . . . . 55 A1
Old Bound Rd BH16. . . . . . 64 C2
Old Brewery The [10]
  BH15. . . . . 90 C2
Old Bridge Rd BH6. . . . . . . 75 A2
Old Christchurch La [12]
  BH1. . . . . 112 B2
Old Christchurch Rd
  Bournemouth BH1 . . . . . . 112 B2
  Everton SO41 . . . . 85 B3
Old Coach Mews BH14 . . 92 A4
Old Coastguard Rd
  BH13. . . . . 106 A4
Old Farm Cl BH24. . . . . 7 A2
Old Farmhouse Mews
  SO41. . . . . 111 A4
Old Farm Rd BH15 . . . . . . 67 B2
Old Farm Wlk SO41 . . . . 110 C2
Old Forge Ct SO41 . . . . . 110 C1
Old Forge Rd BH21 . . . . . . 22 C2
Old Generator Ho The
  BH12. . . . . 70 A1
Old Ham La BH21 . . . . 33 A4
Old Highway Mews
  BH21. . . . . 31 A4
Old Kiln Rd BH16 . . . . 65 A2
Old Lifeboat House* . . . .
  BH15. . . . . 90 C1
Old Maltings The
  SO41. . . . . 110 C2
Old Manor Cl BH21 . . . . . . 31 A4
Old Market Rd BH21 . . . . . 36 A4
Old Mill Ho BH24 . . . . 13 A2
OLD MILTON 81 B4
Old Milton Gn BH25. . . . . 81 C4
Old Milton Rd BH25. . . . . 82 A4
Old Mulberry Cl BH10. . . . 50 A1
Old Orchard BH15 . . . . 90 C1
Old Orchards SO41 . . . . . 111 A1
Old Pines Cl BH22 . . . . . . 35 B4
Old Priory Rd BH6 . . . . 99 C3
Old Rd BH21. . . . . 22 B1
Old Rectory Cl BH21 . . . . . 37 A4
Old Ropewalk BH15. . . . . . 90 A1
Old Rope Wlk The
  BH15. . . . . 89 C1
Old St John's Mews
  BH9. . . . . 51 C3
Old Sandpit La BH16 . . . . 44 A2
Old Sawmill Cl BH31. . . . . . 2 B2
Old School Cl
  Ferndown BH22. . . . . 26 C1
  Poole BH16. . . . . 92 A4
Old Stacks Gdns BH24 . . . 14 A2
OLD TOWN 90 C2
Old Town Mews [8]
  BH15. . . . . 90 C2
Old Vicarage Cl BH10 . . . . 43 B2
Old Vicarage La SO41 . . . 107 C1
Old Wareham Rd
  Corfe Mullen BH16,
  BH21. . . . . 44 A3
  Poole BH12. . . . . 68 A3
Oliver Rd SO41 . . . . 110 B2
Olivers Rd BH21 . . . . 24 A2
Olivers Way BH21. . . . . . . 24 A2
Onslow Gdns BH21 . . . . . . 23 A2
Onslow Ho BH21. . . . . 23 A2
Ophir Gdns [1] BH8 . . . . . 96 C4
Ophir Rd BH8. . . . . 96 B4
Oratory Gdns BH13 . . . . . 104 C4
Orchard Ave BH14 . . . . . . 91 C2
Orchard Cl
  Christchurch BH23 . . . . . . 76 A1
  Corfe Mullen BH21. . . . . . 37 A3
  Ferndown BH22. . . . . 27 B1
  Ringwood BH24 . . . . 13 B4
Orchard Ct BH31. . . . . 3 A1
Orchard Gr BH25 . . . . 82 A3
Orchard La BH21 . . . . 37 A3
Orchard Leigh [2] BH21 . . 37 A4
Orchard Mead [3] BH24 . . 13 B4
Orchard Mews [2] BH23 . . 76 A1

Orchard Mount [3]
  BH24. . . . . 13 B4
Orchard St BH2. . . . . 112 A1
Orchard The
  Bournemouth BH11 . . . . . 41 A2
  Bransgore BH23 . . . . . . 109 B2
  Milford on S SO41 . . . . . . 87 A2
Orchard Wlk [15] BH2 . . . 112 A2
Orcheston Rd BH8. . . . . . . 72 C1
Orchid Way BH23 . . . . 76 C2
Orestes Gate BH23. . . . . . 102 A4
Orford Cl BH23 . . . . 55 A3
Ormonde Rd BH13. . . . . . 94 A2
Osborne Ct [7] SO41. . . . . 86 C2
Osborne Rd
  Bournemouth BH9 . . . . . . 71 B4
  New Milton BH25 . . . . . . 62 B1
  Poole BH14. . . . . 92 B3
  Wimborne Minster BH21 . . 31 A4
Osbourne Ho [4] BH25. . . 62 A1
Osprey Cl BH23 . . . . 102 A4
Osterley Ct BH23 . . . . 76 A3
Ostlers The SO41 . . . . 84 A2
Oswald Cl BH9 . . . . 51 B2
Oswald Rd BH9 . . . . 51 C2
Otterbourne [14] BH2 . . . 95 A4
Otter Cl Upton BH16 . . . . 64 B2
  Verwood BH31 . . . . 3 A1
Otter Rd BH15 . . . . 67 C2
Otters Wlk BH15 . . . . 62 C3
Overbury Manor BH12 . . . 70 B1
Overbury Rd BH14 . . . . . . 92 C3
Overcliffe Mans BH1. . . . . 96 C2
Overcombe Cl BH17 . . . . . 47 B2
Over Links Dr BH14. . . . . . 93 A2
Overstand Cres SO41 . . . . 87 A3
Ovington Ave BH7 . . . . . . 74 C2
Ovington Gdns BH7. . . . . . 74 C2
Owlshotts BH13 . . . . 104 C3
Owls Rd
  Bournemouth BH5 . . . . . . 97 B2
  Verwood BH31 . . . . 3 A1
Oxey Cl BH25 . . . . 82 A3
Oxford Ave BH6. . . . . 98 B4
Oxford La BH11 . . . . 42 B2
Oxford Rd BH8 . . . . 96 B3
Oxford Terr SO41 . . . . . . 107 C3

P

Paddington Cl BH11 . . . . . 49 A4
Paddington Gr BH11. . . . . 49 A4
Paddock Cl
  Ferndown BH22. . . . . 26 A3
  Poole BH12. . . . . 68 B3
  St Leonards BH24 . . . . . . 19 A4
Paddock Gdns SO41 . . . . 110 C2
Paddock Gr BH31. . . . . 3 A1
Paddocks The BH10. . . . . . 51 A4
Paddock The BH24. . . . . . 28 C4
Padfield Cl BH6 . . . . 75 B3
Padget Rd BH24 . . . . .7 A1
Paget Cl BH21. . . . . 24 A1
Paget Rd BH11 . . . . 50 A4
Paisley Rd BH6 . . . . 98 C4
Palfrey Rd BH10 . . . . 43 A1
Palma Ct BH23 . . . . 80 A1
Palmer Pl BH25. . . . . 62 A1
Palmer Rd BH15 . . . . 66 C3
Palmerston Ave BH23. . . . 77 A1
Palmerston Cl BH16 . . . . . 65 A2
Palmerston Rd
  Bournemouth BH1 . . . . . . 97 B3
  Poole BH14. . . . . 93 A4
  Upton BH16 . . . . 64 C2
PAMPHILL 21 B4
Pamphill CE Fst Sch
  BH21. . . . . 21 B4
Pamplyn Cl SO41 . . . . . . 110 B3
Panorama Rd BH13 . . . . . 106 A4
Pans Cnr BH22 . . . . 35 C2
Parade The
  [4] Bournemouth BH6 . . . 99 B4
  New Milton BH25 . . . . . . 63 A4
  Old Milton BH25 . . . . 81 C4
  Poole BH17. . . . . 46 B2
Paradise St [4] BH15 . . . . 90 B4
Pardys Hill BH21. . . . . 37 A4
Parham Cl BH25 . . . . 61 B4
Parham Rd BH10 . . . . 50 C2

Parish Ct SO41 . . . . 111 A3
Parish Rd BH15 . . . . 91 B3
Park Ave
　Bournemouth BH10 . . . . . 42 C2
　Lymington SO41 . . . . . . 110 C3
Park Cl Burton BH23 . . . . 56 C2
　Milford on S SO41 . . . . . 87 B2
　New Milton BH25 . . . . . . 62 C3
Park Ct
　14 Milford on S SO41 . . . . 86 C2
　12 Poole BH13 . . . . 94 B3
Park Dr BH31 . . . . 2 B3
Parker Rd BH9 . . . . 71 C3
Parkers Cl BH24 . . . . 7 A1
Park Gate BH25 . . . . 82 A4
Park Gate Mews 7
　BH2 . . . . 112 A2
Park Gdns BH23 . . . . 77 B2
Park Homer Dr BH21 . . . 24 A2
Park Homer Rd BH21 . . . 23 C2
Park La
　Bournemouth BH10 . . . . . 51 C4
　Milford on S SO41 . . . . . 87 A2
　Wimborne Minster BH21 . . 30 C4
Park Lake Rd BH15 . . . . . 91 B2
Parkland Dr BH25 . . . . . . 81 C3
Parkland Pl BH25 . . . . . . 82 A4
Parklands 11 BH4 . . . . . . 94 C3
Park Pl BH14 . . . . 91 C4
Park Rd
　Bournemouth BH8 . . . . . . 96 A4
　Lymington SO41 . . . . . . 110 C3
　Milford on S SO41 . . . . . 87 B2
　New Milton BH25 . . . . . . 62 C3
　Old Milton BH25 . . . . . . 81 C4
　Poole BH15, BH14 . . . . . 91 C3
Parkside
　Christchurch BH23 . . . . . . 79 A4
　Ringwood BH24 . . . . 13 B2
Parkside Gdns BH10 . . . 51 B2
Parkside Rd BH14 . . . . . 92 C4
Parkstone Ave BH14 . . . . 93 A4
Parkstone Gram Sch
　BH17 . . . . 46 B1
Parkstone Hts
　Poole BH14 . . . . 67 C1
　Poole BH14 . . . . 68 A1
Parkstone Rd BH15 . . . . 91 B3
Parkstone Sta BH14 . . . . 92 B3
Park The
　Barton on S BH25 . . . . . . 80 C2
　Wimborne Minster BH21 . . 32 A1
Parkview BH2 . . . . 112 A3
Park View
　New Milton BH25 . . . . . . 82 A4
　7 Poole BH15 . . . . 91 B3
Park View Ct BH8 . . . . . . 72 C2
Park View Mews BH25 . . 82 A4
Park Way BH22 . . . . 16 C2
Parkway Dr BH8 . . . . 73 B3
Parkwood La 1 BH5 . . . . 98 B4
Parkwood Rd
　Bournemouth BH5 . . . . . . 98 A3
　Wimborne Minster BH21 . . 30 C4
Parley Cl BH22 . . . . 35 C1
Parley Cross BH22 . . . . . 43 B4
Parley Fst Sch BH22 . . . 35 A3
Parley Rd BH9 . . . . 52 A1
Parmiter Dr BH21 . . . . . . 31 B4
Parmiter Rd BH21 . . . . . 31 B4
Parmiter Way BH21 . . . . 31 B4
Parr Ho 1 BH14 . . . . 92 A4
Parr St BH14 . . . . 92 A4
Parsonage Barn La
　BH24 . . . . 13 C3
Parsonage Ct 9 BH8 . . . 96 A4
Parsonage Rd BH1 . . . . . 96 A2
Partridge Cl BH23 . . . . . 102 A4
Partridge Dr BH14 . . . . . 92 C1
Partridge Gn BH25 . . . . . 62 B4
Partridge Wlk BH14 . . . . 92 B1
Pascoe Cl BH14 . . . . 92 A4
Patchins Rd BH16 . . . . . 88 B4
Patchins The BH14 . . . . 103 C4
Pauncefote Rd BH5 . . . . . 98 A4
Pauntley Rd BH23 . . . . . 101 B4
Pavan Gdns BH10 . . . . . . 50 C2
Pavilion The 22 BH4 . . . . 94 C2
Pavilion Theatre*
　BH2 . . . . 112 B1

Payne Cl BH22 . . . . 8 C1
Peace Cl BH23 . . . . 108 C2
Pearce Ave BH14 . . . . . . 92 A1
Pearce Gdns BH14 . . . . . 92 A1
Pearce Rd BH16 . . . . 64 B2
Pearce-Smith Ct BH25 . . 81 B2
Pear Cl BH12 . . . . 94 B4
Pearl Gdns BH10 . . . . . . 50 C4
Pearl Rd BH10 . . . . 50 C4
Pearmain Dr 6 SO41 . . . 111 A1
Pearman Ct SO41 . . . . . . 110 B1
Pearson Ave BH14 . . . . . 68 B1
Pearson Gdns BH10 . . . . 43 A2
Pear Tree Cl BH23 . . . . . 109 A2
Peartree Ct 7 SO41 . . . . 111 A1
Peckham Ave BH25 . . . . 82 A4
Pedlars Wlk BH24 . . . . . 13 A3
Peeks Mews BH6 . . . . . . 99 C4
Peel Cl Poole BH12 . . . . 68 C1
　Verwood BH31 . . . . 2 B3
Pegasus Ave SO41 . . . . . 84 B1
Pegasus Ct
　Bournemouth BH1 . . . . . . 96 A4
　8 New Milton BH25 . . . . 62 A1
Pegasus Lodge BH22 . . . 27 A1
Pelham 8 BH13 . . . . 94 A4
Pelham Cl BH23 . . . . 77 A1
Pelican Mead BH14 . . . . 14 A2
Pembroke Ct 4 BH23 . . . 80 B2
Pembroke Rd
　Bournemouth BH4 . . . . . . 94 B2
　Poole BH12 . . . . 69 A3
Pen Craig 2 BH13 . . . . . . 94 B3
Penelope Ct 12 BH23 . . . 80 B2
Pengelly Ave BH10 . . . . . 43 B1
Pennant Way BH23 . . . . 77 C2
Penn Cl BH25 . . . . 81 B4
Penn Ct BH22 . . . . 16 B2
Penn Hill Ave BH14 . . . . 93 A3
Pennine Ct 8 BH23 . . . . . 77 C3
Pennine Way BH31 . . . . . 2 C1
Pennington CE Jun Sch
　SO41 . . . . 110 B2
Pennington Cl
　Lymington SO41 . . . . 110 B1
　West Moors BH22 . . . . . . 16 B1
Pennington Cres BH22 . . 16 B2
Pennington Cross
　SO41 . . . . 110 C1
Pennington Ho 6 BH4 . . . 94 C2
Pennington Inf Sch
　SO41 . . . . 110 B2
Pennington Oval
　SO41 . . . . 110 A1
Pennington Rd BH22 . . . . 16 B2
Penny Hedge BH25 . . . . 82 B2
Penny's Cnr SO41 . . . . . . 63 C2
Penny's Ct BH22 . . . . . . 27 A1
Penny's Wlk BH22 . . . . . 27 A1
Penny Way BH23 . . . . . . 78 C1
Pennywell Gdns BH25 . . 63 A2
Penrith Cl BH31 . . . . 2 C1
Penrith Rd BH5 . . . . 98 A3
Penrose Rd BH22 . . . . . . 27 A2
Peppercorn Cl BH23 . . . 77 B3
Percy Rd BH5 . . . . 97 C3
Peregrine Rd BH23 . . . . 102 A4
Pergin Cres BH17 . . . . . . 66 B3
Pergin Way BH17 . . . . . . 66 B3
Perryfield Gdns BH17 . . 74 B3
Perry Gdns BH15 . . . . . . 90 C1
Persley Rd BH10 . . . . 51 B4
Perth Cl BH23 . . . . 75 B4
Peter Grant Way BH22 . . 26 C1
Peters Cl BH16 . . . . 64 C2
Petersfield Pl BH7 . . . . . 74 B2
Petersfield Rd BH7 . . . . 74 B2
Petersham Rd BH17 . . . . 66 A4
Peters Rd BH22 . . . . 35 C3
Petit Rd BH9 . . . . 52 A2
Petwyn Cl BH22 . . . . 28 A2
Peverell Rd BH16 . . . . . . 88 B4
Peveril Cl BH24 . . . . 11 A2
Phelipps Rd BH21 . . . . . 37 B2
Phyldon Cl BH12 . . . . 68 B1
Phyldon Rd BH12 . . . . . . 68 B2
Pickard Rd BH22 . . . . . . 27 C3
Pickering Cl BH18 . . . . . 46 A2
Pickford Rd BH9 . . . . 51 B1
Pig Shoot La BH23 . . . . . 53 C4

PILFORD 24 A4
Pilford Heath Rd BH21 . . 24 B3
Pilgrim Park Homes
　BH24 . . . . 14 A4
Pilgrim Pl SO41 . . . . . . 111 A2
Pilgrim's Cl BH25 . . . . . 62 C1
Pilgrims Way BH17 . . . . 66 A3
Pilot Hight Rd BH11 . . . 50 A4
Pilsdon Dr BH17 . . . . . . 47 B3
Pimpern Cl BH17 . . . . . . 47 C2
Pine Ave
　Bournemouth BH6 . . . . . . 98 C3
　Poole BH12 . . . . 69 C2
Pinebeach Cl BH13 . . . . 105 A4
Pine Cl Barton on S BH25 . 81 B3
　Ferndown BH22 . . . . 26 C3
Pinecliffe Ave BH6 . . . . . 98 C3
Pinecliffe Rd BH25 . . . . . 80 C2
Pinecliff Rd BH13 . . . . . . 105 A4
Pine Cres BH23 . . . . 79 B3
Pine Dr Poole BH13 . . . . . 93 C3
　St Leonards BH24 . . . . . . 19 A4
Pine End BH22 . . . . 35 C3
Pine Glen Ave BH22 . . . . 26 C4
Pine Grange 4 BH1 . . . . 96 A2
Pine Ho BH25 . . . . 62 A1
Pineholt Cl BH24 . . . . . . 11 B1
Pinehurst 10 SO41 . . . . . 86 C2
Pinehurst Ave BH23 . . . . 101 C4
Pinehurst Pk BH22 . . . . . 27 C4
Pinehurst Rd BH22 . . . . 17 A1
Pine Lodge 10 BH13 . . . 104 C3
Pine Manor Rd BH24 . . . 10 B1
Pine Mans 3 BH1 . . . . . 97 A3
Pine Park Mans 16
　BH13 . . . . 94 A4
Pine Rd
　Bournemouth BH9 . . . . . . 72 A3
　East End BH21 . . . . 29 C1
Pineside BH9 . . . . 72 A3
Pinesprings Dr BH18 . . . 45 B2
Pines The BH13 . . . . 94 A2
Pinetops Cl SO41 . . . . . . 110 A2
Pine Tree Cl BH21 . . . . . . 23 A1
Pine Tree Glen BH4 . . . . 94 C3
Pinetree Wlk BH17 . . . . 65 C4
Pine Vale Cres BH10 . . . 51 C3
Pine View Cl
　Upton BH16 . . . . 64 C2
　Verwood BH31 . . . . 2 A3
Pine View Rd BH31 . . . . . 2 A3
Pine Wlk Verwood BH31 . . 3 B1
　West Moors BH22 . . . . . . 16 C3
Pinewood Ave BH10 . . . . 43 C1
Pinewood Cl
　Bournemouth BH10 . . . . . 43 A1
　Upton BH16 . . . . 64 A3
　Walkford BH23 . . . . 60 A1
Pinewood Ct BH22 . . . . . 16 B2
Pinewood Gdns BH22 . . 27 A3
Pinewood Rd
　Christchurch BH23 . . . . . . 79 C4
　Ferndown BH22 . . . . 26 C3
　Hordle SO41 . . . . 63 C1
　Poole BH13 . . . . 94 B1
　St Leonards BH24 . . . . . . 19 A4
　Upton BH16 . . . . 64 B3
Pinnacle The 7 BH1 . . . . 96 A2
Pipers Ash BH24 . . . . . . 14 A4
Pipers Dr BH23 . . . . 78 A2
Pippin Cl
　Christchurch BH23 . . . . . . 55 B1
　8 Lymington SO41 . . . . . 111 A1
Pittmore Rd BH23 . . . . . 56 C1
Pitts Pl BH25 . . . . 83 A4
Pitwines Cl BH15 . . . . . . 91 A2
Plantagenet Cres BH11 . 41 A1
Plantation SO41 . . . . 85 C2
Plantation Ct
　Lymington SO41 . . . . 110 C3
　Poole BH17 . . . . 46 C1
Plantation Dr BH23 . . . . 60 A1
Plantation Rd BH17 . . . . 46 C1
Plant Park Rd BH24 . . . . 20 A2
Plassey Cres BH10 . . . . 42 C1
Playfields Dr BH12 . . . . . 69 B2
Pleasance Way BH25 . . . 61 C2
Plecy Cl BH21 . . . . 35 A2
Plemont Cl BH12 . . . . . . 49 B1
Pless Rd SO41 . . . . 86 B3

Plover Dr SO41 . . . . 87 C2
Plumer Rd BH17 . . . . 46 A1
Point The BH5 . . . . 97 B2
POKESDOWN 98 A3
Pokesdown Com Prim Sch
　BH5 . . . . 98 A4
Pokesdown Sta BH7 . . . 98 A4
Pomona Cl BH22 . . . . . . 27 A2
Pompey's Cnr BH21 . . . . 34 A4
Pompey's La BH22 . . . . . 34 B2
Pond Cl BH25 . . . . 62 A1
Ponsonby Rd BH14 . . . . 93 A4
Pony Dr BH11 . . . . 65 A3
POOLE 90 B3
Poole Aquarium &
　Serpentarium*
　BH15 . . . . 90 C1
Poole Commerce Ctr
　BH12 . . . . 69 C1
Poole Gram Sch BH17 . . 47 A2
Poole High Sch BH15 . . . 90 C4
Poole Hill BH2 . . . . 95 A3
Poole Hospl BH15 . . . . . 91 A3
Poole La BH11 . . . . 42 B1
Poole Rd
　Bournemouth BH4 . . . . . . 94 C3
　Poole BH13 . . . . 94 A4
　Upton BH16 . . . . 65 A3
　Wimborne Minster BH21 . . 30 C4
Poole Sta BH15 . . . . 90 C3
Pool Lane Rdbt BH11 . . . 49 B4
Popes Rd BH15 . . . . 67 A2
Poplar Cl
　Bransgore BH23 . . . . 109 B2
　Christchurch BH23 . . . . . . 80 B3
　3 Poole BH15 . . . . 90 B1
　Wimborne Minster BH23 . . 23 A1
Poplar Cres BH24 . . . . . . 13 C3
Poplar La BH23 . . . . 109 B2
Poplar Rd BH25 . . . . 63 A2
Poplar Way BH24 . . . . . . 13 C3
Poppy Cl BH23 . . . . 78 C3
Portadene 1 BH4 . . . . . . 95 A2
Portarlington Cl BH4 . . . 95 A2
Portarlington Ct 44
　BH4 . . . . 94 C3
Portarlington Rd BH4 . . . 94 C2
Portchester Ct 3 BH8 . . 96 B4
Portchester Pl BH8 . . . . 96 B4
Portchester Rd BH8 . . . 96 A4
Portchester Sch BH7 . . 74 A2
Portelet Cl BH12 . . . . 49 A2
Porter Rd BH17 . . . . 66 B3
Porters La BH21 . . . . . . 24 C2
Portesham Gdns BH9 . . . 52 B3
Portesham Way BH17 . . . 47 B3
Portfield Cl BH21 . . . . . . 76 A2
Portfield Rd BH23 . . . . . 76 A2
Portfield Sch BH21 . . . . . 76 A1
Portiere Ho BH11 . . . . . . 50 A4
Portland Pl BH2 . . . . . . 112 B3
Portland Rd BH9 . . . . . . 72 A3
Portman Cres BH5 . . . . . 98 B3
Portman Rd BH7 . . . . . . 97 C4
Portman Terr BH5 . . . . . 98 B3
Portmore Cl BH18 . . . . . 32 C3
Portswood Dr 2 BH10 . . 52 A3
Post Office Bldgs BH9 . 71 C4
Post Office La BH24 . . . . 11 B1
Post Office Rd 18 BH1 . 112 B2
Potterne Way BH21 . . . . 5 A4
Potterne Wood Cl BH31 . . 5 C4
Potters Way BH14 . . . . . 92 C2
Pottery Junc BH14 . . . . . 69 B1
Pottery Rd BH14 . . . . 92 B2
POULNER 14 B4
Poulner Hill BH24 . . . . . 14 C4
Poulner Inf & Jun Schs
　BH24 . . . . 7 A2
Poulner Pk BH24 . . . . . . 7 A1
Pound Cl Poole BH15 . . . 67 C1
　Ringwood BH24 . . . . 13 B4
Pound La
　1 Christchurch BH23 . . . 76 B1
　Poole BH15 . . . . 67 B1
Pound Rd SO41 . . . . 110 A1
Powell Rd BH14 . . . . 92 B3
Powerscourt Rd BH5 . . . 81 B2
Powis Cl BH25 . . . . 62 B1
Powlett Rd SO41 . . . . . . 111 A2

Preston Cl BH16 . . . . 64 C3
Preston La BH23 . . . . 57 A2
Preston Rd BH15 . . . . . . 66 C2
Preston Way BH23 . . . . . 79 A3
Prestwood Cl BH25 . . . . 81 C4
Priestlands La SO41 . . . 110 B2
Priestlands Pl SO41 . . . . 110 C1
Priestlands Sch SO41 . . 110 C1
Priestley Rd BH10 . . . . . 50 B1
Priest's House Mus &
　Gdns* BH21 . . . . 30 B4
Primrose Gdns BH17 . . . 45 C1
Primrose Way
　Christchurch BH23 . . . . . . 78 C3
　Corfe Mullen BH21 . . . . . . 37 B3
Prince Of Wales Rd
　BH4 . . . . 94 C4
Princes Ct 8 BH13 . . . . 94 A4
Prince's Ct BH22 . . . . . . 27 A1
Prince's Pl BH25 . . . . 62 C1
Princes Rd BH22 . . . . 27 A1
Princess Ave BH23 . . . . 76 B1
Princess Rd
　Bournemouth BH4 . . . . . . 94 B4
　Poole BH13 . . . . 94 A4
Pringles Cl BH22 . . . . . . 27 B1
Pringles Dr BH22 . . . . . . 27 B1
Priors Cl BH23 . . . . 78 C2
Priors Wlk 3 BH21 . . . . 22 B1
Priory CE Prim Sch The
　BH23 . . . . 76 B1
Priory Gdns BH22 . . . . . . 28 A4
Priory Ho BH23 . . . . 100 C3
Priory Ind Pk BH23 . . . . 78 B2
Priory Quay BH23 . . . . . 100 C3
Priory Rd
　Bournemouth BH2 . . . . . 112 A1
　West Moors BH22 . . . . . . 28 A4
Priory View Ct 4 BH23 . . 76 B1
Priory View Pl 3 BH9 . . 52 A2
Priory View Rd
　Bournemouth BH9 . . . . . . 52 A2
　Burton BH23 . . . . 56 C1
Private Rd SO41 . . . . . . 111 A4
Privet Rd BH9 . . . . 71 C4
Promenade BH23 . . . . . 102 B4
Prosperous St 1 BH15 . . 90 C1
Prunus Cl BH22 . . . . 26 B3
Prunus Dr BH22 . . . . 26 B3
Puddletown Cres BH17 . 47 C2
Pullman Bsns Pk BH24 . . 13 C2
Pullman Ct BH22 . . . . . . 16 B2
Pullman Way BH24 . . . . 13 C2
Purbeck Ave BH15 . . . . . 89 B1
Purbeck Cl BH16 . . . . . . 64 B1
Purbeck Ct
　Bournemouth BH5 . . . . . . 98 B2
　3 Christchurch BH23 . . . 77 C3
Purbeck Dr BH31 . . . . 2 C1
Purbeck Gdns BH14 . . . 67 C1
Purbeck Hts BH14 . . . . . 68 B1
Purbeck Rd
　Barton on S BH25 . . . . . . 81 A2
　Bournemouth BH2 . . . . . 112 A1
Purchase Rd BH12 . . . . . 70 C3
Purdy Ho BH11 . . . . 50 A4
PUREWELL 77 A2
Purewell BH23 . . . . 77 A1
Purewell Cl BH23 . . . . . . 77 B1
Purewell Cross BH23 . . . 77 B1
Purewell Cross Rd
　BH23 . . . . 77 A2
Purewell Ct 2 BH23 . . . . 77 B2
Purewell Rdbt BH23 . . . 77 B1
Pye Cl BH21 . . . . 30 B4
Pye Cnr BH21 . . . . 30 B4
Pye La BH21 . . . . 30 B4
Pyrford Gdns 3 SO41 . . . 111 A1
Pyrford Mews SO41 . . . . 111 A1

Q

Quadrant Ctr The BH1 . 112 B2
Quaker Ct BH24 . . . . 13 A2
Quantock Ct 7 BH23 . . . 77 C3

Quarr Ho SO41 . . . . 107 A4
Quarry Chase **4** BH4 . . . 94 C3
Quarry Cl BH21 . . . . 24 B3
Quarry Dr BH21 . . . . 24 B3
Quarry Rd BH21 . . . . 24 B3
Quarterjack Mews **1**
BH21 . . . . 30 C4
Quay Hill SO41 . . . . 111 B3
Quayle Dr BH11 . . . . 41 C2
Quay Point **8** BH15 . . . . 90 C1
Quay Rd
  Christchurch BH23 . . . . . . 76 B1
  Lymington SO41 . . . . 111 B3
Quay St SO41 . . . . 111 B3
Quay The BH15 . . . . 90 C1
Queen Anne Dr
  Oakley BH21 . . . . 39 B4
  Wimborne Minster BH21 . . 32 A1
Queen Elizabeth Ave
  SO41 . . . . 110 C3
Queen Elizabeth Ct
  BH21 . . . . 30 B4
Queen Elizabeth's Sch
  BH21 . . . . 21 C2
Queen Katherine Rd
  SO41 . . . . 111 B2
Queen Mary Ave BH9 . . . . 51 C2
Queen's Ave BH23 . . . . . 100 B4
Queensbury Mans **9**
  BH1 . . . . 96 A2
Queens Cl BH22 . . . . 16 B1
Queens Ct
  18 Bournemouth BH4 . . . 95 A4
  Bournemouth, Charminster
  BH8 . . . . 72 B3
  New Milton BH25 . . . . 63 A1
Queens Gdns BH22 . . . . . . 95 A4
Queens Gr BH25 . . . . 62 C2
Queensland Rd BH5 . . . . . 98 A4
Queensmead
  Burton BH23 . . . . 76 A4
  4 Wimborne Minster
  BH21 . . . . 22 C1
Queen's Park Ave BH8 . . . 73 A3
Queen's Park Gdns
  BH8 . . . . 73 A2
Queen's Park Inf Sch
  BH8 . . . . 72 C4
Queen's Park Jun Sch
  BH8 . . . . 72 B4
Queen's Park Rd BH8 . . . . 73 A2
Queen's Park South Dr
  BH8 . . . . 73 A2
Queen's Park West Dr
  BH8 . . . . 73 A2
Queens Rd BH22 . . . . 27 A3
Queen's Rd
  Bournemouth BH3 . . . . . . 95 A4
  Christchurch BH23 . . . . . . 77 B1
  Corfe Mullen BH21 . . . . . . 37 A1
  Poole BH14 . . . . 93 A4
Queen St SO41 . . . . 110 C2
Queensway BH25 . . . . 61 B2
Queens Way BH24 . . . . 13 C3
Queenswood Ave BH8 . . . 73 B4
Queenswood Dr BH22 . . . 27 A3
Quince La BH21 . . . . 23 B2
Quintin Cl BH23 . . . . 79 C3
Quomp The BH24 . . . . 13 B3

R

Rachel Cl BH12 . . . . 68 C3
Radipole Rd BH17 . . . . 48 A2
Raglan Gdns BH11 . . . . 50 A2
Raleigh Cl
  Christchurch BH23 . . . . . 101 C4
  New Milton BH25 . . . . 61 C2
  Ringwood BH24 . . . . 14 A4
Raleigh Rd BH12 . . . . 49 B1
Ralph Jessop Ct BH12 . . . 69 A3
Ralph Rd BH21 . . . . 37 B3
Ramley Rd SO41 . . . . 110 A2
Rampart The SO41 . . . . . 110 C4
Ramsey Cl BH25 . . . . 61 C2
Randolph Rd
  2 Bournemouth BH1 . . . 97 B3

Randolph Rd continued
  Poole BH14 . . . . 68 C1
Ranelagh Rd BH23 . . . . . . 79 C2
Raptor & Reptile Ctr*
  BH24 . . . . 14 A1
Rashley Mews SO41 . . . . 111 A2
Ravana Ct **4** BH8 . . . . . . 96 A4
Ravenscourt Rd
  Bournemouth BH6 . . . . . . 98 C4
  Lymington SO41 . . . . 110 C1
Ravensdale Cl BH12 . . . . . 68 C2
Ravenshall **7** BH22 . . . . 95 A2
Ravens Way SO41 . . . . 87 A2
Raven Way BH23 . . . . 102 A4
Ravine Ct BH13 . . . . 104 C3
Ravine Gdns **5** BH13 . . 104 C3
Ravine Rd
  Bournemouth BH5 . . . . . . 98 B3
  Poole BH13 . . . . 104 C4
Raymond Cl BH31 . . . . 3 B2
Rayners Dr BH12 . . . . 69 A2
Rayscliff **21** BH4 . . . . . . 94 C2
Rebbeck Rd BH7 . . . . 74 A1
Recreation Rd BH12 . . . . . 69 B2
Rectory Ave BH21 . . . . 29 A1
Rectory Rd BH15 . . . . 66 C2
Redan Cl BH23 . . . . 79 C2
Redbreast Rd BH9 . . . . 52 A2
Redbreast Rd N BH9 . . . . . 52 A2
Redcliffe Cl BH23 . . . . 56 C2
Redcotts La BH21 . . . . 22 B1
Redcotts Rd BH21 . . . . 22 B1
RED HILL 43 C1
Redhill Ave BH9 . . . . 51 C3
Redhill Cl BH10 . . . . 51 B3
Redhill Cres BH9 . . . . 51 C3
Redhill Ct **1** BH10 . . . . . 51 C3
Redhill Dr BH10 . . . . 51 B3
Redhill Park Homes **1**
  BH10 . . . . 51 C4
Redhill Rdbt BH10 . . . . 51 C4
Redhoave Rd BH17 . . . . . . 47 B2
Red Horn Cl BH16 . . . . 88 C4
Red House Mews
  SO41 . . . . 111 A2
Red House Mus & Gdns*
  BH23 . . . . 76 B1
Red La BH21 . . . . 36 A4
Redlands
  Christchurch BH23 . . . . . . 78 A2
  Poole BH12 . . . . 69 C1
Redmans View BH31 . . . . . . 2 B2
Red Oaks Cl BH22 . . . . 26 B3
Redsails BH13 . . . . 106 A3
Redshank Cl BH17 . . . . 45 C1
Redvers Cl SO41 . . . . 110 C1
Redvers Rd BH23 . . . . 77 B2
Redwood Cl
  Lymington SO41 . . . . 110 C4
  Ringwood BH24 . . . . 13 C3
Redwood Dr BH22 . . . . 26 C4
Redwood Rd BH16 . . . . 64 A4
Regency Cres BH23 . . . . . . 75 C3
Regency Pl BH24 . . . . 13 B4
Regent Dr BH7 . . . . 73 C3
Regent Way BH23 . . . . 76 B1
Reid St BH23 . . . . 76 A3
Rempstone Rd BH21 . . . . . 39 A4
Renault Dr BH18 . . . . 46 A1
Renouf Cl SO41 . . . . 110 B2
Restharrow BH1 . . . . 96 A3
Restynge Ho BH31 . . . . 2 C3
Retreat Rd BH21 . . . . 31 A4
Reynard Ct BH15 . . . . 91 C3
Rhiners Cl SO41 . . . . 107 B3
Ribble Cl BH18 . . . . 46 A2
Ribbonwood Hts BH14 . . . 92 B4
Ricardo Cres BH23 . . . . . . 78 A1
Rice Gdns BH16 . . . . 89 A4
Rice Terr BH16 . . . . 89 A4
Richard Cl BH16 . . . . 64 B4
Richmond Ct
  12 Milford on S SO41 . . . 86 C2
  7 New Milton BH25 . . . . 62 A1
Richmond Gdns BH11 . . . 112 B2
Richmond Hill BH2 . . . . . . 112 B2
Richmond Hill Dr BH2 . . . 112 B2
Richmond Park Ave
  BH8 . . . . 72 C2
Richmond Park Cl BH8 . . . 73 A1

Richmond Park Cres
  BH8 . . . . 72 C2
Richmond Park Rd
  BH8 . . . . 72 C2
Richmond Rd
  Poole BH14 . . . . 92 C4
  Wimborne Minster BH21 . . 31 A4
Richmond Rise BH8 . . . . . . 73 A1
Richmond Wood Rd
  BH8 . . . . 72 C2
Ridgefield Gdns BH23 . . . . 79 A3
Ridgemount Gdns
  BH15 . . . . 89 B3
Ridgeway
  Broadstone BH18 . . . . 46 B4
  Corfe Mullen BH21 . . . . . . 37 A4
  Ferndown BH22 . . . . 43 B4
Ridley Rd BH9 . . . . 71 C4
Ridout Cl BH10 . . . . 50 B1
Riggs Gdns BH11 . . . . 49 C2
Rigler Rd BH15 . . . . 90 A2
Rimbury Way BH23 . . . . . . 76 A3
RINGWOOD 14 A3
Ringwood CE Inf Sch
  BH24 . . . . 13 B3
Ringwood Jun Sch
  BH24 . . . . 13 B3
Ringwood Rd
  Bournemouth BH11 . . . . . . 49 B4
  Bransgore BH23 . . . . 59 A4
  Ferndown BH22 . . . . 34 C4
  Poole BH12 . . . . 68 B3
  Ringwood BH24 . . . . 12 A2
  St Leonards BH24 . . . . 18 B2
  Three Legged Cross BH21 . . 9 C3
  Walkford BH23 . . . . 80 B4
  West Moors BH22 . . . . 28 A4
Ringwood Rd Nature
  Reserve BH11 . . . . 41 B1
Ringwood Road Ret Pk
  BH11 . . . . 49 B3
Ringwood Sch BH24 . . . . . 13 B3
Ringwood Trad Est
  BH24 . . . . 13 B2
Ringwood Waldorf Sch
  BH24 . . . . 12 B2
Ripley Ct BH22 . . . . 27 C3
Ripon Rd BH9 . . . . 72 A4
Ritchie Pl BH22 . . . . 16 B4
Ritchie Rd BH11 . . . . 50 B4
River Cl BH21 . . . . 22 C2
River Ct SO41 . . . . 111 B3
Riverdale La BH23 . . . . 76 A1
River Gdns SO41 . . . . 87 B2
Riverland Ct **4** BH23 . . . 76 A1
Riverlea Rd BH23 . . . . 76 A1
Rivermead Gdns BH23 . . . 55 B1
River Pk BH6 . . . . 75 C1
Riversdale **8** BH21 . . . . . 30 C4
Riversdale Rd BH6 . . . . . . 100 A3
Riverside
  4 Bournemouth
  BH10 . . . . 51 C4
  Ringwood BH24 . . . . 13 A2
Riverside Ave BH7 . . . . 74 C4
Riverside Bsns Pk
  SO41 . . . . 111 B3
Riverside Ct
  7 Bournemouth BH4 . . . 95 A4
  West Moors BH22 . . . . 16 B3
Riverside La BH6 . . . . 99 C4
Riverside Pk BH23 . . . . . . 100 A4
Riverside Pk Ind Est
  BH21 . . . . 31 A3
Riverside Rd
  Bournemouth BH6 . . . . . . 99 C4
  West Moors BH22 . . . . 16 B3
Riverslea Mews BH23 . . . . 77 A1
Riversmeet Ct BH23 . . . . . 77 A1
Rivers Reach SO41 . . . . . 111 B2
River Way BH23 . . . . 55 A1
Riviera **11** BH1 . . . . 96 B2
Riviera Ct
  Bournemouth BH2 . . . . . . 95 A3
  3 Poole BH23 . . . . 78 A3
R L Stevenson Ave BH4 . . 94 B3
RNLI Mus* BH15 . . . . 90 C2
Roberts Cl SO41 . . . . 85 C3
Roberts La BH17 . . . . 65 C3

Roberts Rd
  Bournemouth BH7 . . . . . . 74 A1
  Poole BH17 . . . . 46 B1
Robin Cres BH25 . . . . 61 A4
Robin Gdns BH23 . . . . 76 A3
Robin Gr BH25 . . . . 61 C1
Robins Ct **7** BH21 . . . . . 30 C4
Robins Way BH23 . . . . . . 102 B4
Robinswood Dr BH22 . . . . 27 A3
Robsall Cl BH12 . . . . 69 B3
Robville Ct **3** BH7 . . . . . 74 B1
Rochester Rd BH11 . . . . . . 50 B4
Rockbourne Gdns
  BH25 . . . . 81 A3
Rockford Cl BH6 . . . . 99 C2
Rockley Mews BH15 . . . . . 89 B2
Rockley Pk Cvn Est BH15,
  BH16 . . . . 88 B3
Rockley Rd BH15 . . . . 89 B1
Rodbourne SO41 . . . . 85 B2
Rodney Cl BH12 . . . . 70 A4
Rodney Ct
  Christchurch BH23 . . . . . . 78 A1
  7 Poole BH15 . . . . 90 C1
Rodney Dr BH23 . . . . 77 C1
Rodway BH21 . . . . 30 C4
Rodwell Cl BH10 . . . . 42 C2
Roebuck Cl BH25 . . . . 62 B1
Roeshot Cres BH23 . . . . . . 79 B4
Roeshot Hill BH23 . . . . 79 A4
Roi-mar Home Pk BH8 . . . 53 A3
Rolls Dr BH6 . . . . 100 B2
Roman Hts BH21 . . . . 37 B4
Roman Rd BH18 . . . . 37 B1
Romney Cl BH10 . . . . 51 B3
Romney Ct **31** BH4 . . . . 94 C3
Romney Rd BH10 . . . . 51 B4
Rookcliff **13** SO41 . . . . . 86 C2
Rookcliff Way SO41 . . . . . 86 C2
Rookes La SO41 . . . . 111 A1
Rook Hill Rd BH23 . . . . 78 B1
Rookwood **3** SO41 . . . . . 86 C2
Roosevelt Cres BH11 . . . . . 42 B2
Ropers La BH16 . . . . 65 A3
Ropley Rd BH7 . . . . 74 C2
Rosamund Ave BH21 . . . . . 31 B1
Roscrea Cl BH6 . . . . 100 B3
Roscrea Dr BH6 . . . . 100 B3
Rosebery Cl BH31 . . . . 3 C1
Rosebery Rd BH5 . . . . 98 A4
Rosebud Ave **1** BH9 . . . . 52 A1
Rosecrae Cl BH25 . . . . 61 C3
Rose Cres BH15 . . . . 67 C2
Rose Ct BH15 . . . . 91 B3
Rosedale Cl **3** BH23 . . . . 77 B1
Rose Farm Cl BH22 . . . . . . 34 B3
Rose Gdns BH9 . . . . 52 A2
Rose Gdn The BH23 . . . . . . 75 A4
Rosehill Cl BH23 . . . . 109 A3
Rosehill Dr BH23 . . . . 109 A3
Rosemary Ct **8** BH23 . . . 80 B2
Rosemary Gdns BH12 . . . . 68 B3
Rosemary Rd BH12 . . . . . . 68 C3
Rosemount Rd BH4 . . . . . . 94 B2
Rosewood Gdns BH25 . . . . 61 C3
Roslin Gdns BH3 . . . . 71 A3
Roslin Rd BH3 . . . . 71 B3
Roslin Rd S BH3 . . . . 71 B3
Ross Gdns BH11 . . . . 40 C1
Ross Glades BH3 . . . . 71 B2
Rossiters Quay BH23 . . . . 76 C1
Rossley Cl BH23 . . . . 59 B1
ROSSMORE 69 B3
Rossmore Com Coll
  BH12 . . . . 69 A4
Rossmore Par BH12 . . . . . 68 B4
Rossmore Rd BH12 . . . . . . 69 A3
Ross Rd BH24 . . . . 7 A1
Rotary Cl BH21 . . . . 23 C3
Rothbury Pk BH25 . . . . 82 B4
Rotherfield Rd
  Bournemouth BH5 . . . . . . 98 B2
  Walkford BH23 . . . . 80 A4
Rothesay Dr BH23 . . . . 79 B2
Rothesay Rd BH4 . . . . 70 C1
Rotterdam Dr BH23 . . . . . . 77 A2
Roumelia La BH1, BH5 . . . 97 B3
Roundhaye Gdns BH11 . . . 41 C2
Roundhaye Rd BH11 . . . . . 41 C2
Roundhouse Ct SO41 . . . . 110 C2

Roundways BH11 . . . . 49 C3
Rowan Cl
  Christchurch BH23 . . . . . . 79 A3
  St Leonards BH24 . . . . 18 B4
  Sway SO41 . . . . 107 B2
Rowan Dr
  Broadstone BH17 . . . . 45 B1
  Christchurch BH23 . . . . . . 79 A3
  Verwood BH31 . . . . 5 B4
Rowans Pk SO41 . . . . 110 C3
Rowbarrow Cl BH17 . . . . . 47 B2
Rowe Gdns **6** BH22 . . . . 69 C3
Rowena Rd BH6 . . . . 99 C4
Rowland Ave BH15 . . . . . . 67 B2
ROWLANDS 22 C1
Rowlands Hill BH21 . . . . . . 23 A2
Rownhams Rd BH8 . . . . 53 A2
Roxborough **47** BH4 . . . . 94 C3
Royal Arc **5** BH1 . . . . . . 97 B3
Royal Bournemouth Gen
  Hospl The BH7 . . . . 74 B4
Royal Oak Rd BH10 . . . . . . 42 C1
Royal Victoria Mews
  BH4 . . . . 95 A3
Royster Cl BH17 . . . . 46 C1
Royston Dr BH21 . . . . 23 A1
Royston Pl BH25 . . . . 82 B2
Rozelle Rd BH14 . . . . 92 C4
Rozel Manor BH13 . . . . 94 B2
Ruben Dr BH15 . . . . 89 A2
Rubens Cl BH25 . . . . 62 B1
Rufford Gdns BH6 . . . . 99 B4
Rugby Rd BH17 . . . . 46 A1
Runnymede Ave BH11 . . . 41 B2
Runton Rd BH12 . . . . 69 C1
Runway The BH23 . . . . 78 B2
Rushall La SO41 . . . . 36 A1
Rushcombe Fst Sch
  BH21 . . . . 37 A1
Rushcombe Way BH21 . . . 37 B2
Rushford Warren
  BH23 . . . . 101 C3
Rushmere Rd BH6 . . . . 75 A2
Rushton Cres BH3 . . . . 71 C2
Ruskin Ave BH9 . . . . 52 B2
Russell Cotes Art Gall &
  Mus* BH1 . . . . 96 A1
Russell Cotes Rd BH1 . . . . 96 A1
Russell Ct **2** BH25 . . . . . 62 A1
Russell Dr BH23 . . . . 77 A1
Russell Gdns
  Hamworthy BH16 . . . . 88 C4
  St Leonards BH24 . . . . 11 C1
Russel Rd BH10 . . . . 42 C2
Russet Cl
  Ferndown BH22 . . . . 27 A2
  3 Lymington SO41 . . . . 111 A1
Rutland Manor **10**
  BH13 . . . . 94 B4
Rutland Rd
  Bournemouth BH9 . . . . . . 72 B3
  Christchurch BH23 . . . . . . 75 C4
Ryall Rd BH17 . . . . 47 A1
Ryan Cl BH22 . . . . 26 C3
Ryan Gdns
  Bournemouth BH11 . . . . . . 42 B2
  Ferndown BH22 . . . . 26 C3
Rydal Cl BH23 . . . . 55 A3
Rydal Ho **2** BH4 . . . . 94 C2
Rydal Mews BH21 . . . . 23 A1
Ryecroft Ave BH11 . . . . 41 B1

S

Saddle Cl BH21 . . . . 24 C2
Saffron Ct BH11 . . . . 49 A3
Saffron Dr BH23 . . . . 78 B3
Saffron Way BH11 . . . . 49 A3
St Aldiem's CE Comb Sch
  BH12 . . . . 70 A2
St Alban's Ave BH8 . . . . . . 72 C2
St Alban's Cres BH8 . . . . . 72 B3
St Alban's Rd BH8 . . . . 72 B2
St Aldhelm's BH14 . . . . 93 C4
St Aldhelm's Cl BH13 . . . . 93 C4
St Aldhelm's Pl BH13 . . . . 93 C4
St Aldhelm's Rd BH13 . . . . 93 C4
St Andrews **3** BH23 . . . . 76 A1
St Andrews Rd BH18 . . . . . 38 A1
St Anne's Ave BH6 . . . . 99 B4

St Annes Gdns SO41 . . . 110 C2
St Anne's Rd BH16 . . . . . . 64 B3
St Ann's Ct ■ BH1 . . . . . . 97 B4
St Ann's Hospl BH13. . . 104 B2
St Anthony's Rd BH22 . . 71 C1
St Antony's ⑥ BH4 . . . . . 95 A2
St Aubyns Ct BH15 . . . . . 90 B2
St Aubyns La BH24 . . . . . 7 C1
St Augustin's Rd BH2 . . 71 C1
St Barbe Mus* SO41 . . . 111 A3
St Brelades Ave BH12 . . 49 A1
St Catherines BH21 . . . . 30 C4
St Catherine's Par
BH23 . . . . 75 C4
St Catherine's RC Prim
Sch BH21 . . . . 24 B2
St Catherine's Rd BH6 . . 99 C2
St Catherine's Way
BH23 . . . . 55 A2
St Clair Rd BH13 . . . . . . 104 C3
St Cleeve Way BH22 . . . 34 C3
St Clement's Gdns BH1 . 97 A4
St Clements Rd BH15 . . 68 A3
St Clement's Rd BH1 . . . 97 A4
St Clement's & St John's
CE Inf Sch BH1 . . . . 71 C1
St Cyres Memorial Cotts
SO41 . . . . 111 B4
St David's Ct ③ BH1 . . . 97 B4
St David's Rd BH16 . . . . 64 B3
St Denys ② BH25 . . . . . . 82 B3
St Edward's RC/CE Sch
BH15 . . . . 67 C3
St George's Almshos ⑥
BH15 . . . . 90 B1
St George's Ave
Bournemouth BH8 . . . . . 72 C3
Poole BH12 . . . . 68 B4
St George's Cl
Bournemouth BH8 . . . . . 72 C3
Christchurch BH23 . . . . . 79 A3
St Georges Ct BH22 . . . . 27 B1
St George's Ct ② BH1 . . 97 B4
St George's Ct BH12 . . . 68 B4
St George's Dr
Bournemouth BH11 . . . . 49 A3
Bransgore BH23 . . . . . . 109 A2
St George's Dr BH22 . . . 34 C4
St Georges Mans ⑤
BH5 . . . . 97 C3
St Helier Rd BH12 . . . . . 49 A1
ST IVES 11 B1
St Ives End La BH24 . . . . 19 B4
St Ives Gdns BH24 . . . . . 11 C1
St Ives Gdns BH2 . . . . . . 71 C1
St Ives Pk BH24 . . . . 11 B1
St Ives Wood BH24 . . . . 12 A1
St James' CE Prim Sch
BH7 . . . . 74 B1
St James Cl ② BH15 . . . 90 B1
St James Rd
Ferndown BH22 . . . . 26 A2
Sway SO41 . . . . 107 C3
St James's ■ BH15 . . . . 97 B2
St James's Sq BH5 . . . . . 98 A4
ST JOHNS 112 A2
St Johns CE Fst Sch
BH21. . . . . 31 A4
St John's Cl BH21 . . . . . . 31 A4
St John's Ct ④ BH1 . . . . 97 B4
St John's Gdns ② BH9 . . 51 C1
St John's Hill BH21 . . . . . 23 A1
St John's Rd
Bournemouth BH5 . . . . . 97 B3
Christchurch BH23 . . . . . 76 A1
Poole BH15 . . . . 91 A4
St Joseph's RC Comb Sch
BH12 . . . . 69 B3
St Joseph's RC Prim Sch
BH23 . . . . 78 A3
St Just Cl BH22 . . . . 34 C3
St Katharine's CE Prim
Sch BH6 . . . . 100 B3
St Ledger's PI BH8 . . . . . 73 A1
St Ledger's Rd BH8 . . . . 73 A1
ST LEONARDS 18 A4
St Leonards Farm Pk
BH22 . . . . 28 A4
St Leonards Hospl
BH24 . . . . 18 A1

St Leonard's Rd BH8 . . . 72 B1
St Leonards Way BH24 . . 18 B4
St Luke's CE Prim Sch
Bournemouth BH9 . . . . . 71 C4
Sway SO41 . . . . 107 B2
St Luke's Rd BH3 . . . . . . 71 C3
St Maradox La BH9 . . . . 51 C2
St Margarets BH2 . . . . . . 71 C1
St Margaret's Almshouses
BH21 . . . . 22 A1
St Margaret's Ave
BH23 . . . . 100 B4
St Margarets Cl BH21 . . 22 A1
St Margarets Hill BH21 . 22 A1
St Margaret's Rd BH21 . 22 A2
St Margaret's Rd
Bournemouth BH10 . . . . 50 C2
Poole BH15 . . . . 91 A4
St Mark's CE Prim Sch
BH10 . . . . 50 C1
St Marks Rd SO41 . . . . 110 A2
St Mark's Rd BH11 . . . . . 50 B3
St Martins Rd BH16 . . . . 64 A3
St Mary Gr SO41 . . . . . . 84 B1
St Marys Cl BH23 . . . . . 109 B2
St Mary's Ct BH6 . . . . . . 99 B2
St Mary's Maternity Hospl
BH15 . . . . 91 A3
St Mary's Mews BH22 . . 35 A4
St Mary's RC Comb Sch
BH15 . . . . 67 B1
St Mary's Rd
Bournemouth BH1 . . . . . 73 A1
Ferndown BH22 . . . . 27 A1
Poole BH15 . . . . 91 B4
St Merrin's Cl BH10 . . . . 50 C4
St Michael's Ave
BH21 . . . . 23 B1
St Michael's CE Mid Sch
BH2 . . . . 95 A3
St Michael's CE Prim Sch
BH2 . . . . 95 A3
St Michaels Cl
Hamworthy BH15 . . . . . . 89 B3
Verwood BH31 . . . . 2 C1
St Michaels Ct ■ BH6 . . 98 C3
St Michael's Mews ⑨
BH2 . . . . 112 A2
St Michael's Pl ⑪
BH2 . . . . 112 A2
St Michaels Rd BH31 . . . 4 C4
St Michael's Rd BH2 . . 112 A1
St Michael's Rdbt BH4 . 95 A3
St Osmund's Rd BH14 . . 93 A3
St Paul's La BH8 . . . . 96 B3
St Paul's Pl BH8 . . . . 96 B3
St Paul's Rd BH8 . . . . . . 96 B3
St Peters Ct ③ BH1 . . . . 96 A2
St Peter's Ct ③ BH14 . . 92 A4
St Peter's Gate ⑬
BH1 . . . . 112 A2
St Peter's RC Comp Sch
BH6 . . . . 99 C3
St Peter's RC Sch BH7 . . 74 B3
St Peter's Rd
Bournemouth BH1 . . . . . 96 A2
Poole BH14 . . . . 92 A4
St Peter's Rdbt BH1 . . . . 96 A2
St Peter's Wlk BH1 . . . . 112 B2
St Saviours Cl BH7 . . . . . 74 C2
Saints Cl BH21 . . . . 8 C4
St Stephen's Ct BH2 . . 112 A3
St Stephens La BH31 . . . 3 A3
St Stephen's Rd BH2 . . 112 A2
St Stephen's Way ④
BH2 . . . . 112 B2
St Swithun's Rd BH1 . . . 96 B3
St Swithun's Rdbt BH1 . 96 B2
St Swithun's Rd S BH1 . 96 B3
St Thomas Cl BH10 . . . . 51 A2
St Thomas Garnet's RC
Sch BH5 . . . . 98 A4
St Thomas Pk SO41 . . . 110 C2
St Thomas's St SO41 . . 111 A2
St Valerie Rd BH2 . . . . . . 71 C1
St Walburga's RC Prim
Sch BH9 . . . . 72 B4
St Winifred's Rd BH1 . . . 71 C1
Salerno Pl BH15 . . . . 89 A2
Salisbury Rd
Bournemouth BH1 . . . . . 97 B3

Salisbury Rd continued
Burton BH23 . . . . 57 A1
Poole BH14 . . . . 68 C1
Ringwood BH24 . . . . 13 A4
Sopley, Winkton BH23 . . 56 A4
Salterne Ho ② SO41 . . . 111 A1
Salterns Ct BH14 . . . . . . 103 B4
Salterns Point BH14 . . . 103 B4
Salterns Quay BH14 . . . 103 B4
Salterns Rd BH14 . . . . . . 92 A3
Salterns Way BH14 . . . . 103 B4
Salter Rd BH13 . . . . 106 B3
Saltings Rd BH16 . . . . . . 64 B2
Samantha Cl BH10 . . . . . 51 B3
Samber Cl SO41 . . . . . . 110 B3
Sammy Miller Motorcycle
Mus* BH25 . . . . 61 B4
Samphire Cl SO41 . . . . 111 A4
Samples Way BH17 . . . . 67 C4
Samson Rd BH15 . . . . . . 89 A2
Sancreed Rd BH12 . . . . . 69 B3
Sancroft Ho BH21 . . . . . 32 A1
SANDBANKS 106 B3
Sandbanks Bsns Ctr
BH13 . . . . 106 A3
Sandbanks Rd BH14,
BH15 . . . . 92 A2
Sandbourne Rd
Bournemouth BH4 . . . . . 94 C1
Poole BH15 . . . . 91 A4
Sandecotes Rd BH14 . . 92 C3
Sanderlings BH24 . . . . . 14 A2
Sandford Cl BH9 . . . . . . 52 C2
Sandford Way BH18 . . . 45 C2
Sandhills Cl BH17 . . . . . . 47 A2
Sandhurst Dr BH21 . . . . 9 B3
Sandmartin BH25 . . . . . . 81 C2
Sandown Rd BH23 . . . . . 77 B1
Sandpiper Cl BH17 . . . . . 45 C1
Sandringham Cl BH9 . . 52 B3
Sandringham Ct BH8 . . 72 C1
Sandringham Gdns
BH9 . . . . 52 B3
Sandringham Rd BH14 . 92 C3
Sandy Cl BH21 . . . . 24 A4
Sandyhurst Cl BH17 . . . . 46 C1
Sandy La
Bournemouth BH6 . . . . . 98 B4
Christchurch BH23 . . . . . 55 B1
St Leonards BH24 . . . . . 11 B1
Three Legged Cross BH21 . . 4 B2
Upton BH16 . . . . 64 B2
Verwood BH31 . . . . 3 A2
Wimborne Minster BH21 . . 24 A4
Sandy Mead Rd BH8 . . . 73 C4
Sandy Plot BH23 . . . . . . 76 C3
Sandy Way BH10 . . . . . . 51 B4
San Remo Twrs ④ BH5 . 97 B2
Santoy BH13 . . . . 104 A1
Sarah Cl BH7 . . . . 74 B3
Sarah Sands Cl BH23 . . . 77 A3
Sark Rd BH12 . . . . 69 A4
Sarum Ave BH22 . . . . . . 16 C4
Sarum Ct BH14 . . . . 92 C4
Sarum St ⑫ BH15 . . . . . 90 B1
Saulfland Dr BH23 . . . . . 79 A3
Saulfland Ho BH23 . . . . . 79 A3
Saulfland Pl BH23 . . . . . 79 A3
Saville Ct BH21 . . . . 31 A3
Saxonbury Rd BH6 . . . . . 99 B4
Saxonford Rd BH23 . . . . 78 C2
Saxon Hts BH6 . . . . 99 B4
Saxonhurst Cl BH10 . . . . 43 B1
Saxonhurst Gdns BH10 . 51 B4
Saxonhurst Rd BH10 . . . 51 B4
Saxon King Gdns BH6 . . 100 B3
Saxon Sq Sh Ctr BH23 . . 76 B1
Scarf Rd BH17 . . . . 67 C3
School Cl BH31 . . . . 3 A3
School La
Bournemouth BH11 . . . . 42 B2
Lymington SO41 . . . . . . 111 A3
Milford on S SO41 . . . . . 87 B4
Poole BH15 . . . . 66 C1
Ringwood BH24 . . . . 13 B3
St Leonards BH24 . . . . . 19 B4
Three Legged Cross BH21 . . 9 A3
Wimborne Minster BH21 . . 22 B1
Scott Cl BH12 . . . . 69 C1
Scotter Rd BH7 . . . . 74 B1

Scott Rd Poole BH12 . . . 49 C1
Poole BH12 . . . . 69 C4
Scott's Gn BH23 . . . . 77 C3
Scotts Hill La BH23 . . . . 77 A2
Seabank Cl BH16 . . . . . . 64 A3
Seabourne Pl ⑤ BH5 . . 98 B4
Seabourne Rd BH5 . . . . 98 B4
Seabreeze Way SO41 . . . 86 A4
Seacliff Ct BH6 . . . . 99 A2
Seacombe Rd BH13 . . . 106 A3
Seacroft Ave BH25 . . . . . 81 B3
Seafield Cl BH25 . . . . 81 C2
Seafield Dr BH6 . . . . 99 B4
Seafield Rd
Barton on S BH25 . . . . . . 81 B3
Bournemouth BH6 . . . . . 99 A3
Christchurch BH23 . . . . . 78 C2
Seagrim Rd BH8 . . . . 52 C2
Seagull Rd BH8 . . . . 72 C4
Seamoor La BH4 . . . . 94 B3
Seamoor Rd BH4 . . . . . . 94 B3
Sea Pines ⑨ SO41 . . . . . 86 C2
Sea Point ⑧ BH13 . . . . 104 C3
Sea Rd Barton on S BH25 . . 81 B3
Bournemouth BH5 . . . . . 97 B3
Bournemouth, Southbourne
BH6. . . . . 99 C2
Milford on S SO41 . . . . . 87 B2
Seaton Cl
Christchurch BH23 . . . . . 80 B3
Lymington SO41 . . . . . . 111 A4
Seaton Rd BH23 . . . . 80 B3
Seatown Cl BH17 . . . . . . 48 A1
Seaview Rd
Barton on S BH25 . . . . . . 81 A2
Walkford BH23 . . . . 80 C4
Sea View Rd
Poole BH15 . . . . 68 A2
Upton BH16 . . . . 64 A3
Sea Vixen Ind Est BH23 . 78 A3
Seaward Ave
Barton on S BH25 . . . . . . 81 C2
Bournemouth BH6 . . . . . 98 B3
Seaway BH25 . . . . 82 B2
Seaway Ave BH23 . . . . . 78 C2
Seawinds SO41 . . . . 86 A3
Seddon Cl BH25 . . . . 82 B2
Sedgley Rd BH9 . . . . 71 B4
Seed Warehouse The ③
BH15 . . . . 90 C1
Selby Cl BH18 . . . . 46 A3
Seldown BH15 . . . . 91 A3
Seldown Bridge BH15 . . 91 A2
Seldown La BH15 . . . . . . 91 A3
Seldown Rd BH15 . . . . . 91 A3
Self Rd BH15 . . . . 90 A2
Selfridge Ave BH6 . . . . 100 B3
Selfridge Cl BH6 . . . . . . 100 B2
Seliot Cl BH15 . . . . 67 A1
Selkirk Cl BH21 . . . . 31 B1
Sellwood Way BH25 . . . 81 A3
Selwood Pk BH10 . . . . . . 42 C3
Selworthy Cl BH14 . . . . . 92 A2
Sentinal Ct BH15 . . . . . . 91 B3
Serpentine Rd BH15 . . . 90 C3
Setley Gdns BH8 . . . . . . 53 B2
Set Thorns Rd SO41 . . . 107 C3
Sevenoaks Dr BH7 . . . . . 74 A3
Severn Rd BH22 . . . . 28 A1
Seymour Gdns BH24 . . . 6 C1
Seymour Rd BH24 . . . . . 6 C1
Shackleton Sq BH23 . . 109 A3
Shaftesbury Cl BH22 . . . 17 A2
Shaftesbury Ct BH3 . . . . 71 C2
Shaftesbury Rd
Bournemouth BH8 . . . . . 72 C1
Poole BH15 . . . . 91 A3
West Moors BH22 . . . . . 17 A2
Shakespeare Rd
Bournemouth BH6 . . . . . 75 A2
Wimborne Minster BH21 . . 22 C2
Shamrock Ct ② BH21 . . 30 C4
Shapland Ave BH11 . . . . 41 B1
Shapwick Rd BH15 . . . . . 90 A1
Shard Cl BH31 . . . . 3 A2
Sharlands Cl BH18 . . . . . 46 B3
Sharp Rd BH12 . . . . 70 A3
Sharvells Rd SO41 . . . . . 86 C3
Shaves La BH25 . . . . 62 A3
Shawford Gdns BH8 . . . 53 A1

Shawford Rd BH8 . . . . . . 53 A2
Shaw Rd BH24 . . . . 7 A2
Shears Brook Cl BH23 . 109 A3
Sheiling Sch The BH24. . 12 A2
Shelbourne Cl BH8 . . . . 73 A1
Shelbourne Rd BH8 . . . . 72 B1
Sheldrake Gdns SO41 . . 84 B2
Sheldrake Rd BH23 . . . 102 A4
Shelley Cl
Bournemouth BH1 . . . . . 97 B4
Christchurch BH23 . . . . . 78 C2
St Leonards BH24 . . . . . 10 C1
Shelley Ct
Bournemouth BH4 . . . . . 94 C3
Ferndown BH22 . . . . 27 A1
Shelley Gdns BH1 . . . . . . 97 B4
Shelley Hamlets BH23 . . 79 A2
Shelley Hill BH23 . . . . . . 79 A2
Shelley Ho ⑨ BH25 . . . . 82 A4
Shelley Rd
Bournemouth BH1 . . . . . 97 B4
Poole BH12 . . . . 69 A1
Shelley Rd E BH7 . . . . . . 97 C4
Shelley Way SO41 . . . . . 87 A3
Shelton Rd BH6 . . . . 74 C1
Shenstone Ct ② BH25 . . 82 A1
Shepherd Cl BH23 . . . . . 79 C4
Shepherds Way
Bournemouth BH7 . . . . . 74 A2
Everton SO41 . . . . 85 B3
Sheppards Field ④
BH21 . . . . 22 B2
Sherborn Cres BH17 . . . 48 A2
Sherborne Dr BH22 . . . . 35 A4
Sherfield Cl BH18 . . . . . . 53 A1
Sheringham Rd BH12 . . 69 C1
Sherrin Cl BH15 . . . . 67 A1
Sherwood Ave
Ferndown BH22 . . . . 34 C3
Poole BH14 . . . . 92 A3
Sherwood Ct BH23 . . . . 75 C2
Sherwood Dr BH31 . . . . . 3 B2
Shetland View BH31 . . . . 3 A2
Shillingstone Dr BH9 . . . 52 B2
Shillingstone Gdns ③
BH12 . . . . 69 C3
Shillito Rd BH12 . . . . 69 B1
Shingle Bank Dr SO41 . . 87 A2
Shipstal Cl BH16 . . . . 88 C4
Shires Copse BH6 . . . . . . 99 C2
Shires Mead BH31 . . . . . 3 A2
SHIRLEY 108 C4
Shirley Cl
Bransgore BH23 . . . . . . 109 A3
West Moors BH22 . . . . . 16 C2
Shirley Rd
Bournemouth BH9 . . . . . 72 A4
Poole BH12 . . . . 68 B2
Upton BH16 . . . . 64 C3
Shoreacres BH13 . . . . . 106 B3
Shore Ave BH16 . . . . 64 C2
Shore Cl
Milford on S SO41 . . . . . 87 A2
Upton BH16 . . . . 64 C2
Shorefield Country Pk
SO41 . . . . 86 A4
Shorefield Cres SO41 . . 86 C2
Shorefield Rd SO41 . . . . 86 A4
Shorefield Way SO41 . . 86 C2
Shore Gdns BH16 . . . . . . 64 B2
Shore La BH16 . . . . 64 C2
Shore Rd BH13 . . . . 104 A2
Short Cl BH12 . . . . 70 A4
Shorts Cl BH23 . . . . 76 C4
Shottsford Rd BH15 . . . . 66 C1
Shrubb's Ave SO41 . . . . 111 A3
Sidney Gdns ② BH9 . . . 52 B3
Sidney Smith Ct BH17 . . 47 B2
Sidney St SO41 . . . . 84 A1
Silchester Cl BH7 . . . . . . 71 C1
Silver Birch Cl BH13 . . . 94 A4
Silver Bsns Pk BH23 . . . 77 C2
Silverdale BH25 . . . . 82 B1
Silverdale Cl BH18 . . . . . 45 B4
Silver St
⑤ Christchurch BH23 . . 76 B1
Hordle SO41 . . . . 84 C4

Silver Way BH23 . . . . 79 B2
Silverwood Cl BH21. . . 31 A2
Simmonds Cl BH15 . . . . 67 A1
Sinclair Ct 4 BH14 . . . 92 A4
Singleton Dr BH10. . . . 50 C2
Siskin Cl BH22. . . . . 26 B3
Sixpenny Cl BH12. . . . . 69 C3
Skinner St BH15 . . . . . . 90 C1
Skipton Cl BH18 . . . . . . 46 A2
Sky End La SO41. . . . . . 84 A1
Slade Cl SO41 . . . . 84 A2
Slader Bsns Pk BH17 . . 47 B1
Slades Farm Rd BH10. . 51 A2
Slade's La BH10 . . . . . . 70 C4
Sleepbrook Cl BH31 . . . .2 B2
SLEIGHT. 29 A1
Sleight La BH21 . . . . . . 36 C4
Slepe Cres BH12. . . . . . 69 C4
Slinn Rd BH23 . . . . 77 B2
Slip Way BH15. . . . . 90 B2
Slough La BH14 . . . . 64 A2
Smithfield Pl BH9 . . . . 51 C1
Smithson Cl BH12 . . . . 70 C4
Smugglers La BH21. . . . 23 B3
Smugglers La N BH23. . 79 B4
Smugglers La S BH23 . . 79 B3
Smugglers Reach
  BH23. . . . . 102 A4
Smugglers Wood Rd
  BH23. . . . . 79 A4
Snails La BH24 . . . . 6 C3
Snowdon Rd BH4 . . . . . 94 C4
Snowdrop Gdns BH23. . 78 B4
Soberton Rd BH8 . . . . . 73 A1
Solar Ct BH13 . . . . 94 A2
Solent Cl SO41 . . . . . . 111 C2
Solent Cl SO41 . . . . . . 111 B2
Solent Ct 6 SO41 . . . . 86 C2
Solent Dr BH25. . . . . . . 82 A1
Solent Lo 5 BH25 . . . . 82 A3
Solent Mead SO41 . . . 111 A2
Solent Pines 2 SO41. . . 86 B2
Solent Rd
  Barton on S BH25. . . . 81 A2
  Bournemouth BH6 . . . 100 A2
  Walkford BH23 . . . . . . 60 B1
Solent View BH6 . . . . . 100 A2
Solent Way SO41 . . . . . 87 C2
Solly Cl BH12 . . . . 69 B3
Solomon Way BH15. . . 89 A2
Somerby Rd BH15 . . . . 67 A2
SOMERFORD 77 B2
Somerford Ave BH23. . 78 B3
Somerford Bsns Pk
  BH23. . . . . 78 A2
Somerford Ct BH23 . . . 79 B2
Somerford Prim Com Sch
  BH23. . . . . 78 A2
Somerford Rd BH23. . . 77 C2
Somerford Rdbt BH23. . 77 C2
Somerford Way BH23 . . 77 B1
Somerley Rd BH9 . . . . . 72 A3
Somerley View 1
  BH24. . . . . 13 B4
Somerset Rd
  Bournemouth BH7 . . . 98 A4
  Christchurch BH23 . . . 75 B3
Somerton Cl BH25 . . . . 63 A1
Somerville Ct BH25 . . . 61 C2
Somerville Rd
  Bournemouth BH2 . . . 95 A3
  Ringwood BH24 . . . . . . 14 A4
Sonning Way BH8 . . . . 52 B1
Sopers La
  Christchurch BH23 . . . 76 A1
  Poole BH17. . . . . 46 B1
Sopley Cl BH25 . . . . 81 A3
Sopwith Cl BH23. . . . . . 78 B1
Sopwith Cres BH21 . . . 31 B2
Sorrel Gdns BH18 . . . . 45 C2
Sorrell Ct BH23 . . . . . . 78 B3
Sorrell Way BH23 . . . . . 78 B3
Southampton Rd
  Lymington SO41 . . . . . 110 C4
  Ringwood BH24 . . . . . . 13 C4
South Ave BH25 . . . . . . 82 B4

SOUTH
  BOCKHAMPTON 57 B3
SOUTHBOURNE. 99 C3
Southbourne Coast Rd
  BH6. . . . . 99 B2
Southbourne Cross Roads
  5 BH6 . . . . 99 B2
Southbourne Gr BH6 . . 98 C3
Southbourne Lane Central
  6 BH6 . . . . 98 C3
Southbourne Lane E 5
  BH6. . . . . 98 C3
Southbourne Lane W
  BH6. . . . . 98 B3
Southbourne Overcliff Dr
  BH6. . . . . 99 A2
Southbourne Rd
  Bournemouth BH6 . . . 98 C3
  Lymington SO41 . . . . . 110 B2
Southbourne Sands
  BH6. . . . . 99 A2
Southbrook Cl BH17 . . 48 A2
Southcliffe Rd
  Barton on S BH25. . . . 81 A2
  Christchurch BH23 . . . 78 C1
South Cliff Rd BH2 . . . 112 B1
Southcote Rd BH1 . . . . 96 C3
South Ct SO41 . . . . 87 B2
Southdown Ct 1 BH23. . 77 C3
Southdown Way BH22 . . 17 A1
South Dr BH24 . . . . 28 B3
Southern Ave BH22 . . . 17 B1
Southernhay Rd BH31 . . .3 B2
Southern La
  Barton on S BH25. . . . 81 C3
  Old Milton BH25 . . . . . 81 C4
Southern Oaks BH25 . . 81 C4
Southern Rd
  Bournemouth BH6 . . . 98 C3
  Lymington SO41 . . . . . 110 C2
Southey Rd BH23 . . . . . 77 C2
Southfield BH24 . . . . . . 13 B2
Southfield Mews 6
  BH24. . . . . 13 B2
South Gr SO41. . . . . . . 111 B2
South Haven Cl BH16 . . 88 B3
Southill Ave BH12 . . . . 68 C2
Southill Gdns BH9 . . . . 72 A4
Southill Rd
  Bournemouth BH9 . . . 72 A4
  Poole BH12. . . . . 69 A3
Southlands SO41 . . . . . 110 B1
Southlands Ave
  Bournemouth BH6 . . . 99 C3
  Corfe Mullen BH21. . . 37 A2
Southlands Cl BH21. . . 37 A2
Southlands Ct BH18 . . 46 A3
Southlawns Wlk BH25 . . 81 C4
Southlea Ave BH6 . . . . 99 C3
South Lodge BH13 . . . 105 A3
South Park Rd BH12 . . 70 A4
South Rd
  Bournemouth BH1 . . . 97 B4
  Corfe Mullen BH21. . . 37 B2
  Poole BH15. . . . . 90 C2
South Road Comb Sch
  BH15. . . . . 90 C2
South St SO41 . . . . . . 110 B1
South Sway La SO41 . . 107 C1
South View BH2 . . . . . . 71 C1
South View Pl 10 BH2 . . 112 A2
South View Rd BH23. . . 76 A1
Southville Rd BH5 . . . . 98 B4
South Western Cres
  BH14. . . . . 92 B2
Southwick Pl BH6 . . . . 74 C2
Southwick Rd BH6. . . . 74 C1
Southwood Ave
  Bournemouth BH6 . . . 98 C3
  Walkford BH23 . . . . . . 80 B4
Southwood Cl
  Ferndown BH22 . . . . . 26 C2
  Walkford BH23 . . . . . . 80 A4
Sovereign Bsns Ctr
  BH15. . . . . 66 B2
Sovereign Cl BH7 . . . . 73 C2
Sovereign Ctr 6 BH7 . . 97 B3
Sovereign Pl BH24. . . . 13 A3
Sparkford Cl BH7 . . . . 74 B3

Spartina Dr SO41 . . . . . 111 A4
Speedwell Dr BH23 . . . 78 B3
Spencer Ct 1 BH25. . . . 82 B4
Spencer Rd
  Bournemouth BH1 . . . 96 C3
  New Milton BH25 . . . . 82 B4
  Poole BH13. . . . . 104 C4
Spetisbury Cl BH9 . . . . 52 B2
Spicer La BH11 . . . . 41 B1
Spinacre BH25 . . . . 82 B2
Spindle Cl BH18 . . . . . . 45 C2
Spindlewood Cl 10
  BH25. . . . . 82 A3
Spinners Cl BH22 . . . . . 16 C1
Spinney Cl BH24 . . . . . . 18 B4
Spinneys La BH22. . . . . 27 A1
Spinney The BH24 . . . . 11 A2
Spinney Way BH25. . . . 82 B4
Spittlefields BH24 . . . . 13 C3
Springbank Rd BH7. . . 73 C3
SPRINGBOURNE. 96 C4
Springbourne Ct BH1. . 97 A4
Springbourne Mews
  BH1. . . . . 96 C4
Spring Cl BH31 . . . . 2 C1
Spring Ct BH12 . . . . 69 A1
Springdale Ave BH18 . . 37 C1
Springdale Fst Sch
  BH18. . . . . 45 B4
Springdale Gr BH21. . . 45 B4
Springdale Rd BH18,
  BH21. . . . . 45 B4
Springfield Ave
  Bournemouth BH6 . . . 100 A3
  Christchurch BH23 . . . 55 A1
Springfield Cl
  Lymington SO41 . . . . . 111 C2
  Verwood BH31 . . . . . . 2 C1
Springfield Cres BH14 . . 92 B4
Springfield Gdns BH25. . 83 A4
Springfield Rd
  Poole BH14. . . . . 92 A4
  Verwood BH31 . . . . . . 2 C1
Spring Gdns BH12 . . . . 69 A1
Spring La BH25. . . . . . . 83 A4
Spring Rd
  Bournemouth BH1 . . . 97 A4
  Lymington SO41 . . . . . 111 C1
Springvale Ave BH7. . . 73 C3
Springwater Cl BH11 . . 50 A3
Springwater Ct BH23 . . 77 A1
Springwater Dr BH23 . . 77 A1
Springwater Rd BH11. . 50 A3
Spruce Cl BH17. . . . . . . 45 B1
Spur Cl BH21 . . . . 24 C2
Spurgeon Rd BH7 . . . . 74 B1
Spur Hill Ave BH14. . . . 93 A3
Spur Rd BH14 . . . . 93 A3
Square Cl BH21. . . . . . . 33 C3
Square The
  Bournemouth BH2 . . . 112 B2
  Lymington SO41 . . . . . 110 B2
  West Moors BH24 . . . . 28 B4
  Wimborne Minster BH21. . 22 B1
Squirrel's Cl BH23 . . . . 55 A1
Squirrel Wlk BH31 . . . . 2 C1
Stables The BH23 . . . . . 75 C2
Stacey Cl BH21 . . . . 68 C3
Stacey Gdns BH8 . . . . . 53 C1
Stadium Way BH15 . . . 90 C3
Stafford Rd BH1 . . . . . . 96 A3
Stag Bsns Pk BH24 . . . 13 B1
Stag Cl BH25 . . . . 61 B3
Stagswood BH31 . . . . . 2 A1
Stalbridge Dr BH22 . . . 35 A4
Stalbridge Rd BH17. . . 66 A3
Stalham Rd BH17 . . . . . 69 C2
Stallards La BH24. . . . . 13 A3
Stamford Rd BH6 . . . . . 99 A4
Stanfield Cl BH12 . . . . 69 A3
Stanfield Rd
  Bournemouth BH9 . . . 71 B4
  Ferndown BH22 . . . . . 26 C2
  Poole BH12. . . . . 69 A3
Stanford Gdns SO41 . . 110 C1
Stanford Hill SO41 . . . 110 C2
Stanford Rd SO41. . . . . 110 C2
Stanford Rise SO41 . . . 107 B3
Staniforth Ct BH23. . . . 77 A1
Stanley Cl BH31 . . . . . . 3 A1

Stanley Ct
  Bournemouth BH1 . . . 96 C4
  Poole BH15. . . . . 66 C2
STANLEY GREEN. 66 C2
Stanley Green Cres
  BH15. . . . . 66 C1
Stanley Green Fst Sch
  BH15. . . . . 66 C1
Stanley Green Ind Est
  BH15. . . . . 66 C1
Stanley Green Rd
  Poole BH15. . . . . 66 C1
  Poole BH15. . . . . 66 C2
Stanley Pearce Ho
  BH17. . . . . 46 C1
Stanley Pk (Cvn & Chalet
  Site) BH25. . . . . 62 C4
Stanley Rd
  Bournemouth BH1 . . . 96 C4
  Christchurch BH23 . . . 80 A3
  Lymington SO41 . . . . . 111 C1
  Poole BH15. . . . . 90 C2
Stannington Cl BH25. . 82 B4
STANPIT. 101 C4
Stanpit BH23 . . . . 101 B4
Stanton Lacy 12 BH13 . . 104 C3
Stanton Rd BH10 . . . . . 50 C2
STAPEHILL. 25 B1
Stapehill Cres BH21. . . 24 C1
Stapehill Mus & Gdns*
  BH21. . . . . 25 B1
Stapehill Rd BH21 . . . . 33 C4
Staple Close La BH15 . . 66 C2
Staple Cross BH17 . . . . 77 B3
Staplecross La BH23 . . 77 A3
Stapleford Ave BH22 . . 27 C2
Star La BH24 . . . . 13 A3
Starlight Farm Cl BH31 . . 3 A3
Station App BH18. . . . . 46 A4
Station Rd
  Christchurch BH23 . . . 76 A2
  Christchurch, Highcliffe
    BH23. . . . . 59 B1
  New Milton BH25 . . . . 82 A4
  Poole, Lower Hamworthy
    BH15. . . . . 90 A1
  Poole, Lower Parkstone
    BH14. . . . . 92 B4
  Sway SO41 . . . . 107 B2
  Verwood BH31 . . . . . . 2 A3
  West Moors BH22 . . . . 16 B2
  Wimborne Minster BH21. . 31 A3
Station St SO41. . . . . . 111 B3
Station Terr BH31 . . . . . 31 A4
Staunton BH2 . . . . 112 B1
Stedman Rd BH5 . . . . . 98 B4
Steepdene BH14 . . . . . 92 B3
Steeple Cl BH17 . . . . . . 47 A3
Steepleton Rd BH18 . . 46 C3
Stella Ct 15 BH23 . . . . . 80 B2
Stem La BH25 . . . . 61 B3
Stenhurst Rd BH15 . . . 67 B2
Stephen Langton Dr
  BH11. . . . . 41 A1
Stephens Wlk BH24. . . 13 A3
Stepnell Reach BH16 . . 65 A1
STERTE. 90 B3
Sterte Ave BH15 . . . . . 90 B4
Sterte Avenue W BH15. . 90 B4
Sterte Cl BH15. . . . . . . 90 C4
Sterte Ct BH15. . . . . . . 90 C4
Sterte Espl BH15. . . . . 90 C3
Sterte Ind Est BH15. . . 90 B4
Sterte Rd BH15 . . . . . . 90 C4
Stevenson Cres BH14 . . 93 B3
Stevenson Rd BH6. . . . 100 A2
Stevensons Cl 3 BH21. . 30 C4
Stewart Cl 5 BH8 . . . . 96 C4
Stewart Rd BH8 . . . . . . 72 B1
Stewarts Way BH22. . . 27 B3
Stibbs Way BH23 . . . . . 109 B3
Stillmore Rd BH11 . . . . 49 A3
Stillwater Pk BH24. . . . 7 A2
Stinsford Cl BH9 . . . . . 52 B3
Stinsford Rd BH17 . . . . 47 A1
Stirling Bsns Pk BH21 . . 25 C3
Stirling Cl BH25 . . . . . . 62 B1
Stirling Ct
  3 Bournemouth BH4 . . 94 C2
  1 New Milton BH25 . . . 62 B1

Stirling Rd BH3. . . . . . . 71 B3
Stirling Way BH23 . . . . 78 B1
Stirrup Cl Upton BH16 . . 65 A3
  Wimborne Minster BH21. . 24 C2
Stoborough Dr BH18. . 46 A2
Stockbridge Cl BH17. . 48 B2
Stokes Ave BH15. . . . . 91 A4
Stoke Wood Rd BH3 . . 71 C2
STONE. 22 A2
Stonechat Cl BH22. . . . 26 B4
Stonechat Ct BH23. . . . 77 C2
Stonecrop Cl BH18 . . . 45 B2
Stone Gdns BH8 . . . . . 54 A1
Stone La BH21. . . . . 22 A2
Stone Lane Ind Est
  BH21. . . . . 22 B2
Stoneleigh 3 BH13. . . 104 C4
Stoneleigh Ave SO41. . 63 C2
Stony La Burton BH23. . 56 C1
Stony La BH23. . . . . 76 C2
Stony Lane S BH23. . . . 77 A1
Stopples La SO41 . . . . 63 C1
Story La BH18 . . . . 46 B4
Stourbank Rd BH23 . . . 76 A1
Stour Cl BH21 . . . . 33 A4
Stourcliffe Ave BH6 . . . 98 C3
Stourcroft Dr BH23 . . . 75 B4
Stour Ct 6 BH13 . . . . . 94 A4
Stourfield Inf & Jun Schs
  BH6. . . . . 75 A1
Stourfield Rd BH5 . . . . 98 B3
Stourpaine Rd BH17 . . 47 A2
Stour Pk BH10. . . . . 43 B2
Stour Rd
  Bournemouth BH8 . . . 73 A1
  Christchurch BH23 . . . 76 A1
Stour Rdbt BH23. . . . . . 99 C4
Stourton Ct 21 BH4 . . . 94 C3
Stourvale Ave BH23 . . . 75 A3
Stourvale Pl 8 BH5 . . . 98 B4
Stourvale Rd BH6. . . . . 74 C1
Stour View Gdns BH21. . 29 B1
Stour Way BH23 . . . . . . 75 A4
Stour Wlk
  Bournemouth BH8 . . . 53 A3
  Wimborne Minster BH21. . 31 A3
Stourwood Ave BH6. . . 99 A3
Stourwood Mans 4
  BH6. . . . . 98 C3
Stourwood Rd BH6 . . . 99 A3
Stouts La BH23 . . . . 109 A3
Strand St BH15 . . . . . . 90 C1
Stratfield Pl BH25 . . . . 61 B2
Stratford Pl SO41. . . . . 110 C4
Strathmore Dr BH31 . . . 3 B2
Strathmore Rd BH9 . . . 52 A3
Stratton Rd BH9 . . . . . . 52 C2
Strete Mount 1 BH23. . . 77 B2
Stretton Ct BH14 . . . . . 92 B4
Strides La BH24 . . . . . . 13 A3
Strode Gdns BH24 . . . . 11 C1
Stroud Cl BH21 . . . . 24 A2
STROUDEN. 73 B4
Strouden Ave BH8 . . . . 72 C3
Strouden Rd BH9 . . . . . 72 A4
Stroud Gdns BH23 . . . . 77 B1
Stroud La BH23. . . . . . . 77 C1
Stroud Park Ave BH23 . . 77 B1
Struan Cl BH24 . . . . 11 A2
Struan Ct BH24 . . . . 11 B2
Struan Dr BH24. . . . . . . 11 B2
Struan Gdns BH24 . . . . 11 A2
Stuart Cl BH16. . . . . 64 B3
Stuart Rd BH23 . . . . 80 B3
Student Village BH12 . . 71 A4
Studland Ct 20 BH4 . . . 94 C3
Studland Dr SO41. . . . . 86 C3
Studland Rd BH4 . . . . . 94 C1
Studley Cl BH23 . . . . . . 80 C3
Studley Ct BH25 . . . . . . 81 A3
Sturminster Rd 1 BH9. . 52 B3
Suffolk Ave BH23 . . . . . 55 C1
Suffolk Cl BH21. . . . . . . 24 C2
Suffolk Rd BH2 . . . . 112 A2
Suffolk Rd S BH2 . . . . . 95 A3
Summercroft Way
  BH22. . . . . 16 C3
Summerfield Cl BH23. . 56 C1
Summer Field Cl BH21. . 32 A4
Summerfields BH7 . . . . 73 C2

Summer Flds BH31 ...... 4 C4
Summerlands BH22.... 27 A2
Summers Ave BH11.... 42 B2
Summers La BH23 ..... 77 A4
Summertrees Ct BH25 .. 63 A2
Sunbury Cl BH11 ...... 42 A2
Sunbury Rd
 [1] Bournemouth
  BH2.....................112 A2
 [2] Bournemouth BH4 .. 94 C3
Sunderland Dr BH23 .. 78 B2
Sundew Cl
 Christchurch BH23 .... 78 C4
 New Milton BH25 ..... 63 A2
Sundew Rd BH18 ..... 45 B2
Sunningdale
 [4] Bournemouth BH4 .. 94 C3
 Christchurch BH23 .... 75 C1
 [6] Poole BH15 .... 91 B3
Sunningdale Cres
 BH10.................. 50 C4
Sunningdale Gdns
 BH18.................. 38 A1
Sunnybank Dr BH21 ... 24 B2
Sunnybank Rd BH21 ... 24 B2
Sunnybank Way BH21... 24 B2
Sunnyfield Rd BH25.... 82 A2
Sunny Hill Ct BH12..... 69 A1
Sunnyhill Rd BH6...... 98 C4
Sunny Hill Rd BH12 .... 69 A1
Sunnylands Ave BH6... 99 C3
Sunnymoor Rd BH11... 50 A1
Sunnyside Pk BH24 .... 12 A1
Sunnyside Rd BH12 .... 69 A2
Sunridge Cl BH12...... 70 A2
Sunrise Ct BH22 ...... 27 A1
Sunset Lo BH13....... 94 A2
Surrey Cl BH23 .... 55 C1
Surrey Gdns BH4 ..... 94 C4
Surrey Lo [8] BH4 ..... 95 A4
Surrey Rd BH4, BH12 ... 94 B4
Surrey Rd S BH4...... 94 C4
Sussex Cl BH9 .... 52 B3
Sutherland Ave BH18 ... 37 B1
Sutton Cl BH17 ...... 48 B2
Sutton Rd BH9 .... 72 B4
Swallow Cl BH17 ..... 65 C4
Swallow Dr SO41..... 87 B2
Swallow Way BH21.... 24 A3
Swan Gn [3] BH23 .... 100 A4
Swan Mead BH24..... 14 A2
Swanmore Cl BH7 .... 74 B2
Swanmore Rd BH7.... 74 B2
Swansbury Dr BH8.... 54 B1
SWAY 107 B2
Sway Cl SO41........ 107 C1
Sway Gdns BH8...... 53 A1
Sway Park Ind Est
 SO41.................107 B2
Sway Rd BH25, SO41.... 62 C4
Sway Sta SO41 ....107 B2
Sweep The BH24 ..... 13 A3
Swift Cl BH17........ 65 C4
Swordfish Dr BH23 ... 78 B2
Sycamore Cl
 Broadstone BH17...... 45 C1
 Christchurch BH23 .... 75 A3
 Milford on S SO41..... 86 C3
Sycamore Ct BH24.... 7 A2
Sycamore Pl BH21.... 25 A1
Sycamore Rd SO41.... 63 C2
Sydling Cl BH17 ..... 48 B2
Sydney Rd
 Broadstone BH18...... 46 A3
 Christchurch BH23 .... 75 B4
Sylmor Gdns BH9..... 52 A1
Sylvan Cl Hordle SO41 ... 84 B1
 St Leonards BH24 .... 18 B4
Sylvan Fst Sch BH22... 68 B2
Sylvan Rd BH12...... 68 B2
Symes Rd BH15...... 89 B4

T

Tadden Cotts BH21 ... 21 A3
Tadden Wlk BH18..... 45 C2
Tait Cl BH17 .... 67 B3
Talbot Ave BH3 ...... 71 B3
Talbot Comb Sch BH12 . 70 B4
Talbot Ct BH9 .... 51 C1

Talbot Dr
 Christchurch BH23..... 59 C1
 Poole BH12........... 70 B4
TALBOT HEATH 70 B3
Talbot Heath Sch BH4 .. 70 C1
Talbot Hill Rd BH9 .... 71 A4
Talbot House Prep Sch
 BH9................... 71 B3
Talbot Manor BH3 .... 71 A4
Talbot Mdws BH12.... 70 B4
Talbot Mews BH10.... 50 B1
Talbot Rd BH9 .... 71 B3
Talbot Rdbt BH3 ...... 71 A3
Talbot Rise BH10 ..... 50 C2
TALBOT VILLAGE 50 C1
TALBOT WOODS 71 B3
Tamar Cl BH22........ 28 A1
Tamworth Rd BH7 .... 97 C4
Tanglewood Ct [1]
 BH25.................. 62 B1
Tanglewood Lo BH17 ... 65 C4
Tangmere Cl BH23 .... 78 B1
Tangmere Pl BH17.... 67 B3
Tan Howse Cl BH7 .... 74 B3
Tapper Ct BH21....... 31 B4
Tarn Dr BH17........ 65 C4
Tarrant Cl BH17....... 47 B2
Tarrant Rd BH9 ...... 52 B2
Tarrants The [12] BH2 .. 95 A4
Tasman Cl BH23 ..... 75 C3
Tatnam Cres BH15 .... 90 C3
Tatnam Rd BH15..... 90 C4
Taverner Cl BH15 .... 91 A2
Taylor Dr BH8 .... 53 A3
Taylor's Bldgs [6] BH15.. 90 C1
Taylor Way BH31...... 3 A2
Teak Cl BH13 ....105 B4
Teasel Way BH22 ..... 16 C1
Tebourba Cotts SO41 ... 107 B2
Technology Rd BH17... 66 A4
Tedder Cl BH11....... 50 B3
Tedder Gdns BH11.... 50 B3
Tedder Rd BH11 ..... 50 B3
Telford Pl SO41....... 87 B2
Telford Rd BH21 ..... 26 A4
Temple Mews BH1.... 73 A1
Templer Cl BH11...... 49 C1
Temple Trees [45] BH4.. 94 C3
Tennyson Rd
 Bournemouth BH9 .... 51 C2
 [1] Poole BH14........ 92 A3
 Wimborne Minster BH21.. 22 C2
Tenon Ct BH23........ 76 B2
Tensing Rd BH23 ..... 77 B3
Terence Ave BH17 .... 46 C1
Terence Rd BH21..... 36 C1
Tern Ct BH6 .... 75 A1
Terrace Rd BH2.......112 A2
Terrington Ave BH23... 79 B4
Thames Cl BH21...... 28 A2
Thames Mews [1] BH15 . 90 B1
Thames St BH15...... 90 B1
Thatchers La BH23.....108 B3
THE MARSH 64 A3
Thessaly Ct [4] BH5 ... 97 C3
Thetchers Cl BH25.... 62 B3
Thetford Rd BH12..... 69 C1
Thistlebarrow Rd BH7 .. 73 B1
Thistle Cl BH23 ...... 78 C3
Thomas Lockyer Cl
 BH31.................. 3 A1
Thoresby Ct BH25.... 61 B2
Thornbury [18] BH4 .... 94 C3
Thornbury Rd BH6.... 100 A3
Thorncombe Cl
 Bournemouth BH9 .... 52 B3
 Poole BH17........... 47 B2
Thorne Cl BH31........ 2 B2
Thorne Way BH21 .... 9 C2
Thornfield Dr BH23 ... 79 C4
Thornham Rd BH25 ... 63 A1
Thornley Rd BH10 .... 51 A4
Thorn Rd BH17....... 47 A3
Thornton Cl BH21..... 36 C1
Thorogood Ct [4] BH15 . 91 B4
Three Acre Dr BH25.... 81 C3
Three Cross Rd BH21 ... 8 C2
THREE LEGGED CROSS. 9 A4
Three Legged Cross Fst
 Sch BH21............ 4 B1

Three Lions Cl [9] BH21 . 22 B1
THROOP 53 B3
Throop Cl BH8....... 54 A1
Throop Rd
 Bournemouth, Holdenhurst
  BH8................. 54 A1
 Bournemouth, Throop
  BH8................. 53 B3
Throopside Ave BH9 ... 53 A3
Thrush Rd BH12 ...... 48 C1
Thursby Rd BH23 .... 79 C4
Thwaite Rd BH12 .... 70 B1
Tidemill Cl BH23 ..... 76 A3
Tiffany Cl SO41....... 63 C2
Tilbury Rd BH23 ..... 77 A2
Tiller Gdns BH11 ..... 42 A1
Timothy Cl BH10...... 43 A1
Tincleton Gdns BH9 ... 52 B3
Tithe Barn SO41.......111 A4
Tiverton Cl [34] BH4... 94 C3
Todber Cl BH11....... 49 A3
Tollard Cl BH12...... 69 B4
Tollerford Rd BH17 ... 47 A2
Tolpuddle Gdns BH9 ... 52 B3
Tolstoi Rd BH14...... 68 A2
Tonge Rd BH11...... 42 B2
Topiary The BH14 .... 67 C1
Top La BH24.......... 13 B3
Torbay Rd BH14 ..... 92 C3
Torvain Pk BH14 ..... 68 A1
Totland Ct [8] SO41 ... 86 C2
Totmel Rd BH17 ..... 48 A2
Tourney Rd BH11..... 41 B2
Towans The BH13 .....106 B3
Tower Ct BH2......... 112 A1
Tower La BH21........ 23 A2
Tower Park Rdbt BH15 . 67 C3
Tower Rd
 Bournemouth BH1 .... 97 B4
 Poole BH13........... 94 B2
Tower Rd W BH13 .... 94 A1
Towers Farm BH21.... 37 A3
Towers Way BH21.... 37 A3
Towngate Bridge BH15. 90 C3
Towngate Sh Ctr [1]
 BH15.................. 90 C2
Townsend Cl BH11.... 42 B2
Townsend Prim Sch
 BH8.................. 54 A1
Townsville Rd BH9.... 52 B1
Tozer Cl BH11 .... 49 C2
Tracey Ct [6] BH23 ... 80 A2
Trafalgar Ct BH23.....101 C4
Trafalgar Pl SO41......111 B3
Trafalgar Rd BH9 .... 71 C3
Tranmere Cl SO41 .....111 B1
Treebys Cl BH23 ..... 77 A4
Tree Hamlets BH16 ... 64 C1
Treeside BH23........ 58 C1
Treetops [9] BH13 .....104 C3
Trefoil Way BH23 .... 78 C3
Tregonwell Ct [18] BH2..112 A2
Tregonwell Rd BH2....112 A1
Treloen Ct [3] BH8.... 96 A4
Trentham Ave BH7.... 74 B3
Trentham Cl BH7 .... 74 B3
Trent Way BH22 ..... 28 A2
Tresillian Cl BH23.... 60 B1
Tresillian Way BH23... 60 B1
Trevone [5] BH25...... 62 B1
Triangle The
 Bournemouth BH2 .....112 A2
 Upton BH16........... 64 B3
TRICKETT'S CROSS .. 27 C3
Tricketts La BH22..... 27 C2
Trigon Rd BH15....... 67 A3
Trinidad Cres BH12 ... 68 C4
Trinidad Ho BH12.... 68 C4
Trinity [2] BH1....... 96 A3
Trinity CE Fst Sch BH31.. 2 C4
Trinity Ind Est BH21.... 31 B3
Trinity Rd BH1....... 96 A3
Troak Cl BH23 .... 77 B3
Troon Rd BH18 ...... 38 A1
Trotters La BH21..... 24 B2
Truman Rd BH11..... 42 B2
Truscott Ave BH9 .... 72 A2
Trystworthy [3] BH2...112 A2
Tuckers La BH15..... 89 C1
Tucks Cl BH23 ....108 C2

TUCKTON 99 C4
Tuckton Cl BH6....... 99 A3
Tuckton Rd
 Bournemouth,
  Southbourne BH6..... 99 C4
 Bournemouth, West
  Southbourne BH6..... 99 B3
Tuckton Rdbt BH6 .... 99 C4
Tudor Ct
 Bournemouth BH1 .... 96 A4
 Poole BH15........... 67 B2
Tudor Rd BH18 ...... 46 B4
Turbary Cl BH12 ..... 69 A4
Turbary Ct
 Bournemouth BH12 ... 50 A1
 Ferndown BH22 ...... 27 C2
 Upton BH16........... 64 C4
Turbary Hts BH11.... 49 C2
Turbary Park Ave BH11.. 50 A2
Turbary Rd
 Ferndown BH22 ...... 27 C2
 Poole BH12........... 50 A1
Turbary Ret Pk BH11 ... 49 B3
Turf Croft Ct BH23 ... 60 B1
Turk's La BH14 ...... 92 A1
TURLIN MOOR 88 B4
Turlin Moor Com Fst Sch
 BH16................. 88 C4
Turlin Moor Com Mid Sch
 BH16................. 88 C4
Turlin Rd BH16....... 88 C4
Turnberry Cl BH23 ... 75 C1
Turners Farm Cres
 SO41................. 84 A1
Turnworth Cl BH18 ... 46 C3
Tweedale Rd BH9 .... 52 C2
Twemlow Ave BH14... 91 C3
Twin Oaks Cl BH18.... 46 A3
Twyford Cl BH8....... 53 A1
Twyford Ho BH22 .... 27 C2
Twyford Way BH17.... 48 A2
Twynham Ave BH23 ... 76 A2
Twynham Rd BH6..... 99 C3
Twynham Sch BH23.... 76 A1
Tylers Cl SO41 ....110 C4
Tynedale Cl BH9 ..... 52 B3
Tyneham Ave BH12 ... 68 C4
Tynham Ct BH23 ..... 76 C1
Tyrrell Gdns BH8 .... 54 A1
Tyrrells Ct BH23 .....109 A3
Tytherley Gn BH8 .... 53 A1

U

Ubsdell Cl BH25 ..... 62 A1
Uddens Dr BH21...... 25 A3
Uddens Trad Est BH21 .. 25 B2
Ullswater Rd BH21.... 30 C2
Undercliff Dr BH1 .... 96 C1
Undercliff Rd BH5 .... 97 B2
Undershore Rd SO41...111 C3
Underwood Cl BH17 ... 46 B1
University Rdbt BH10 .. 70 C4
Uplands Ave BH25 ... 82 A2
Uplands Cl BH22...... 28 A2
Uplands Gdns BH8.... 52 C1
Uplands Rd
 Bournemouth BH8 .... 52 C1
 West Moors BH22 .... 17 B1
Uplands Sch BH14..... 92 C3
Uplyme Cl BH17 ..... 48 A2
Upper Golf Links Rd
 BH18.................. 38 B1
Upper Gordon Rd BH23 . 80 A4
Upper Hinton Rd BH1 ..112 B2
Upper Norwich Rd [6]
 BH2.................112 A2
UPPER PARKSTONE.. 68 B3
Upper Rd BH12....... 69 A2
Upper Terrace Rd
 BH2..................112 A2
Uppleby Rd BH12.... 68 C2
UPTON 65 A3
Upton Cl BH16........ 64 B3
Upton Cross Mobile Home
 Pk BH16.............. 65 A2
Upton Ct BH16........ 64 B3
Upton Ctry Pk* BH17... 65 C2
Upton Heath Est BH16 . 65 A3
Upton Ind Est BH16.... 65 A2

Upton Inf Sch BH16.... 64 A3
Upton Jun Sch BH16.... 64 A3
Upton Rd BH17 ...... 65 C3
Upton Way BH18...... 45 C3
Upwey Ave BH15..... 89 B3
Utrecht Ct BH23 ..... 77 A2

V

Vaggs La SO41....... 63 B4
Vale Cl BH14 .... 93 B4
Vale Lodge BH1 ..... 97 A4
Vale Mans [4] BH1 ... 97 A3
Valencia Cl BH23 .... 55 A3
Vale Rd
 Bournemouth BH1 .... 97 A3
 Poole BH14........... 93 B4
Valette Rd BH9 ...... 52 A2
Valiant Way BH23 .... 78 B2
Valley Cl BH23 ...... 55 B2
Valley Rd BH8 .... 53 C2
Valley View BH12 .... 70 B3
Valleys Cl BH15 ...... 91 A1
Vanguard Rd
 Bournemouth BH8 .... 73 B4
 [6] Poole BH15........ 90 C2
Vantage Way BH12.... 48 B2
Vecta Cl BH23 .... 78 C1
Vectis Rd BH25 ...... 81 A2
Velvet Lawn Rd BH25 ... 61 C3
Venator Pl BH21...... 22 C2
Venning Ave BH11 ... 41 B1
Ventry Cl BH13 ...... 93 C4
Ventura Ctr The BH16... 65 A2
Ventura Pl BH16...... 65 A2
Verity Cres BH17 .... 48 A1
Vernalls Cl BH10..... 43 A2
Vernalls Ct BH25..... 62 C3
Vernalls Gdns BH10... 43 A1
Verne Rd BH31 .... 3 A1
Verney Cl BH11...... 50 B3
Verney Rd BH11 ..... 50 A3
Verno La BH23....... 78 C4
Verona Ave BH6 ..... 99 A4
Verulam Pl [8] BH1....112 B2
Verulam Rd BH14..... 91 C4
VERWOOD............ 4 B3
Verwood CE Fst Sch
 BH31.................. 2 B1
Verwood Cres BH6.... 100 B3
Verwood Ind Est BH31 .. 3 A2
Verwood Rd
 Ringwood BH24 ..... 12 A4
 Three Legged Cross BH21.. 4 C1
Vetch Cl BH23 .... 78 C3
Vian Ct BH25 .... 61 C2
Vicarage Cotts BH8.... 53 C2
Vicarage Gdns SO41 ... 84 A1
Vicarage La SO41..... 84 A1
Vicarage Rd
 Bournemouth BH9 .... 51 C1
 Poole BH15........... 66 C2
 Verwood BH31 .... 2 C2
Vicarage Way BH23 ... 57 A1
Vickers Cl BH8........ 54 B1
Vickery Way BH23 ... 77 A3
Victoria Ave BH9 .... 51 B1
Victoria Cl BH21...... 37 A1
Victoria Cres BH12.... 69 A2
Victoria Gdns
 Ferndown BH22 ...... 27 A2
 Ringwood BH24 ..... 13 B2
Victoria Hospl BH21 ... 22 A1
Victoria Park Pl [4]
 BH9.................. 51 C1
Victoria Park Rd BH9 ... 51 B1
Victoria Pl
 Bournemouth BH1,
  BH8.................. 96 C4
 [4] Lymington SO41 .....111 A1
 Wimborne Minster BH21.. 22 B1
Victoria Rd
 Bournemouth BH1 .... 96 C4
 Christchurch BH23 .... 101 B4
 Ferndown BH22 ...... 27 A2
 Milford on S SO41..... 86 C2
 Poole BH12........... 68 C2

Victoria Rd continued
Wimborne Minster BH21. . . **22** B1
Victoria St BH13 . . . . **93** C4
Victory Cl BH21. . . . . 9 C2
Viewside Cl BH21. . . . . **36** C1
Viking Cl BH6 . . . . **100** A3
Viking Way
Bournemouth BH6 . . . . . . **100** A3
Christchurch BH23. . . . . . **102** A4
Villas The BH25 . . . . **61** B4
Villette Cl BH23. . . . . **76** A4
Vince Cl BH11 . . . . **42** B1
Vincent Cl 2 BH24 . . . . **82** A4
Vincent Rd 1 BH25. . . . . . . **82** A4
Vine Cl BH7 . . . . **74** A2
Vine Farm Cl BH12. . . . . . . **70** C4
Vine Farm Rd BH12 . . . . . . **70** B4
Vinegar Hill SO41. . . . . **87** A3
Vine Hill BH21 . . . . **21** B1
Vineries Cl BH21. . . . . **23** C2
Vineries The BH21 . . . . **23** C2
Vinery The BH25 . . . . **82** B4
Vinneys Cl BH23 . . . . **56** C1
Violet Farm Cl BH21 . . . . . . **37** A4
Violet La BH25. . . . . **62** A2
Virginia Cl BH12 . . . . **68** C3
Viscount Cl BH11 . . . . **41** A1
Viscount Ct BH11 . . . . **41** A1
Viscount Dr BH23. . . . . **78** B2
Viscount Wlk BH11 . . . . **41** A1
Vista Marina BH13 . . . . . . **104** A2
Vitre Gdns SO41 . . . . **111** A1
Vixen Wlk BH25. . . . . **62** B3
Vulcan Way BH23 . . . . **78** B2

W

Wagtail Dr BH25. . . . . **61** C1
Wainsford Cl SO41. . . . . . **110** A1
Wainsford Ct SO41. . . . . . **110** B1
Wainsford Rd SO41 . . . . . . **85** C4
Wakefield Ave BH10 . . . . . . **43** B1
Wakely Gdns BH11. . . . . . . **42** A1
Wakely Rd BH11 . . . . **42** B1
Walcheren Pl BH15 . . . . **88** C3
Walcott Ave BH23. . . . . **75** C4
Walditch Gdns BH17 . . . . . . **47** B2
Waldren Cl BH15 . . . . **91** B2
Walford Cl BH21. . . . . **22** C2
Walford Gdns BH21 . . . . . . **22** C2
Walford Mill Craft Ctr*
BH21. . . . . **22** B2
WALHAMPTON **111** C3
Walhampton Hill
SO41. . . . . **111** B4
WALKFORD **80** C4
Walkford La BH25 . . . . **61** A2
Walkford Rd BH23 . . . . **60** C1
Walkford Way BH23. . . . . . **80** B4
Walking Field La BH15 . . **91** A2
Walkwood Ave BH7 . . . . . . **74** B3
Wallace Ct BH18. . . . . **46** A3
Wallace Rd BH18 . . . . **46** A3
Walliscott Rd BH11 . . . . **50** A1
WALLISDOWN **50** A1
Wallisdown Rd BH10. . . . . . **70** C4
Wallisdown Rdbt BH12. . . . **50** A1
Wallis Rd BH10 . . . . **50** B1
Walnut Cl BH25. . . . . **61** C2
Walpole Rd BH1 . . . . **97** B4
Walsford Rd BH7 . . . . **70** C1
Walsingham Dene BH7 . . . . **73** C3
Waltham Rd BH7 . . . . **74** B1
Walton Rd
Bournemouth BH10 . . . . . . **50** C2
Poole BH15. . . . . **68** A2
Wanstead Cl BH24. . . . . 6 C1
Warbler Cl BH16. . . . . **64** B4
Warburton Rd BH17 . . . . . . **67** B4
Wareham Ct
Bournemouth BH7 . . . . . . **74** B1
Hamworthy BH15. . . . . . . **89** B2
Wareham Rd BH21 . . . . **37** A1
Warland Way BH21 . . . . **37** A2
War Meml Hospl SO41. . . **87** B2
Warmwell Cl
Bournemouth BH9 . . . . . . **52** B3

Warmwell Cl continued
Poole BH17. . . . . **47** C2
Warnford Rd BH7 . . . . **74** B2
Warren Ave BH23. . . . . . . **101** C4
Warren Cl BH24 . . . . **12** B1
Warren Dr BH24 . . . . **12** B1
Warren Edge Cl BH6. . . . . . **99** C2
Warren Edge Ct BH6 . . . . . . **99** C2
Warren Edge Rd BH6 . . . . . **99** C2
Warren La BH24 . . . . **12** B1
Warren Pk SO41. . . . . **86** A4
Warren Rd
Bournemouth BH4 . . . . . . **94** B2
Poole BH14. . . . . **93** A4
Warren Wlk BH22. . . . . **26** B3
Warwick Ave BH25. . . . . . . **62** B1
Warwick Pl 1 BH7 . . . . **98** A4
Warwick Rd
Bournemouth BH7 . . . . . . **98** A4
Poole BH14. . . . . **92** C3
Washington Ave BH1 . . . . . **73** A1
Watcombe Rd BH6. . . . . **99** A4
WATERDITCH **58** B4
Waterditch Rd BH23 . . . . . . **58** A3
Waterford Cl
Lymington SO41 . . . . **111** B2
Poole BH14. . . . . **92** A2
Waterford Gdns BH23. . . . . **80** A2
Waterford La SO41. . . . . . **111** B1
Waterford Lodge BH23. . . . **78** B1
Waterford Pl BH23. . . . . **80** B2
Waterford Rd
Christchurch BH23 . . . . . . **80** B2
New Milton BH25 . . . . **62** C1
Waterfront Mus* BH15. **90** B1
Watergardens BH8 . . . . **96** A4
Water La BH6 . . . . **75** A2
Water Lane Farm BH10 . **43** B2
WATERLOO **46** B1
Waterloo Ho BH17. . . . . **46** B1
Waterloo Rd
Bournemouth BH9 . . . . . . **71** C3
Corfe Mullen BH21. . . . . . **36** B1
Lymington SO41 . . . . **111** B3
Poole BH17. . . . . **66** C4
Waterloo Way BH24. . . . . . **13** B2
Watermead 5 BH23 . . . . . **100** A4
Watermill Rd BH23 . . . . **76** A3
Waters Edge BH13 . . . . . . **104** A2
Watership Dr BH24 . . . . **14** B2
Waterside BH23 . . . . **101** C3
Waterside Cl BH24. . . . . 6 C1
Watersmeet Ct BH23. . . . . **100** B4
Waterston Cl BH17. . . . . **47** A1
Water Tower Rd BH18. . . **46** C4
Watery La
Christchurch BH23 . . . . . . **78** A3
Upton BH16 . . . . **64** A3
Watkin Rd 6 BH5 . . . . **97** C3
Watton Cl BH18. . . . . **54** A1
Wavell Ave BH17. . . . . **46** A1
Wavell Rd BH11 . . . . **50** B4
Wavendon Ave BH25. . . . . . **81** B3
Waverley 14 BH4 . . . . **94** C3
Waverley Cres BH15 . . . . . . **67** A2
Waverley Ho 9 BH25. . . . . . **82** B4
Waverley Rd BH25 . . . . **82** B4
Wayground Rd BH21. . . . . . **29** B1
Wayman Rd BH21. . . . . **37** B2
Wayne Rd BH12 . . . . **68** B2
Wayside Cl SO41. . . . . **87** A3
Wayside Rd BH6. . . . . **99** B3
Waytown Cl BH17. . . . . **47** A1
Weavers Cl BH22 . . . . **16** C1
Webbs Cl BH24 . . . . **10** B2
Webbs Way BH24 . . . . **10** C2
Webb's Way BH11 . . . . **49** C1
Webster Rd BH9 . . . . **52** A2
Wedgwood Dr BH14 . . . . . . **92** A2
Wedgwood Gdns
BH23. . . . . **109** B3
Weldon Ave BH11. . . . . **41** B1
Welland Rd BH21 . . . . **31** A4
Well Cl BH25 . . . . **61** C1
Wellesley Ave BH23 . . . . . . **78** C2
Wellington Ave BH23 . . . . . **78** C2
Wellington Ct
7 Bournemouth, Dean
Park BH8 . . . . **96** A4

Wellington Ct continued
Bournemouth, Westbourne
BH2. . . . . **95** A3
New Milton BH25 . . . . **62** A1
Wellingtonia Gdns
SO41. . . . . **63** C2
Wellington Rd
Bournemouth BH8 . . . . . . **96** A4
Lymington SO41 . . . . **111** C1
Well La BH15 . . . . **90** C4
Wendover Cl BH25. . . . . **81** C4
Wendy Cres BH22. . . . . **35** C3
Wenlock Ct 9 BH23 . . . . . . **77** C3
Wentwood Glen BH25 . . . . . **83** A4
Wentworth BH14 . . . . **103** C3
Wentworth Ave BH5 . . . . . . **98** B3
Wentworth Cl BH5. . . . . **98** B3
Wentworth Coll BH5. . . . . **98** A3
Wentworth Dr
Broadstone BH18. . . . . **38** B1
Christchurch BH23 . . . . . . **75** C1
Wentworth Grange
BH22. . . . . **27** A3
Wescott Way BH11. . . . . . . **49** B4
Wesley Cl 8 BH8 . . . . **96** C4
Wesley Grange 4B BH4. . . **94** C3
Wesley Ho BH22 . . . . **27** C2
Wesley Rd Poole BH12. . . . . **68** C1
Wimborne Minster BH21. . . **23** B1
Wessex Ave BH25. . . . . **82** A4
Wessex Cl BH23 . . . . **78** C2
Wessex Est BH24 . . . . **14** A4
Wessex Gate BH25 . . . . **72** C1
Wessex Gate Ret Pk
BH15. . . . . **66** B2
Wessex Rd Poole BH14. . . . . **92** A3
Ringwood BH24 . . . . **13** C4
Wessex Trade Ctr
BH12. . . . . **68** A3
Wessex Way
Bournemouth,
Springbourne BH8 . . . . . . **96** C4
Bournemouth, Westbourne
BH2, BH4 . . . . **95** A3
West Ave BH21 . . . . 8 C4
Westbeams Rd SO41. . . . . **107** B2
West Borough BH21 . . . . . . **22** B1
WESTBOURNE. **94** C3
Westbourne Cl BH4. . . . . . . **94** C3
Westbourne Gate 15
BH4. . . . . **94** C3
Westbourne Park Rd
BH4. . . . . **94** B2
Westbrook Cl BH10 . . . . **51** A2
Westbury Cl
Barton on Sea BH25. . . . . . **82** B2
Bransgore BH23 . . . . **108** C1
Christchurch BH23 . . . . . . **79** A4
Westbury Ct 1 BH14. . . . . . **92** B4
Westbury Rd BH23 . . . . **13** C3
Westby Rd BH5 . . . . **97** C3
West Cl
Lymington SO41 . . . . **110** A1
Verwood BH31 . . . . 2 A2
WEST CLIFF **94** C1
West Cliff BH2 . . . . **112** B3
West Cliff Cotts BH2 . . . . . **112** A1
West Cliff Ct 40 BH4 . . . . . . **94** C2
West Cliff Gdns BH2 . . . . . **112** A1
Westcliff Ho 8 BH4 . . . . **94** C2
West Cliff Mews BH2 . . . . . **112** A1
Westcliff Palms 18
BH4. . . . . **94** C2
West Cliff Rd BH4. . . . . **94** C2
West Close Ho BH6 . . . . . . **100** A3
Westcroft Par 7 BH25 . . . . **82** B4
Westcroft Pk BH18. . . . . **46** C4
Westdown Rd BH11. . . . . . . **42** A1
West Dr BH24 . . . . **28** B4
Westerham 7 BH13 . . . . . . **94** B3
Westerham Rd BH4. . . . . . . **94** B3
Westerleigh 12 BH4. . . . . . . **94** C2
Western Ave
Barton on Sea BH25. . . . . . **81** A3
Bournemouth BH10 . . . . . . **51** A4
Poole BH13. . . . . **93** C2
Western Cl BH10 . . . . **51** A4
Westergate 13 BH13 . . . . . . **94** B3
Western Rd
Lymington SO41 . . . . **110** C3

Western Rd continued
Poole BH13. . . . . **94** A2
Poole, Canford Cliffs
BH13. . . . . **104** C3
Westfield 10 BH21 . . . . **22** B1
Westfield Cl BH21 . . . . **22** B1
Westfield Rd
Bournemouth BH6 . . . . . . **99** B3
Lymington SO41 . . . . **111** C1
Westgate Pk BH4 . . . . **94** B3
Westham Cl BH17. . . . . **47** B3
West Hayes SO41. . . . . . . **111** B2
Westheath Rd BH18. . . . . . . **46** B4
West Hill Pl 8 BH2. . . . . . . **112** A2
West Hill Rd BH2 . . . . **112** A1
WEST HOWE **49** B4
West Howe Cl BH11. . . . . . . **50** A4
West Howe Ind Est
BH11. . . . . **49** B3
West La SO41. . . . . **85** C3
Westlands Ct BH23 . . . . . . **108** C2
Westlands Dr BH13 . . . . . . **104** C3
West Mans 3 BH4. . . . . **94** C3
Westminster Ct BH25 . . . . . **81** C2
Westminster Rd
Milford on S SO41 . . . . . . **86** A2
Poole BH13. . . . . **94** B1
Westminster Rd E
BH13. . . . . **94** B1
WEST MOORS **16** C3
West Moors Mid Sch
BH22. . . . . **17** A1
West Moors Rd
Ferndown BH22 . . . . **27** A3
Three Legged Cross BH21. . 8 C3
West Moors BH22 . . . . 8 B1
West Moors St Mary's CE
Fst Sch BH22 . . . . **16** B3
Westmoreland Ct SO41 . . **63** C1
Weston Dr BH1 . . . . **96** B2
Weston Rd BH21 . . . . **23** C3
West Overcliff Dr BH4. . . . . **95** A1
Westover La BH24 . . . . **12** B1
Westover Rd
Bournemouth BH1 . . . . . . **112** B2
Milford on S SO41 . . . . . . **87** A2
Westover Retail Pk
BH9. . . . . **52** A3
WEST PARLEY **35** B1
West Quay Rd BH15. . . . . . **90** B2
Westray Hall BH4 . . . . **94** C1
West Rd
Bournemouth BH5 . . . . . . **98** B3
Bransgore BH23. . . . . **108** C2
Milford on S SO41 . . . . . . **86** A3
West Row BH21. . . . . **30** B4
West Row Mews BH21. . . . . **30** B4
WEST SOUTHBOURNE . . **99** A4
West St Poole BH15. . . . . . . **90** B2
Ringwood BH24 . . . . **12** C3
Wimborne Minster BH21. . **22** B1
West Station Terr BH4. . . . . **95** A3
West Street Ct 8 BH21 . . . . **22** B1
West Undercliff Prom
BH2. . . . . **95** A1
West View Rd
Christchurch BH23 . . . . . . **77** B1
Poole BH15. . . . . **90** C4
West Way
Bournemouth BH9 . . . . . . **52** B1
Broadstone BH18. . . . . **45** C3
Lymington SO41 . . . . **110** B1
West Way Cl BH9 . . . . **72** B4
Westwood Ave BH22 . . . . . . **27** A2
Wetherby Cl BH18 . . . . **46** A2
Weyman's Ave BH10 . . . . . . **42** C2
Weymans Dr BH10 . . . . **42** C2
Weymouth Rd BH14. . . . . . . **68** C1
Wharf Cl BH12. . . . . **69** B2
Wharfdale Rd
Bournemouth BH4 . . . . . . **95** A4
Poole BH12. . . . . **69** B2
Wharncliffe Ct BH23 . . . . . . **79** C2
Wharncliffe Gdns BH23 . . . **80** A2
Wharncliffe Rd
Bournemouth BH5 . . . . . . **97** A3
Christchurch BH23 . . . . . . **80** A2
Whatleigh Cl BH15. . . . . **90** C1
Wheaton Grange 4
BH4. . . . . **95** A4

Wheaton Rd BH7 . . . . **98** A4
Wheatplot Park Homes 2
BH10. . . . . **51** C4
Wheelers La BH11 . . . . **41** A2
Whimbrel Ct BH23 . . . . **78** A1
Whincroft Cl BH22. . . . . **27** B3
Whincroft Dr BH22 . . . . **27** B2
Whitaker Cres SO41 . . . . . **110** B2
Whitby Ave BH18 . . . . **46** A2
Whitby Cl BH23 . . . . **55** A3
Whitby Cres BH18 . . . . **46** A2
Whitby Ct 4 SO41. . . . . **86** B2
Whitby Rd SO41 . . . . **86** B2
Whitchurch Ave BH18. . . . . **46** C3
White Barn Cres SO41 . . . . **84** A2
Whitebeam Way BH31 . . . . 3 B1
White Cl BH15. . . . . **68** A3
Whitecliff Cres BH14. . . . . . **92** A2
Whitecliff Rd BH14 . . . . **91** C2
Whitecross Cl BH17. . . . . . . **47** B3
White Farm Cl BH10 . . . . . . **71** A4
Whitefield Rd
New Milton BH25 . . . . **82** A4
Poole BH14. . . . . **92** A2
Whitehall BH23. . . . . **76** B1
Whitehart Fields BH24 . . . . **14** A4
Whitehayes Cl BH23 . . . . . . **57** A1
Whitehayes Rd BH23. . . . . . **76** C4
White Horse Dr BH15 . . . . . **66** C1
White Horses BH25 . . . . **81** B2
White Ho SO41 . . . . **87** A1
Whitehouse Rd BH21 . . . . . . **31** A2
White Knights BH25 . . . . . . **81** C2
Whitelegg Way BH10 . . . . . **43** C1
White Lion Ctyd BH24 . . . . **13** A3
Whiteways BH21. . . . . **23** B2
Whitfield Pk BH24 . . . . **11** C1
Whitingham Ct 1 BH5. . . . . **98** B4
Whitley Way BH25 . . . . **62** B3
Whitsbury Cl BH8. . . . . **53** A1
Whittle Rd BH21. . . . . **25** C3
Whittles Way BH15 . . . . **90** B2
WICK **100** B3
Wick 1 Ind Est BH25. . . . **61** B1
Wick 2 Ind Est BH25. . . . **61** B1
Wick Cl BH25. . . . . **61** B1
Wick Dr BH25 . . . . **61** B1
Wicket Rd BH10 . . . . **42** C1
Wick Farm BH6. . . . . **100** B4
Wickfield Ave BH23 . . . . . . **76** B1
Wickfield Cl BH23 . . . . **76** B1
Wickford Ho BH23 . . . . **76** A1
Wickham Ct BH22 . . . . **27** B2
Wickham Dr BH21 . . . . **45** A4
Wickham Rd BH7. . . . . **98** A4
Wick La
Bournemouth BH6 . . . . . **100** A4
Christchurch BH23 . . . . . . **76** B1
Wicklea Rd BH6. . . . . **100** B3
Wickmeads Rd BH6. . . . . . **100** A4
Wick Point Mews
BH23. . . . . **100** B4
Widbury Rd SO41. . . . . . . **110** B3
Widden Cl SO41 . . . . **107** B3
Widdicombe Ave BH14. . . . **93** B2
Widget Cl BH11. . . . . **50** B2
Widworthy Dr BH18. . . . . . . **37** C1
Wight Wlk BH22 . . . . **35** B2
Wilderton Rd BH13 . . . . **93** C3
Wilderton Rd W BH13 . . . . . **94** A3
Wildfell Cl BH23 . . . . **76** A4
Wildown Gdns BH6 . . . . . . **100** A2
Wildown Rd BH6 . . . . **100** A2
Wilfred Rd BH5. . . . . **97** C3
Wilkinson Dr BH8. . . . . **54** B1
Wilkins Way BH15 . . . . **90** B2
Willett Rd BH21. . . . . **30** A2
William Cl BH23 . . . . **60** A1
William Ct 11 BH23 . . . . . . **80** B2
William Rd
Bournemouth BH7 . . . . . . **73** C2
Lymington SO41 . . . . **111** A4
William's Ind Pk BH25 . . **61** B1
Willis Way BH15 . . . . **66** B2
Willow Cl
Bournemouth BH4 . . . . . . **70** B1
St Leonards BH24 . . . . **18** B4
Upton BH16 . . . . **65** A1
Willow Ct BH1 . . . . **74** C1
Willowdene Cl BH25 . . . . . . **62** C1

Willow Dr
Christchurch BH6 . . . . **100** A4
Ringwood BH24 . . . . **13** B1
Wimborne Minster BH21 . . **24** C2
Willow Lo **1** BH1 . . . . **97** A3
Willow Mead BH8 . . . . **53** A3
Willow Pk BH12 . . . . **92** A3
Willow Pl BH23 . . . . **76** C1
Willows The BH25 . . . . **82** B2
Willow Tree Ho SO41 . . **110** B1
Willow Tree Rise BH11 . . **50** B3
Willow View BH16 . . . . . . **88** C4
Willow Way
Christchurch BH23 . . . . . . **100** A4
Ferndown BH22 . . . . **27** A3
Willow Wlk BH23 . . . . **82** B1
Wills Cl BH21 . . . . **45** A4
Wills Rd BH12 . . . . **93** C4
Willwood Cl BH17 . . . . . . **47** B3
Wilmur Cres BH15 . . . . . . **67** B2
Wilson Rd
Bournemouth BH1 . . . . **73** B1
Poole BH14 . . . . **92** C4
Wilton Cl BH23 . . . . **75** A4
Wilton Gdns BH25 . . . . . . **61** C2
Wilton Pl **10** BH4 . . . . . . **94** C2
Wilton Rd BH7 . . . . **97** C4
Wiltshire Gdns BH23 . . **108** B2
Wiltshire Rd BH23 . . . . **108** B2
Wilverley Ave BH8 . . . . . **53** C1
Wilverley Cl SO41 . . . . . . **110** A1
Wilverley Rd BH23 . . . . . **78** A2
Wimborne Fst Sch
BH21 . . . . **22** B1
Wimborne Ho BH22 . . . . . . **27** C3
WIMBORNE MINSTER . . **22** A2
Wimborne Minster Model
Town & Gdns * BH21 . . **30** B4
Wimborne Rd
Bournemouth, Dean Park
BH9 . . . . **71** C1
Bournemouth, Kinson
BH11 . . . . **42** C2
Bournemouth, Moordown
BH9 . . . . **71** C4
East End BH21 . . . . **29** C1
Poole, Longfleet BH15 . . . . **91** A4
Poole, Oakdale BH15 . . . . . **67** A2
Wimborne Minster BH21 . . **23** B2
Wimborne Rd E
Ferndown BH22 . . . . **26** B2
Trickett's Cross BH22 . . . . . **27** B3
Wimborne Rd W
Ferndown BH21 . . . . **25** B2
Wimborne Minster BH21 . . **32** B4
Winchelsea Specl Sch
BH12 . . . . **49** A1
Winchester Pl **8** BH9 . . **90** C2
Winchester Rd BH25 . . . . **62** C2
Wincombe Cl BH22 . . . . . . **35** A3
Wincombe Dr BH22 . . . . . . **35** A4

Windermere Rd BH3 . . . . **72** A2
Windgreen Est BH21 . . . . **37** B3
Windham Mews BH1 . . . . **97** A4
Windham Rd BH1 . . . . **97** A4
Windmill Cl
5 Milford on S SO41 . . . . **87** A3
St Leonards BH24 . . . . **20** B4
Windmill La BH24 . . . . **20** B4
Windsor Cl Hordle SO41 . . **63** B2
St Leonards BH24 . . . . **19** A4
Windsor Ct
3 Christchurch BH23 . . . **80** A2
Poole BH14 . . . . **92** B3
Windsor Mans **1** BH6 . . **99** B2
Windsor Rd
Bournemouth BH5 . . . . **97** B3
Christchurch BH23 . . . . . . **75** B2
Poole BH14 . . . . **92** B3
Winfrith Cres BH12 . . . . . **69** B4
Wingfield Ave
Christchurch BH23 . . . . . . **79** A4
Poole BH15 . . . . **67** A2
Wingfield Ct BH1 . . . . **96** C2
Winifred Rd BH15 . . . . **67** B1
WINKTON **56** C4
Winkton Cl BH23 . . . . **56** C2
Winkton Gn BH23 . . . . **56** C4
Winkton Ho BH23 . . . . **56** C3
Winnards Cl BH22 . . . . **35** B2
Winsford Cl BH23 . . . . **79** A4
Winsley Ave BH6 . . . . **98** C3
Winspit Cl BH15 . . . . **89** B3
Winston Ave BH12 . . . . . . **70** A2
Winston Ct
1 Christchurch BH23 . . . **76** A2
4 Old Milton BH25 . . . . . **82** A3
Winston Gdns BH12 . . . . . **70** A2
Winston Par **6** BH25 . . **82** A3
Winston Pk BH12 . . . . **70** A2
Winston Rd BH9 . . . . **52** A2
Winston Way BH24 . . . . . . **13** C4
Winterbourne Cl BH15 . . **91** A4
Winterbourne Rd BH15 . . **67** A1
Winterhayes Cl BH17 . . . . **47** B3
WINTON **71** C3
Winton Boys' Sch BH10 . . **51** A1
Winton Cl SO41 . . . . **111** B2
Winton Prim Sch BH9 . . **51** B2
Winton Way
Bournemouth BH10 . . . . . . **51** A1
New Milton BH25 . . . . **62** B3
Wisbech Way SO41 . . . . . . **63** C1
Wishart Gdns BH9 . . . . . . **52** B4
Wistaria Ho **7** BH10 . . . . **51** C4
Wisteria Dr BH31 . . . . **5** C4
Witchampton Rd BH18 . . **45** C2
Withermoor Rd BH9 . . . . . **71** B4
Withingham Rd BH13 . . . . **93** C3
Witley BH14 . . . . **103** C3
Witney Rd BH17 . . . . **47** A1
Wivenhoe Ho BH22 . . . . . . **27** C2

Woking Rd BH14 . . . . **92** C4
Wolfe Cl BH23 . . . . **77** A2
Wollaston Rd BH6 . . . . **99** C2
Wollaton Cres BH22 . . . . . **34** C3
Wollaton Rd BH22 . . . . . . **34** C3
Wollstonecraft Rd **1**
BH5 . . . . **97** C2
Wolseley Rd BH12 . . . . . . **69** A2
Wolsey Way SO41 . . . . **87** A3
Wolterton Rd BH12 . . . . . **70** A1
Wolverley Ct **19** BH4 . . . **94** C3
Wolverton Rd BH7 . . . . . . **97** C4
Wonderholm Par BH11 . . **50** B2
Woodacre Gdns BH22 . . . **35** B4
Woodbury BH1 . . . . **96** A1
Woodbury Ave BH8 . . . . . **53** C1
Woodbury Ct BH23 . . . . . . **55** B2
Woodcock La SO41 . . . . . . **84** B3
Woodcocks Cres BH7 . . . . **74** A3
Woodcote Dr BH16 . . . . . . **64** B2
Woodend Rd BH9 . . . . **71** B4
Wood End Rd BH24 . . . . . . **14** C1
Woodfield Gdns BH23 . . . **79** A4
Woodfield Rd BH11 . . . . . . **42** A1
Woodford Ct BH24 . . . . . . **14** A3
Woodford Rd BH1 . . . . **96** C3
Woodgreen Dr BH11 . . . . . **49** A4
Woodhayes Ave BH20 . . . **59** B1
Wood Ho **6** BH13 . . . . . . **94** B3
Wood La
Bournemouth BH11 . . . . . . **41** B2
Milford on S SO41 . . . . . . **86** C2
Woodlake Cl BH17 . . . . . . **47** A1
Woodland Ave BH5 . . . . . . **98** A3
Woodland Cl BH31 . . . . **2** B3
Woodland Ct BH7 . . . . **97** C4
Woodland Mans BH14 . . . **68** B1
Woodlands **20** BH13 . . . . **94** A4
Woodlands Ave BH15 . . . . **89** C3
Woodlands Cl BH23 . . . . **108** C2
Woodlands Cres BH15 . . . **89** C3
Woodlands Ct BH12 . . . . . **70** B1
Woodlands Cvn Pk
SO41 . . . . **84** A2
Woodlands Rd BH25 . . . . . **81** B2
Woodlands Way
New Milton BH25 . . . . **62** B3
St Leonards BH24 . . . . **19** A4
Woodland Way
Christchurch BH23 . . . . . . **79** A3
Milford on S SO41 . . . . . . **86** C2
Woodland Wlk
Bournemouth BH5 . . . . **98** A3
Ferndown BH22 . . . . **27** C3
Wood Lawn Cl BH25 . . . . **81** C3
Woodleaze Cl BH18 . . . . . **38** B2
Woodley Gdns SO41 . . . . **110** C4
Woodlinken Cl BH31 . . . . . **5** B4
Woodlinken Dr BH31 . . . . . **3** B1
Woodlinken Way BH31 . . . **5** C4
Woodpecker Cl BH31 . . . . **2** C1

Woodpecker Dr BH17 . . . . **65** C4
Woodrising BH13 . . . . . . **106** A3
Woodrisings The **6**
BH2 . . . . **95** A4
Wood Row BH9 . . . . **53** B3
Woodruff Cl BH23 . . . . . . **78** C3
Woods Edge BH18 . . . . . . **46** A2
Woodside Cl
Ferndown BH22 . . . . **27** B2
10 Lymington SO41 . . . . **111** A1
Woodside Rd
Bournemouth BH5 . . . . **98** B3
Ferndown BH22 . . . . **27** B2
Poole BH14 . . . . **92** C3
West Moors BH22 . . . . **16** B4
Woodstock Cl BH10 . . . . . **52** B3
Woodstock La BH24 . . . . . **13** B2
Woodstock Rd
Burton BH23 . . . . **57** A1
Poole BH14 . . . . **92** A2
Woods View Rd BH9 . . . . . **71** A4
Woodvale Gdns BH25 . . . **62** C2
Wood View BH21 . . . . **24** A4
Woolmer La BH24 . . . . **6** B2
Wool Rd BH12 . . . . **68** B4
WOOLSBRIDGE **9** C2
Woolsbridge Ind Est
BH21 . . . . **9** B2
Woolsbridge Rd BH24 . . . **10** C1
Woolslope Gdns BH22 . . . **17** A1
Woolslope Rd BH22 . . . . . **16** C1
Woolven Cl BH14 . . . . **68** A1
Wootton Gdns BH1 . . . . . **96** A2
Wootton Mount BH1 . . . . **96** A2
Worbarrow Gdns BH12 . . **68** C4
Worcester Pl **1** SO41 . . **111** B1
Wordsworth Ave BH8 . . . **73** B4
Worgret Rd BH15 . . . . **67** A3
Worrell Dr BH12 . . . . **68** C4
Worthington Cres
BH14 . . . . **92** A3
Worthy Rd BH25 . . . . **62** A1
Wortley Rd BH23 . . . . **80** A2
Wraxall Cl BH17 . . . . **47** A1
Wren Cl
Christchurch BH23 . . . . . **102** B4
New Milton BH25 . . . . **61** C1
Ringwood BH24 . . . . **14** A2
Wren Cres BH12 . . . . **70** B1
Wroxham Rd BH12 . . . . . . **69** C1
Wyatts Cl BH21 . . . . **37** A2
Wyatts La BH21 . . . . **36** C2
Wychwood **38** BH4 . . . . . **94** C3
Wychwood Cl BH2 . . . . . **112** B3
Wychwood Dr BH2 . . . . . **112** B3
Wychwood Grange
BH2 . . . . **112** B3
Wycliffe Rd BH9 . . . . **71** C4
Wyelands Ave BH21 . . . . . **25** A1
Wykeham Cl BH17 . . . . . . **67** B4

Wykeham Pl SO41 . . . . . **111** A2
Wyncombe Rd BH5 . . . . . **98** B4
Wyndham Cl BH23 . . . . . . **60** B1
Wyndham Rd
Poole BH14 . . . . **92** B3
Walkford BH23 . . . . **60** B1
Wynford Rd
Bournemouth BH9 . . . . **52** B3
Poole BH14 . . . . **92** C4
Wynne Cl BH18 . . . . **45** C4
Wynter Cl BH17 . . . . **73** C2
Wyvern Cl BH12 . . . . **69** A3

Y

Yaldhurst La SO41 . . . . . **110** A2
Yarmouth Cl BH12 . . . . . . **70** A1
Yarmouth Rd BH12 . . . . . **69** C2
Yarrell Mead SO41 . . . . . **110** A2
Yarrells Cl BH16 . . . . **64** C3
Yarrells Dr BH16 . . . . **64** B3
Yarrells La BH16 . . . . **64** C2
Yarrells Sch BH16 . . . . . . **64** B3
Yarrow Cl BH23 . . . . **78** B3
Yarrow Rd BH12 . . . . **68** A4
Yeatmans Old Mill **10**
BH15 . . . . **90** B1
Yeatminster Rd BH17 . . . **47** C2
Yelverton Rd BH1 . . . . . . **112** B2
Yeomans Ind Pk BH8 . . . **53** C1
Yeomans Lodge **6**
BH25 . . . . **82** B4
Yeomans Rd BH8 . . . . **53** B2
Yeomans Way BH8 . . . . . . **53** B1
Yeovilton Cl SO41 . . . . . . **85** C3
Yerville Gdns SO41 . . . . . **63** C1
Yew La BH25 . . . . **62** C2
Yew Tree Cl BH21 . . . . **23** A1
Yew Tree Cl **5** BH25 . . . **82** B3
Yew Tree Gdns **3**
BH24 . . . . **13** B2
York Cl
Broadstone BH18 . . . . **46** A2
Christchurch BH23 . . . . . . **75** C2
York Pl
Bournemouth BH7 . . . . **98** A4
7 New Milton BH25 . . . . . **62** B1
York Rd
Bournemouth BH1 . . . . **96** B3
Broadstone BH18 . . . . **46** A2
Youngs Rd BH11 . . . . **42** A1

Z

Zamek Cl BH11 . . . . **42** A1
Zetland Ct BH4 . . . . **94** B1
Zinnia Cl BH10 . . . . **51** B2

List of numbered locations

In some busy areas of the maps it is not always possible to show the name of every place.

Where not all names will fit, some smaller places are shown by a number. If you wish to find out the name associated with a number, use this listing.

The places in this list are also listed normally in the Index.

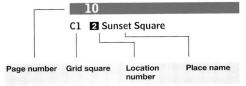

C1 **2** Sunset Square

Page number   Grid square   Location number   Place name

13
B2 **1** Harry Barrow Cl
2 Coxstone La
3 Yew Tree Gdns
4 Mintys Yd
5 Duck Island La
6 Southfield Mews
B4 **1** Somerley View
2 Orchard Mead
3 Orchard Mount
C4 **1** Beechcroft Mews
2 Lumby Drive Mobile Home Pk
3 Cavendish Corner Mobile Home Pk

22
B1 **1** Hamilton Ct
2 Bartley Ct
3 Priors Wlk
4 Crown Ct
5 Kingsmead Ct
6 Church St
7 Cornmarket Cl
8 West Street Ct
9 Three Lions Cl
10 Westfield
11 Moray Ct
B2 **1** Farmers Wlk
2 Cowdrys Field
3 Knobcrook Rd
4 Sheppards Field
5 Culverhayes Cl
C1 **1** Gulliver Ct
2 Helic Ho
3 Marlborough Ct
4 Queensmead
5 Millbank Ho
6 Jessopp Ho

30
C4 **1** Quarterjack Mews
2 Shamrock Ct
3 Stevensons Cl
4 Broadway Pk
5 Coppercourt Leaze
6 Broadway Gdns
7 Robins Ct
8 Riversdale

31
A4 **1** Ingram Wlk
2 Moorhills
3 Meadow Ct
4 Cromwell Rd
5 Harleston Villas

43
A1 **1** Ashridge Ave
2 Ashridge Par
3 Northbourne Pl

51
C1 **1** Evelyn Mews
2 St John's Gdns
3 Norway Cl
4 Victoria Park Pl
5 Lampton Gdns
C4 **1** Redhill Park Homes
2 Wheatplot Park Homes
3 Kingfisher Park Homes
4 Riverside
5 Magnolia Ho
6 Wistaria Ho
7 Wistaria Ho
8 Laburnum Ho

52
A1 **1** Rosebud Ave
2 McWilliam Rd
3 Minterne Rd
4 Malvern Ct
A2 **1** Comber Rd
2 Meadow Ct
3 Priory View Pl
A3 **1** Redhill Ct
2 Portswood Dr
3 Circle The
B3 **1** Sturminster Rd
2 Sidney Gdns

62
A1 **1** Heather Lo
2 Russell Ct
3 Danestead Ho
4 Osbourne Ho
5 Homemill Ho
6 Mallard Bldgs
7 Richmond Ct
8 Pegasus Ct
9 Beau Ct
B1 **1** Tanglewood Ct
2 Alvandi Gdns
3 Ashton Ct
4 Morant Ct
5 Trevone
6 Fremington Ct
7 York Pl
8 Faircourt
9 Merlewood Ct
10 Conway Ct
11 Stirling Ct

69
C3 **1** Greenfields
2 Handley Lodge
3 Shillingstone Gdns
4 Cashmoor Cl
5 Rowe Gdns

74
B1 **1** Lascelles Ct

2 Marlborough Mans
3 Robville Ct

76
A1 **1** Homestour Ho
2 Orchard Mews
3 St Andrews
4 Riverland Ct
A2 **1** Winston Ct
2 Kenilworth Ct
3 Arthur La
4 Mulberry Ct
5 Mitre Ct
B1 **1** Pound La
2 Millhams Street N
3 Cloisters The
4 Priory View Ct
5 Silver St

77
B1 **1** Francesca Lo
2 Gillion Ct
3 Rosedale Ct
B2 **1** Strete Mount
2 Purewell Ct
3 Court Cl
4 Francesca Grange
5 Francesca Ct
C3 **1** Southdown Ct
2 Malvern Ct
3 Purbeck Ct
4 Mendip Ct
5 Chiltern Ct
6 Cotswold Ct
7 Quantock Ct
8 Pennine Ct
9 Wenlock Ct

80
A2 **1** Buckingham Ct
2 Castle Ct
3 Windsor Ct
4 Hurst Ct
5 Bermuda Ct
6 Claire Ct
7 Diana Ct
8 Tracey Ct
9 Carisbrooke Ct
B2 **1** Carisbrooke Ct
2 Merton Ct
3 Balmoral Ct
4 Pembroke Ct
5 Exeter Ct
6 Hertford Ct
7 Frances Ct
8 Rosemary Ct
9 Kenneth Ct
10 Alan Ct
11 William Ct
12 Penelope Ct
13 Stella Ct

82
A3 **1** Keats Ho
2 Shenstone Ct
3 Clifton Ct
4 Winston Ct
5 Solent Lo
6 Winston Par
7 Bouverie Cl
8 Edmunds Cl
10 Spindlewood Cl
A4 **1** Vincent Rd
2 Vincent Cl
3 Charlotte Ct
4 Bursledon Ho
5 Elm Ct
6 Casselles Ct
7 Homefield Ho
8 Eliot Ho
9 Shelley Ho
10 Byron Ho
B3 **1** Hazel Ct
2 St Denys
3 Dudley Pl
4 Cherry Tree Ct
5 Yew Tree Ct
6 Greenwoods
B4 **1** Spencer Ct
2 Orchard Leigh
3 Cornerways Ct
4 Jacmar Ct
5 Ashley Arnewood Ct
6 Yeomans Lodge
7 Westcroft Par
8 Elizabeth Ct
9 Waverley Ho

86
B2 **1** Camden Hurst
2 Solent Pines
3 Maryland Ct
4 Whitby Ct
5 Beatrice Ct
6 Allison Ct
C2 **1** Kivernell Pl
2 Rookwood
3 Haven Ct
4 Hurst Ct
5 Solent Ct
6 Osborne Ct
7 Totland Ct
8 Sea Pines
9 Pinehurst
10 Needles Ct
11 Richmond Ct
12 Rookcliff
13 Park Ct

87
A3 **1** Addington Ct
2 Blandford Ct
3 Dacres Wlk
4 Dryden Pl

5 Windmill Cl
6 Glebefields

90
B1 **1** Barbers Piles
2 St James Cl
3 Poplar Cl
4 Levet's La
5 New St
6 St George's Almshos
7 Cinnamon La
8 Barbers Wharf
9 Barbers Gate
10 Yeatmans Old Mill
11 Thames Mews
12 Sarum St
13 Grand Par
14 Paradise St
C1 **1** Prosperous St
2 Daniel Gdns
3 Seed Warehouse The
4 Drake Ct
5 Gray's Yd
6 Taylor's Bldgs
7 Rodney Ct
8 Quay Point
9 Kiosks The
10 Dolphin Quays
11 East Quay
C2 **1** Towngate Sh Ctr
2 Falkland Sq
3 Dolphin Ctr
4 Kingland Cres
5 Winchester Pl
6 Vanguard Rd
7 Malthouse
8 Old Town Mews
9 Carter's La
10 Old Brewery The
11 Brombys The
12 Emerson Cl
13 Nelson Ct
14 Lagland Ct
15 Grenville Ct

91
B3 **1** Birds Hill Gdns
2 Churchfield Ct
3 Maltings The
4 Lansdell Ct
5 Gardens Ct
6 Sunningdale
7 Park View
B4 **1** Bancroft Ct
2 Crowe Hill Ct
3 Merton Ct
4 Thorogood Ct

92
A3 **1** Tennyson Rd
2 Mentone Rd
3 Clarence Rd

PHILIP'S MAPS

the Gold Standard for drivers

◆ **Philip's street atlases cover every county in England, Wales and much of Scotland**

◆ Every named street is shown, including alleys, lanes and walkways

◆ Thousands of additional features marked: stations, public buildings, car parks, places of interest

◆ Route-planning maps to get you close to your destination

◆ Postcodes on the maps and in the index

◆ Widely used by the emergency services, transport companies and local authorities

BEST BUY • BEST BUY
Auto EXPRESS
BEST BUY • BEST BUY

PHILIP'S
STREET ATLAS
London
The definitive Lond...

PHILIP'S
STREET ATLAS
Devon
Unique comprehensive coverage
BEST BUY
Plus Lyme Regis, Sidlouth and Wellington Exeter and Plymouth city centres at extra-large scale

PHILIP'S
STREET ATLAS
Norfolk
Unique comprehensive coverage
BEST BUY
Plus Brandon, Bungay and Wisbech Norwich city centre at extra-large scale

PHILIP'S
STREET ATLAS
Cumbria
Unique comprehensive coverage
Every named street, road and lane
BEST BUY
Plus town maps of Dumfries and Morecambe, with Carlisle city centre at extra-large scale

PHILIP'S
BRITAIN'S MOST DETAILED ROAD ATLAS
NAVIGATOR Britain
Ultra-large scale mapping
1½ miles to 1 inch

50 fully indexed town plans

'Extremely clear maps with the most detail to far'
Auto Express

Recommended by the Institute of Advanced Motorists

For national mapping, choose
Philip's Navigator Britain
the most detailed road atlas available of England, Wales and Scotland. Hailed by Auto Express as 'the ultimate road atlas', this is the only one-volume atlas to show every road and lane in Britain.

Street atlases currently available

England

Bedfordshire	East Sussex
Berkshire	West Sussex
Birmingham and West Midlands	Tyne and Wear
	Warwickshire
Bristol and Bath	Birmingham and West Midlands
Buckinghamshire	Wiltshire and Swindon
Cambridgeshire	Worcestershire
Cheshire	East Yorkshire Northern Lincolnshire
Cornwall	North Yorkshire
Cumbria	South Yorkshire
Derbyshire	West Yorkshire
Devon	
Dorset	**Wales**
County Durham and Teesside	Anglesey, Conwy and Gwynedd
Essex	Cardiff, Swansea and The Valleys
North Essex	
South Essex	Carmarthenshire, Pembrokeshire and Swansea
Gloucestershire	
Hampshire	Ceredigion and South Gwynedd
North Hampshire	
South Hampshire	Denbighshire, Flintshire, Wrexham
Herefordshire Monmouthshire	Herefordshire Monmouthshire
Hertfordshire	Powys
Isle of Wight	
Kent	**Scotland**
East Kent	Aberdeenshire
West Kent	Ayrshire
Lancashire	Dumfries and Galloway
Leicestershire and Rutland	Edinburgh and East Central Scotland
Lincolnshire	
London	Fife and Tayside
Greater Manchester	Glasgow and West Central Scotland
Merseyside	Inverness and Moray
Norfolk	Lanarkshire
Northamptonshire	Scottish Borders
Northumberland	
Nottinghamshire	**Northern Ireland***
Oxfordshire	County Antrim and County Londonderry
Shropshire	County Armagh and County Down
Somerset	
Staffordshire	Belfast
Suffolk	County Tyrone and County Fermanagh
Surrey	
	*Publishing autumn 2006

How to order Philip's maps and atlases are available from bookshops, motorway services and petrol stations. You can order direct from the publisher by phoning **01903 828503** or online at **www.philips-maps.co.uk**
For bulk orders only, phone 020 7644 6940